BACKCOUNTRY
SKI & SNOWBOARD
ROUTES

CALIFORNIA

BACKCOUNTRY SKI & SNOWBOARD ROUTES

CALIFORNIA

JEREMY BENSON

MOUNTAINEERS
BOOKS

To everyone who has shared their knowledge, passion, and expertise, which has aided in my exploration and fueled my enjoyment. To those who've broken trail through these mountains before me and those who will continue to do so after I am gone. To the loving memory of those we've lost pursuing their passions while living life to the fullest who continue to share these mountains with us in spirit.

MOUNTAINEERS BOOKS

Mountaineers Books is the publishing division of The Mountaineers, an organization founded in 1906 and dedicated to the exploration, preservation, and enjoyment of outdoor and wilderness areas.

1001 SW Klickitat Way, Suite 201, Seattle, WA 98134
800.553.4453, www.mountaineersbooks.org

Printed in the United States of America
Distributed in the United Kingdom by Cordee, www.cordee.co.uk
First edition, 2017

Copyeditor: Kris Fulsaas
Series design: Peggy Egerdahl
Cover design and layout: Jennifer Shontz, www.redshoedesign.com
Cartographer: Pease Press Cartography
The background maps for this book were produced using the online map viewer CalTopo. For more information, visit caltopo.com.

Cover photograph: *Enjoying spring powder at the top of Independence Pass, high above the Owens Valley* (Oscar Havens)
Frontispiece: *Slashing a sunset powder turn down the main Bear Scratch Chute on Herlan Peak* (Anthony Santos)
All photographs by the author unless otherwise noted.

Library of Congress Cataloging-in-Publication Data

Names: Benson, Jeremy, author.
Title: Backcountry ski & snowboard routes: California / Jeremy Benson.
Other titles: Backcountry ski and snowboard routes
Description: First edition. | Seattle, Washington: Mountaineers Books, [2017] | Includes index.
Identifiers: LCCN 2017017062 | ISBN 9781594858994 (paperback) | ISBN 9781594859007 (e-book)
Subjects: LCSH: Cross-country skiing—California—Guidebooks. | Snowboarding—California—Guidebooks. | Cross-country ski trails—California—Guidebooks. | Outdoor recreation—California—Guidebooks. | California—Guidebooks.
Classification: LCC GV854.5.C2 B46 2017 | DDC 796.9309794—dc23
LC record available at https://lccn.loc.gov/2017017062

 Printed on recycled paper

ISBN (paperback): 978-1-59485-899-4
ISBN (ebook): 978-1-59485-900-7

CONTENTS

Kicking up spray on a chalky wind buff in the northeast couloir of Monument Peak (Oscar Havens)

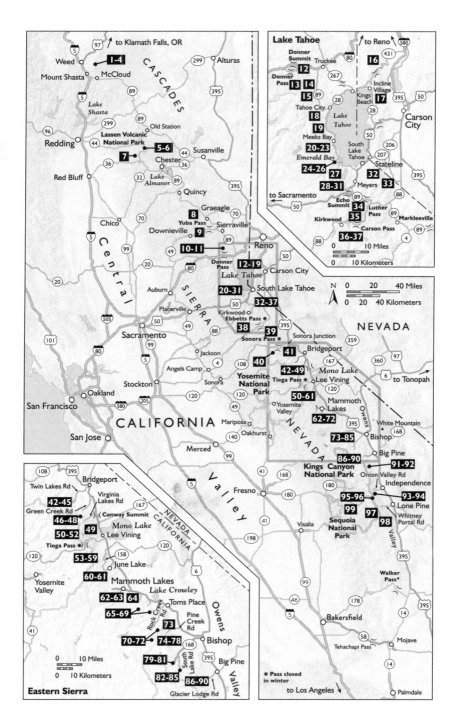

Lake Tahoe

to Reno

to Klamath Falls, OR

1-4

Weed
Mount Shasta
McCloud
Lake Shasta
Redding
Red Bluff
Chico
Sacramento
San Francisco
San Jose

CASCADES

Alturas

Old Station
Lassen Volcanic National Park
5-6
7
Chester
Lake Almanor
Quincy

Graeagle
8
Yuba Pass
Downieville
9
Sierraville
10-11

Donner Pass
12-19
Lake Tahoe
20-31
32-37
Kirkwood
Ebbetts Pass
38
39
Sonora Pass

CALIFORNIA

Auburn
Placerville
Jackson
Angels Camp
Sonora
Stockton
Oakland
Mariposa
Merced

SIERRA

Central

Valley

NEVADA

40
Yosemite National Park
41
Bridgeport
42-49
Tioga Pass
Lee Vining
Mono Lake
50-61
Yosemite Valley
62-72
Mammoth Lakes
73-85
Bishop
86-90
91-92
Kings Canyon National Park
Onion Valley Rd
Independence
95-96
93-94
99
97
Lone Pine
98
Whitney Portal Rd
Sequoia National Park
Visalia
White Mountain
Big Pine

Fresno

Bakersfield
Tehachapi Pass
Mojave

Walker Pass

to Los Angeles
Palmdale

* Pass closed in winter

Lake Tahoe

Donner Summit
Truckee
16
Incline Village
12
Donner Pass
13 14
15
Kings Beach
17
Tahoe City
18
19
Lake Tahoe
Meeks Bay
20-23
South Lake Tahoe
Emerald Bay
24-26
27
32
28-31
Meyers
33
Stateline
Carson City
Echo Summit
34
Luther Pass
Kirkwood
35
Markleeville
36-37
Carson Pass

to Sacramento

0   10 Miles
0   10 Kilometers

N   0   20   40 Miles
    0   20   40 Kilometers

Eastern Sierra

Twin Lakes Rd
Bridgeport
Virginia Lakes Rd
42-45
46-48
Green Creek Rd
50-52
49
Conway Summit
Mono Lake
Lee Vining
Tioga Pass
53-59
158
June Lake
60-61
Yosemite Valley
Mammoth Lakes
62-63 64
Lake Crowley
65-69
Toms Place
73
Pine Creek Rd
70-72
74-78
Rock Creek Rd
79-81
South Lake Rd
82-85
86-90
Glacier Lodge Rd
Bishop
Big Pine

NEVADA
CALIFORNIA

Owens
Valley

0   10 Miles
0   10 Kilometers

9

Powder turns and panoramic views of Lake Tahoe while skiing on Rubicon Peak (Oscar Havens)

TOURS AT A GLANCE

No.	Route	Roundtrip Distance (in miles)	Difficulty Level	Terrain Rating	Aspect	Best Season
PART I. SOUTHERN CASCADES						
MOUNT SHASTA						
1.	Mount Shasta: Avalanche Gulch	11	Very strenuous	3	S-SW-W	Spring, early summer
2.	Green Butte	3	Moderate	2–3	S-SW-W	Winter, spring, early summer
3.	Shastina: Cascade Gulch	10	Strenuous	2	S-SW	Spring, early summer
4.	Mount Shasta: Brewer Creek	11	Very strenuous	3	E	Late spring, early summer
LASSEN VOLCANIC NATIONAL PARK						
5.	Lassen Peak: Northeast Face via Devastated Area	7	Strenuous	3	E-NE-N	Spring, early summer
6.	Lassen Peak: Southeast Face	3 or 12	Moderate or strenuous	2	SE	Late spring, early summer
7.	Brokeoff Mountain	7	Moderate	3	S-SE	Winter, spring
PART II. NORTHERN SIERRA						
THE LOST SIERRA						
8.	Eureka Peak	3.5	Moderate	3	SE-E, NE	Winter
9.	Sierra Buttes: Violet Couloir	4	Moderate	5	N-NE	Winter
THE TRUCKEE AREA						
10.	Castle Peak: North Gullies	4	Moderate	3	N, S-SW	Winter, spring
11.	Castle Peak: Castle Pass and Peter Grubb Hut	5.5 or 7	Moderate	2	All	Winter, spring
12.	Mount Judah: Lake Run	1.75 or 2.8	Easy	2–3	E-NE	Winter, spring
13.	Anderson Peak and Benson Hut	6 or 11	Moderate or strenuous	2–3	E-NE-N, NW	Winter, spring
14.	Billys Peak: Deep Creek	7.5	Moderate	2	N	Winter
15.	Silver Peak and Bradley Hut	6 or 11.6	Moderate	2	NW, NE, E	Winter
PART III. LAKE TAHOE AREA						
NORTH LAKE TAHOE AND WEST SHORE						
16.	Tamarack Peak	2	Easy	2	N, NE, E	Winter, spring
17.	Herlan Peak: Bear Scratch	3	Moderate	3	W, NW	Winter
18.	Twin Peaks	6.5	Moderate	3	NE	Winter, spring
19.	Blackwood Canyon Cliffs: Fourth of July Chutes	2	Easy	3	N	Late spring, early summer
20.	Rubicon Peak	4	Moderate	2	N-NE, E	Winter, spring
21.	Hidden Peak	3	Moderate	2	NE	Winter, spring

No.	Route	Roundtrip Distance (in miles)	Difficulty Level	Terrain Rating	Aspect	Best Season
22.	Jakes Peak: Northeast Side	3	Moderate	2–3	NE-E	Winter, spring
23.	Jakes Peak: South Side	3	Moderate	3	E-SE-S	Winter, spring
SOUTH LAKE TAHOE AND DESOLATION WILDERNESS						
24.	Maggies Peaks	2.5 or 3.5	Easy	3	N, NE, E	Winter, spring
25.	Janines Peak	7	Strenuous	3	E-NE	Winter, spring
26.	Dicks Peak	10	Strenuous	3	N, SE	Winter, spring
27.	Mount Tallac	5	Moderate	3–4	N, NE, E, SE	Winter, spring
28.	Pyramid Peak	6	Strenuous	2	NE, SE	Winter, spring
29.	Ralston Peak	2.5 or 10	Moderate	2	N-NE, SE, SW	Winter, spring
30.	Talking Mountain	4.5	Easy	3	N-NE	Winter, spring
31.	Echo Peak	4.5	Moderate	3	NE-E, E-SE	Winter, spring
32.	Trimmer Peak	5	Strenuous	3	N-NW	Winter, spring
33.	Jobs Peak	8	Very strenuous	3	N-NE-E	Winter
34.	Powderhouse and Waterhouse Peaks	2.25 or 3	Easy	2	N-NE, SE	Winter, spring
35.	Red Lake Peak	3, 4, or 4.5	Easy to moderate	3	N-NE, E-SE	Winter, spring
36.	Elephants Back	4	Easy	2	N, NE-E, SE	Winter, spring
37.	Round Top Mountain	6	Moderate	3–4	N-NE, S	Winter, spring
EBBETTS AND SONORA PASSES						
38.	Mount Reba	3 or 6	Easy to moderate	2	S, SW, W, E	Winter, spring
39.	Silver Peak at Ebbetts Pass	6	Strenuous	4	N-NW-W	Late spring, early summer
40.	Leavitt Peak	5	Moderate	3	N	Late spring, early summer
41.	Mount Emma	4	Moderate	2–3	E, NE, NW	Winter, spring
PART IV. EASTERN SIERRA						
BRIDGEPORT TO LUNDY CANYON						
42.	Monument Peak	10.5	Strenuous	3	N-NE	Winter, spring
43.	Crater Crest	4 or 5	Strenuous	3	N	Winter, spring
44.	Matterhorn Peak	10	Strenuous	3–4	N-NE	Winter, spring
45.	Incredible Hulk and Kettle Peak: Little Slide Canyon	10	Strenuous	3–4	NW, E-NE, N	Winter, spring

No.	Route	Roundtrip Distance (in miles)	Difficulty Level	Terrain Rating	Aspect	Best Season
46.	Dunderberg Peak	3 or 4.25	Moderate	3	S-SE, N	Winter, spring
47.	Black Mountain	2.5 or 3	Easy	2–3	N, NE	Winter, spring
48.	Excelsior Mountain	9	Moderate	3	E-NE	Winter, spring
49.	Gilcrest Peak	5	Moderate	3	N, E	Winter, spring
TIOGA PASS						
50.	North Peak	11.5	Strenuous	3–4	N, SE-E	Late spring
51.	Mount Conness	9 or 12	Strenuous	3	E, N	Late spring, early summer
52.	False White Mountain	6.5	Moderate	2	E	Late spring, early summer
53.	Dana Plateau: Ellery Bowl	2.75 one-way	Easy	3–4	N, NE	Winter, spring, early summer
54.	Dana Plateau: Power Plant Bowl	4 one-way	Easy	3	N, NE	Winter, spring, early summer
55.	Dana Plateau: East Face and East End	5, 6.25, or 7	Moderate to strenuous	3–4	NE, E, SE	Winter, spring, early summer
56.	Mount Dana	5.5	Moderate	4	N-NE	Late spring, early summer
JUNE LAKE AREA						
57.	Mount Gibbs	4 or 7–8	Strenuous	3	SE-E, NE, N	Winter, spring
58.	Mount Lewis	5.75 or 8.5	Strenuous	3	SE-E, NE, N	Winter, spring
59.	Mount Wood	5.25 or 9.5	Strenuous	3	E	Winter, spring
60.	The Negatives	4.5 or 8	Moderate to strenuous	3	NE, E, S	Winter, spring
61.	Carson Peak	4 or 6	Moderate to strenuous	3	N-NE, S-SE	Winter, spring
MAMMOTH LAKES TO ROCK CREEK						
62.	Sherwin Ridge: The Sherwins	2.6–5	Easy	2–3	N-NE	Winter, spring
63.	Mammoth Crest	6 or 7	Easy	2–3	N	Winter, spring
64.	Bloody Mountain	4.8 or 12	Moderate to very strenuous	4	N	Winter, spring
65.	Mount Morrison	4.5 or 7	Strenuous	2 or 4	E, N	Winter, spring
66.	Laurel Mountain	5 or 6	Strenuous	4	E-NE	Winter, spring
67.	Red Slate Mountain	16	Very strenuous	4–5	N	Winter, spring
68.	Esha Peak	6	Strenuous	3	NE, N-NW	Winter, spring

No.	Route	Roundtrip Distance (in miles)	Difficulty Level	Terrain Rating	Aspect	Best Season
69.	Mount Morgan North: Nevahbe Ridge	up to 8 or 12	Strenuous	3	E-NE	Winter, spring
70.	Mount Morgan South	9 or 15	Strenuous	3	N-NE	Winter, spring
71.	Mount Dade	9	Strenuous	2 or 4	N-NE	Spring
72.	Mount Abbott	9	Strenuous	3	NE	Spring
BISHOP AREA						
73.	Wheeler Crest: Scheelite Chute	4	Very strenuous	4	SE	Winter, spring
74.	Mount Tom	7	Very strenuous	4	E-NE	Winter, spring
75.	Basin Mountain	5 or 5.4	Strenuous	3	E-NE	Winter, spring
76.	Mount Humphreys	8.25	Strenuous	4	NE-N	Spring, early summer
77.	Mount Locke: Wahoo Gullies	4	Strenuous	2	NE, SE	Winter, spring, early summer
78.	Mount Emerson	6.5	Strenuous	4	N, NE	Winter, spring
79.	Mount Goethe	15	Very strenuous	4	N-NE	Late spring
80.	Mount Lamarck	10	Strenuous	2 or 4	N-NE, E	Winter, spring
81.	Mount Darwin	14	Very strenuous	3	N-NE, SW	Late spring
82.	Hurd Peak	5	Moderate	3	N	Late spring, early summer
83.	Mount Johnson	6.75	Strenuous	4	N-NE	Late spring
84.	Mount Gilbert	6.5	Strenuous	3 or 4	N-NE, E-NE	Late spring, early summer
85.	Mount Thompson	6.5	Strenuous	3–4	N-NE	Spring
PART V. SOUTHERN SIERRA						
86.	Kid Mountain	4	Strenuous	3	N, NW	Winter, spring
87.	North Palisade: U-notch; Polemonium Peak: V-notch	16	Very strenuous	4	N-NW	Winter, spring, early summer
88.	Thunderbolt Peak	16	Very strenuous	4	N-NW	Winter, spring, early summer
89.	Slide Mountain	6.5	Strenuous	3	E-SE	Winter, spring
90.	Norman Clyde Peak	10	Very strenuous	4	N-NE	Winter, spring
91.	Birch Mountain	7	Very strenuous	3	SE, E	Winter, spring

No.	Route	Roundtrip Distance (in miles)	Difficulty Level	Terrain Rating	Aspect	Best Season
92.	Split Mountain	9	Very strenuous	4–5	NE, E, SE	Winter, spring
93.	Independence Peak	3	Moderate	3	NE	Winter, spring
94.	University Peak	5.5	Strenuous	3	N-NE, E	Spring, early summer
95.	Mount Keith	17	Very strenuous	3	S	Winter, spring
96.	Mount Tyndall	19	Very strenuous	3	N, NE	Winter, spring
97.	Mount Whitney	8.5	Very strenuous	4	E	Winter, spring
98.	Mount Langley	11	Very strenuous	4	NE	Winter, spring
99.	Alta Peak and Pear Lake Hut	11	Strenuous	2–3	SE, N, E, NE; W, NW	Winter, spring

Heading up for another lap on a classic California bluebird day

INTRODUCTION

"Then it seemed to me the Sierra should be called not the Nevada, or Snowy Range, but the Range of Light...it seems to me above all others the Range of Light, the most divinely beautiful of all the mountain-chains I have seen."

—John Muir

YOU NEED ONLY TO READ JOHN MUIR'S *The Mountains of California* to gain a deeply passionate insight into and understanding of the beauty and diversity of the mountains in this great state. From the cone-shaped volcanoes of the southern Cascades in the north to the jagged and precipitous eastern escarpment of the Sierra in the south—and everything in between—an astounding number and incredible variety of mountains stretch uninterrupted for more than 500 miles.

Some of the best backcountry skiing and snowboarding anywhere can be found in the mountains of California. Each winter these ranges are blanketed in a glorious white coat of snow, creating a seemingly limitless backcountry ski and snowboard playground with something to suit everyone. In the north, the volcanoes offer long, wide-open pitches ranging from moderate gullies and bowls to steep faces and chutes. The northern Sierra around Lake Tahoe feature an abundance of bowls, glades, and chutes on pitches as mellow or as steep as you can handle. The High Sierra stretch toward the sky with numerous peaks over 14,000 feet and more terrain and descents than you could ever do in a lifetime.

Adventurous backcountry skiers have been laying tracks down California mountains since the 1960s, possibly even earlier, chronicled in the first published ski guidebook for the Sierra, H. J. Burhenne's *Sierra Spring Ski-Touring*, in 1971. Since then, the sport has continued to evolve and grow in popularity, but skiers still flock to the same mountains first skied over a half century ago.

This guidebook provides what I consider to be many of the finest routes and descents throughout the state. The reality is that these tours are just the tip of the iceberg, as there is no limit to the options and remote wilderness peaks in the sea of mountains that is the Sierra Nevada. Ease of access is one of my goals for including the routes described here, virtually all of which can and have been done in a single day, although many of them are well suited to more casual overnight adventures.

EDUCATION

In many ways, experience is the best teacher. Before you go out and experience the backcountry, however, there are quite a few things you should know. Take the time to educate yourself, and your ski partners, to help reduce your risk in the backcountry. For additional suggestions, see Resources at the back of this book.

- **Take an avalanche education course.** It is your responsibility to keep yourself and your ski partners safe in the backcountry. Therefore it is important that you learn about avalanche safety by taking an avalanche course. Various levels of avalanche education are available for those who are interested in learning more than the basics. Avalanche courses are offered every year throughout the state by various guide services, avalanche educators, even ski areas. Find a course near you and take it; you'll be glad you did.
- **Take a backcountry skills course.** Those just getting into backcountry skiing or snowboarding can usually benefit from an introductory backcountry skills course to learn simple things like using your equipment properly, hiking with backcountry gear, avalanche basics, routefinding, and more.
- **Take a first-aid course.** Injuries can and do happen, and in an uncontrolled backcountry environment, help is often a long way off. Knowing the basics of wilderness first aid could help you save both life and limb.
- **Read some books!** There are many books available to further your education on your own. Mountaineers Books has published numerous books that are excellent resources. *Backcountry Skiing: Skills for Ski Touring*

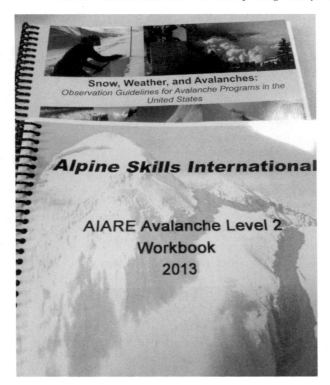

Avalanche education course materials

and Ski Mountaineering by Martin Volken, Scott Schell, and Margaret Wheeler details essential skills like backcountry ski and travel techniques, trip planning, terrain navigation, and avalanche safety. *Staying Alive in Avalanche Terrain* by Bruce Tremper provides detailed information about avalanche safety, including safe travel techniques and snow stability tests and assessment.

- **Practice what you've learned.** Skills like digging snow pits, assessing a snowpack, and searching with avalanche transceivers need to be practiced. Take refresher courses for first aid and avalanche education.

EQUIPMENT

Backcountry skiing equipment has evolved significantly since the 1960s and early 1970s when the sport began to gain popularity throughout the mountains of California. The leather boots, bear-trap bindings, firn gliders, and woolen knickers used back then are a far cry from the technologically advanced boots, bindings, skis, snowboards, and clothing used today. Modern equipment allows us to go farther, higher, and faster than ever before, and it continues to improve. From an equipment standpoint, there has never been a better time to be a backcountry skier or snowboarder. The following sections list gear you will need to get into the backcountry.

The Basics

- **Skis or snowboard:** Virtually any skis will do, but there are many options in various widths, weights, materials, and designs; get some that work for you. Splitboard technology has advanced significantly in recent years, and while some snowboarders still use snowshoes, it is recommended to use a splitboard to access the backcountry.
- **Bindings:** There are a variety of ski bindings with touring capabilities on the market today. Pin style, or "tech," bindings are the most popular and generally the most efficient for travel in the backcountry. Telemark ski bindings allow for uphill travel, and recent models include features for more efficient backcountry travel. Like the splitboards they are designed for, splitboard bindings have improved dramatically in the past several years for greater efficiency while hiking, better power transfer, and faster transitions.
- **Boots:** Almost any ski boot will work for backcountry skiing, assuming you have bindings that work with them; however, backcountry-specific boots with a walk mode, rubber soles, and tech fittings are preferred. Virtually any snowboard boot will work for splitboarding; some newer models have backcountry-specific features that make life easier in the mountains.
- **Poles:** Any poles will get you into the backcountry, although most people prefer adjustable poles with comfortable grips. Adjustable poles allow you to change your pole's length on the fly depending on the terrain you are traveling in. Snowboarders generally prefer poles that can be collapsed small enough to strap onto their packs for the descent.

Hiking toward Cascade Gulch, framed by Shastina (left) and Mount Shasta's west face (right) (Jon Rockwood)

- **Climbing skins:** Climbing skins stick to the bottoms of your skis or splitboard and provide traction so you can walk uphill when you use them correctly. The directional hairs of a climbing skin allow it to slide forward but grip the snow when pushed back. It is essential for your skins to be fitted to the length and width of your skis or splitboard for them to work properly. Skin wax should be applied regularly.
- **Backpack:** A sturdy and properly fitting backpack is an essential piece of backcountry equipment. Backcountry-specific packs typically have pockets or sleeves to organize your avalanche safety equipment and come in various sizes. Most packs also have a way to attach your skis or snowboard and an ice axe, a crucial feature when traveling in steeper terrain that requires boot-packing. Avalanche Airbag backpacks have been increasing in popularity, and while they are expensive, when used correctly they may help reduce your chances of injury or death in the event of an avalanche.
- **Avalanche safety equipment:** This includes an avalanche transceiver, shovel, and probe—and the knowledge to use them. Every member of a backcountry party must have this potentially lifesaving equipment and know how to use it. It could save your life, your friend's life, or that of someone you don't even know. Most avalanche shovels and probes are lightweight and collapse down small enough to fit inside your pack.

- **Clothing:** Waterproof outerwear, wicking base layers, midlayers, an emergency layer, hat, gloves, and properly fitting socks are all important for your comfort in the mountains.
- **Helmet:** It is a personal choice, but I always recommend wearing a helmet anytime you are skiing or snowboarding. Modern helmets are lightweight and stylish—and could save your life.
- **Cell phone:** Most of us don't go anywhere without our cell phones, but in addition to their many uses, they could be potentially lifesaving devices in an emergency. Cell phone coverage is often unreliable and in many cases nonexistent in the mountains of California, but that said, they do work in many places, and I am occasionally surprised by where I can get a signal. I recommend that you and your ski partners carry a cell phone as a form of emergency communication while in the backcountry. Although this form of communication may not be dependable, it could come in handy in an emergency situation.

The Ten Essentials

I consider the above list to be the basic items you will need to get out and enjoy the backcountry of California, but in addition to that, be sure to bring the Ten Essentials, as outlined by The Mountaineers:

1. **Navigation:** map, compass, altimeter, GPS receiver
2. **Sun protection:** sunglasses, sunscreen, goggles
3. **Insulation:** extra clothing
4. **Illumination:** headlamp or flashlight, plus extra batteries
5. **First-aid kit**
6. **Fire:** firestarter, matches or lighter
7. **Repair kit:** including a multitool
8. **Nutrition:** extra food
9. **Hydration:** extra water
10. **Emergency shelter**

Additional Items

- **Snow study kit:** This includes items used for digging snow pits, examining the snowpack, and recording observations—a snow saw, thermometers, a crystal card (a metal card printed with various-size grids that, used with a magnifying glass, helps you determine snow crystal size and type of grains) and loupe (magnifying glass) for examining snow crystals, and a notebook.
- **Crampons and ice axe:** Many routes described in this guidebook may require the use of crampons and/or an ice axe for safety.
- **Ski crampons:** These metal traction devices attach to many models of bindings and provide added grip in some snow conditions on the ascent.
- **Verts:** These small molded-plastic snowshoes are used by some for boot-packing in soft snow.

Crampons are essential to safely climb steep and firm snow like the kind found at the top of Dana Plateau's Cocaine Chute.

- **Voile Straps:** These rubber straps hold your skis together and are among the most useful things you can have in your pack, with applications from first aid to gear repair.
- **Overnight gear:** Several of the routes in this guidebook involve potentially spending the night camping in the mountains. What you bring is up to you, but here is a basic list of things that I bring: tent, sleeping pad, sleeping bag, camp stove, extra clothing layers, extra socks, and lots of food.

BACKCOUNTRY CONDITIONS

In addition to the items listed in the preceding section, it is always important to bring a healthy dose of common sense and good judgment with you every day. Good ski partners who share similar goals are nice to bring along as well. Of course, it is up to you what you ultimately bring with you; use your best judgment based on the weather, snow and avalanche conditions, and your planned route to bring the items you will need on any given foray into the backcountry.

Weather

The mountains of California are known for sunny days and relatively mild temperatures when compared with other mountainous regions of the west. Conditions in the mountains, however, can change very rapidly as the Sierra Nevada and the southern Cascades catch weather systems as they roll off the Pacific Ocean. Winter storms are often quite intense, with heavy snowfall sometimes accompanied by 100-plus-mile-per-hour winds, making backcountry travel difficult, dangerous, and sometimes impossible. The crest and western slope receive the most precipitation, whereas the rain-shadow effect decreases the totals significantly to the east. While temperatures are generally moderate, they vary wildly depending on the storm system, elevation, and your exposure to the sun and/or wind.

Weather plays the ultimate role in the snow conditions throughout the state and, therefore, is one of the main factors that should influence your route selection and decision making in the backcountry. Always check the weather to help you make informed decisions before heading out.

There are many sources for weather forecasts, but the National Weather Service (see Resources) is my primary source of weather information, with local and pinpoint forecasts, a weather discussion, and remote weather data. Regional avalanche forecasts also provide weather information and links to local weather resources.

Spring is a great time for overnight camping deeper into a range. (Oscar Havens)

The Sierra crest is prone to strong storms with high winds.

Avalanche Information

California's snowpack is known for being generally more stable and "safer" than other places in the western United States. While this is often true, it also gives people a false sense of security. Every storm brings with it an avalanche cycle in which natural and human-triggered avalanches may occur, especially during and immediately following storms. Everything from small to catastrophic avalanches are possible and may cause injury or even death.

Snow and avalanche conditions vary significantly throughout the regions and routes described in this book. Regional avalanche centers do their best to provide backcountry users with current avalanche information. Avalanche advisories and observations should be checked regularly as part of your information-gathering and decision-making process.

There are three avalanche centers in the state of California, each providing an avalanche advisory, observations, and weather information for each region (see Resources):

- **Eastern Sierra Avalanche Center:** Covers the region from Lee Vining to Bishop on the eastern side of the Sierra
- **Mount Shasta Avalanche Center:** Covers the greater Mount Shasta area
- **Sierra Avalanche Center:** Covers the Lake Tahoe region from Yuba Pass in the north to Ebbetts Pass in the south

Snowpack

California is known for having a maritime snowpack characterized by frequent heavy storms and relatively warm temperatures, resulting in a deep snowpack with cohesive layers. This very broad generalization is not always the case, as the weather, snowpack depth, and stability vary wildly from year to year and region to region. For example, the winter of 2010–11 had the thickest snowpack in the last 25 years, while the winter of 2014–15 had the lowest snowpack on record, and barely any of the routes in this guidebook were skiable at any point during that season.

The snow line is also an important factor that often comes into play for many of the routes described in this guidebook. The elevation of the snow line is temperature dependent and varies for each storm and season. For example, some years you may be able to drive to the top of Buttermilk Road outside of Bishop to 8000-plus feet all winter long, while in others you may have to wait until late April or early May to reach the same point by vehicle.

Snow Conditions

Perfect snow is one of the reasons to venture into the backcountry, and while that is usually the goal, it isn't always the reality. Snow surface conditions in the backcountry can be quite variable, ranging from deep powder or perfect California corn

The southern portion of the Sierra—10,000 feet from the summit to the Owens Valley far below

It's hard not to get fired up while skiing in the Sierra, especially after a 7000-foot corn run!

to solid ice or breakable wind-board. While some people refer to California's snow as "Sierra cement" due to the often high water content, those who live and play in the mountains throughout the state know that while it is sometimes the case, it often is not. One thing you can usually count on is that the world-renowned corn cycle each spring, and sometimes midwinter during extended periods of high pressure, doesn't get much better.

Many factors influence the snow conditions in the California backcountry, and it is in a constant state of flux due to the effects of precipitation, temperature, solar radiation, and wind. Conditions vary wildly on different aspects (a slope's position facing a particular direction, such as north or south), at different elevations, from day to day, and from one storm to the next. Learn the differences between various aspects and always hope for the best but be prepared for the worst.

ROAD CONDITIONS AND FEES

Road closures occur frequently in the mountains of California during winter storms. Interstate 80, US Highway 50, CA 88, and NV 431 near Lake Tahoe are often subject to chain restrictions or closure during winter weather. Many other roads throughout the state close for the winter and reopen in the spring or early summer. Tioga Pass (CA 120), Sonora Pass (CA 108), and Ebbetts Pass (CA 4) all cross the rugged Sierra Nevada and close seasonally, around the first snowfall of the winter season, and reopen when the snowpack and weather allow, typically late spring or early summer. The Lassen Peak Highway (CA 89) bisects Lassen Volcanic National Park and is closed for the winter between the southwest park entrance and the north park entrance. The California Department of Transportation (see Resources) is the best source of the most current information for all major roads throughout the state.

Other less-major roads and highways used to access routes in this guidebook may be closed or not maintained in the winter, especially around Mount Shasta and the eastern Sierra. Many of these roads have "soft" closures, meaning you can drive to the snow line, even in winter, while others have "firm" closures and locked gates. Many roads in the eastern Sierra are reopened and maintained for the summer season for "Fishmas," opening day of the fishing season, typically the last Saturday in April. Dirt roads used for access are generally not cleared of snow, and access varies greatly from year to year depending on the season's snowpack.

Parking

For the most part, there are no parking fees for the routes described in this guidebook. Several of the routes, however, do start from a Sno-Park, where a permit is required, and this information is detailed in the Getting There section of those routes. Sno-Park permits can be purchased for daily and seasonal rates and are available for purchase online or at various local retailers (see Resources). If you are entering a national park, you will need to pay the entry fee or purchase an annual pass.

Parking has been and continues to be an occasionally contentious issue in the Tahoe area. Parking on area roadways, especially during periods of snow removal, is not allowed from November 1 through May 1. Always park completely off the road and be respectful of private property; do not block any gates or driveways. Parking for some of the routes described in this book is somewhat limited, so please be courteous and leave as much space as possible for others to park so they can enjoy the mountains.

Permits

Permits are required for backcountry travel in certain areas throughout the state of California and for entering wilderness areas in the Sierra year-round. Many of the routes in this book are located in the state's numerous federal wilderness areas. Backcountry permits can be acquired free of charge from the nearest US Forest Service ranger station. See Resources for the relevant USFS website or stop by the nearest ranger station.

Some of this book's routes enter a few of California's national parks, which require entrance fees payable at the park entrance stations. A summit pass is required for anyone traveling above 10,000 feet on Mount Shasta, available at any of the Shasta area's major trailheads.

For overnight and day trips into the Mount Whitney zone (Route 97), permits are required and can be obtained at the Eastern Sierra Interagency Visitor Center located at the junction of US 395 and CA 136, 1 mile south of Lone Pine, California. Between May 1 and October 31, permits are limited by quotas and can be reserved online at www.recreation.gov. Between November 1 and April 30, permits can be self-issued at the kiosk outside the visitor center.

BACKCOUNTRY SKIING ETIQUETTE

Getting into the backcountry means getting away from the rules and restrictions of everyday life; however, with the ever-increasing popularity of backcountry skiing and snowboarding, it is important that we follow basic etiquette to keep ourselves and others safe and happy.

First and foremost, be respectful of others. This involves not only being nice to people, but being aware of others and how your actions could affect them. If you kick off a cornice or cause an avalanche, could it harm people who may be below you? If someone is hiking faster than you, let them pass. Do not boot-pack, snowshoe, or urinate in the skin track. Control your dog and clean up after it as necessary.

Practice the seven principles of Leave No Trace outdoor ethics:

1. Plan ahead and prepare.
2. Travel and camp on durable surfaces (or snow).
3. Dispose of waste properly: if you pack it in, pack it out.
4. Leave what you find.
5. Minimize campfire impacts.
6. Respect wildlife.
7. Be considerate of others.

HOW TO USE THIS BOOK

THE ROUTES DESCRIBED IN THIS GUIDEBOOK are appropriate for both skiers and snowboarders, assuming that snowboarders are using splitboards with skins. With modern backcountry ski and splitboard technology, the two styles of backcountry travel are more similar than they have ever been, and there is no longer a reason to differentiate between the two.

Routes in this guidebook are grouped into parts by mountain ranges or other large landforms and into geographic regions within each part, starting with the Cascades and Mount Shasta in the north and ending with the southwestern Sierra and Alta Peak in Sequoia National Park. Each geographic region's overview outlines skiing opportunities, amenities, access, and general information about the area.

Each route description begins with an information block that includes a summary of information about the route, followed by an overview of the route's highlights, directions to the trailhead or starting point, a detailed route description, and a map.

Starting Point: The ideal starting point and its elevation are listed. In many cases, where you start a route varies based on the current snowpack. Details are listed under Getting There in the route description.

High Point: The summit elevation or high point of the route is given in feet.

Distance: The approximate roundtrip distance is listed in miles from the ideal starting point.

Elevation Gain: The total elevation gain is given in vertical feet from the ideal starting point to the high point.

Time: A rough time estimate is based on my own experience and the experiences of others. This estimate is an average time to complete the route, and it may take you more or less time. Many variables may affect your speed, including weather, snow conditions, rest stops, equipment issues, and the speed of people in your group.

Difficulty Level: A rating representing the effort the route requires is based on a combination of both distance and elevation gain. This rating is, of course, subjective due to factors such as your fitness, hiking speed, the elevation, snow conditions, and weather. Routes may not always fall squarely into these difficulty-rating parameters; in cases where the vertical gain and mileage fall into different ratings, the route is classified generally as the harder of the two. Occasionally a route will have two difficulty ratings, depending where you can start, potentially adding distance and vertical gain to the route. The following are the four difficulty ratings used in this guidebook to differentiate between routes:

Easy: Less than 2000 vertical feet of gain and up to 4 miles.

Moderate: Between 2000 and 3500 vertical feet of gain and 4 to 6 miles.

Strenuous: Between 3500 and 5500 vertical feet of gain and 6 to 10 miles.

Very strenuous: Over 5500 vertical feet of gain and over 10 miles.

Terrain Rating: This difficulty rating is based on the steepness and complexity of the terrain, potential avalanche hazard, exposure, commitment level (distance traveled from the trailhead and difficulty of turning back once you are at a route's high point), technical difficulty, and routefinding. It is a challenge to rate or define the terrain difficulty of any particular route. Difficulty is subjective, differing from person to person and in varying weather and snow conditions. Terrain ratings range from 1 to 5, with 1 being the easiest and 5 the most difficult. Some routes show more than one terrain rating if multiple descent options have differing difficulty levels.

    1: Very moderate terrain with few objective hazards like rocks and trees and generally lower avalanche hazard. Low risk in the event of a fall. Easy routefinding and hiking. Very near the trailhead.

    2: Slightly steeper terrain with more objective hazards like rocks and trees and and increased avalanche potential. More-challenging hiking and some routefinding. Close to the trailhead.

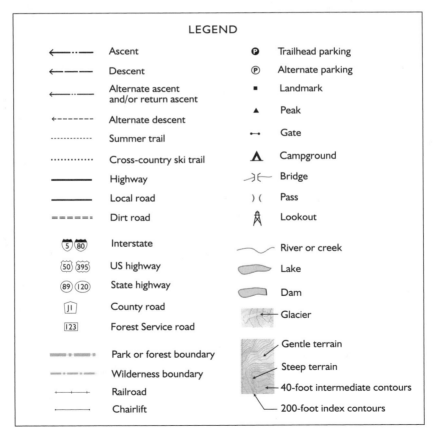

LEGEND

←––··––	Ascent	℗	Trailhead parking
←––––	Descent	℗	Alternate parking
←––··––	Alternate ascent and/or return ascent	■	Landmark
←–––––––	Alternate descent	▲	Peak
·············	Summer trail	↔	Gate
··············	Cross-country ski trail	▲	Campground
––––––	Highway	)⊢	Bridge
––––––	Local road	) (	Pass
======	Dirt road	🔭	Lookout
⑤ ⑧⓪	Interstate	～	River or creek
㊿ ㉟⑨⑤	US highway	⬭	Lake
⑧⑨ ①②⓪	State highway	⬭	Dam
⌷J1⌷	County road		Glacier
⌷123⌷	Forest Service road		
–·–·–·–	Park or forest boundary		Gentle terrain
–·–·–·–	Wilderness boundary		Steep terrain
⊢–––⊢–	Railroad		40-foot intermediate contours
––––––	Chairlift		200-foot index contours

3: The most common terrain, right in the sweet spot of pitch for great skiing and avalanche potential. Larger terrain features include chutes, bowls, cliffs, trees, rocks, cornices, etc. More-difficult hiking, some easy boot-packing, and routefinding skills may be required. Falls may result in injury. Slightly farther from the trailhead.

4: Steeper terrain where a fall would most likely result in injury and possibly even death. Some exposure and complex terrain features; use of ice axe and crampons is probably necessary. Lots of avalanche hazards; farther from the trailhead.

5: Very steep and exposed terrain that requires a very high skill level to negotiate, where a fall would almost certainly be fatal. Many complex terrain features; far from the trailhead. Use of an ice axe and crampons and potentially more-advanced rope or technical skills are typically involved.

Aspect: This provides the cardinal aspect (major compass direction the slope faces) of the primary route. For some routes, this may include several aspects or a range of aspects. Other aspect information may also be listed in the route's description. Aspect is an important piece of information that may assist in route selection based on snow and weather conditions. Aspects separated by hyphens are aspects you may encounter during the ascent/descent of a route. Aspects separated by commas are for separate ascent/descent routes which are likely near each other but may be, for example, separated by a ridge or other feature.

Season: This is approximately the best season to attempt a route.

Maps: The USGS maps (all the 7.5-minute series) of the featured route are listed.

After the information block, a brief summary of the route gives you a general idea of what to expect: highlights of the route and the area, any special challenges, when conditions are best, and the like. Getting There covers detailed directions to reach the ideal trailhead or starting point of the route from the nearest town or major road. And finally, there is a detailed description of the route from the starting point to the end. This section also details alternate ascent and/or descent options and ways to extend the tour (listed under an "Options" heading).

The incredible terrain, climate, snowfall, and weather throughout the state combine to create an ideal environment for exploration and recreation in California's mountains. Consider the routes in this guidebook as a starting point, a list of some of the finest routes the state has to offer, but know that there is virtually no limit to the backcountry skiing possibilities. I hope this guidebook provides you with the information to get out and enjoy the mountains and inspires you to continue to explore.

A NOTE ABOUT SAFETY

Please use common sense. This book is not intended as a substitute for careful planning, professional training, or your own good judgment. It is incumbent upon any user of this guide to assess his or her own skills, experience, fitness, and equipment. Readers will recognize the inherent dangers in skiing, snowboarding, and backcountry terrain and assume responsibility for their own actions and safety.

Changing or unfavorable conditions in weather, roads, trails, waterways, etc., cannot be anticipated by the author or publisher but should be considered by any outdoor participants, as routes may become dangerous or slopes unstable due to such altered conditions. Likewise, be aware of any changes in public jurisdiction, and do not access private property without permission. The publisher and author are not responsible for any adverse consequences resulting directly or indirectly from information contained in this book.

—Mountaineers Books

Opposite: *Topping out above the clouds near the summit of Mount Shasta's east face*

PART I
SOUTHERN CASCADES

THE SOUTHERN END OF THE CASCADE RANGE extends into Northern California, where the impressive cones of Lassen Peak and Mount Shasta are the most obvious examples of these volcanic mountains. Part of the Pacific Ring of Fire, the Cascade volcanoes extend north from California through Oregon and Washington and up into British Columbia, Canada. Mount Shasta stands behind Mount Rainier as the second-highest Cascade volcano, and Shastina, Mount Shasta's subpeak, would be the third highest if it stood on its own.

Mount Shasta last erupted in the late 1700s, while Lassen's most recent eruption was from 1914 to 1917, prompting Congress to create Lassen Volcanic National Park. Volcanically speaking, Lassen Peak is still considered active, while Mount Shasta is thought to be potentially active.

The quality of the ski terrain on these mountains is incredibly high. The peaks of the southern Cascades are also weather magnets, standing high above the surrounding terrain and catching powerful winter storms that create some of the deepest snowpacks in the state. As a result, excellent ski conditions can exist on these mountains all winter long and well into summer in most years. Climbing and skiing on a volcano is a truly unique experience that absolutely should not be missed.

MOUNT SHASTA

Northern California's Mount Shasta is the fifth-highest mountain in the state of California. Rising up to 14,162 feet, Mount Shasta towers more than 10,000 feet above the surrounding terrain and the new-age outdoor mecca of the City of Mount Shasta. Flanked by 12,330-foot Shastina to the northwest, this massive mountain has incredible ski terrain on all sides. Backcountry skiing pilgrimages to Mount Shasta most often occur in the spring and early summer, but excellent early and midwinter skiing can be found here as well. The Everitt Memorial Highway provides year-round access to the Bunny Flat trailhead, so you can always get on the mountain when roads to other trailheads may be snowbound for miles. Access to other wilderness trailheads on Mount Shasta, such as Brewer Creek, opens up as the snow recedes, typically in late spring or early summer.

The City of Mount Shasta sits at the junction of Interstate 5 and CA 89, so getting to and from Mount Shasta is relatively painless. The town is a hotbed for adventurous outdoor enthusiasts, retirees, and new-age enthusiasts. Mount Shasta, considered by many to be an energy vortex, draws people for tours and various spiritual purposes. The City of Mount Shasta has plenty of restaurants, lodging, gas, groceries, outdoor gear stores, and crystal shops for refueling or resting before or after a long day on the mountain.

Mount Shasta is a weather magnet, and strong winter storms are often accompanied by strong and damaging winds. Several feet of snow at a time are quite common, and Mount Shasta's deep snowpack feeds its seven named glaciers. The mountain is known for its legendary winds as well as the UFO-shaped lenticular clouds that often form above or on its summit. That said, there is no lack of calm days to get out and enjoy the mountain.

Before you head up onto Mount Shasta, you must obtain a free wilderness permit at any of the wilderness trailheads. Anyone climbing above 10,000 feet must purchase a summit pass, valid for three days ($25 per person as of 2016), available at any of the trailheads or the Mount Shasta or McCloud US Forest Service ranger stations; an annual pass for $30 is available only at the Mount Shasta or McCloud ranger stations and the Fifth Season store in the City of Mount Shasta—please bring correct change or a personal check. Keep the summit-pass stub with you as well as the green copy of your wilderness permit. There are currently no parking or camping fees and no reservations required for camping or climbing on the mountain except at Horse Camp ($5 per tent payable to the Sierra Club).

Spring and summer weekends on the mountain can be extremely busy, so plan a trip for midweek if possible. While at the trailhead, be sure to use the facilities and grab a human waste kit, as no human waste may be left on the mountain. The human waste kit provided by the Forest Service consists of a resealable plastic bag, some kitty litter, and a paper target to facilitate packing out your feces. As gross as that may sound, just imagine how disgusting the mountain would be if the tens of thousands of climbers per year left their poop on the mountain. Also, for all you dog people, there are no dogs allowed in the Mount Shasta Wilderness.

The Mount Shasta Avalanche Center (see Resources) provides regular avalanche advisories for Mount Shasta and the surrounding area. Shasta Mountain Guides (see Resources) is a local company offering guided single-day or overnight mountaineering and backcountry skiing trips on and around Mount Shasta.

1   Mount Shasta: Avalanche Gulch

Starting Point	Bunny Flat trailhead, 6950 feet
High Point	14,162 feet
Distance	11 miles
Elevation Gain	7200 feet
Time	6 hours to 2 days
Difficulty Level	Very strenuous
Terrain Rating	3
Aspect	South-southwest-west
Seasons	Spring, early summer
Maps	USGS Mount Shasta; McCloud

A late-spring or early summer ski of Mount Shasta's southwest face, or Avalanche Gulch, became an annual rite of passage for me over a decade ago. Since the Everitt Memorial Highway is cleared of snow to the Bunny Flat trailhead year-round, you can count on relatively easy access and a minimal approach no matter when you attempt this route. For the same reason, this route is also one of the most popular for guided and unguided mountaineering trips; on busy weekends during climbing season, you might see several hundred people climbing or glissading the slopes of Avy Gulch. Depending on the season's snowpack and the weather, conditions can be prime anytime from mid-April through June on this side of Mount Shasta. The best corn runs of many people's lives have been experienced on these slopes that rise high above the City of Mount Shasta. Depending on your fitness level and your aversion to pain, a jaunt to the summit of Shasta and back can take as few as six hours or up to two or more days. For a day trip, skiers generally start in the dark, with the goal of descending around midday when the corn is most likely to be ripened to perfection. It is not uncommon for slower groups to start as early as 2:00 AM, while much faster hikers may begin the ascent at first light. People who spend the night on the mountain generally do so at Helen Lake (10,443 feet). This nice, flat camping area is almost exactly halfway up the mountain, splitting up the effort of the ascent very nicely.

GETTING THERE

From the central Mount Shasta exit off Interstate 5, turn northeast onto West Lake Boulevard (Everitt Memorial Highway, A-10). Follow this road through town and past the sports fields, then continue uphill for 11 miles and nearly 3000 vertical feet to the Bunny Flat trailhead.

THE ROUTE

Once you've gotten your permits at the trailhead, the trickiest part of the routefinding, in my opinion, is right out of the parking lot. Starting from the toilets and permit kiosk, head north along the western edge of the "bunny flat"; a low ridgeline is immediately to climber's left. If there is no snow on the ground, the summer trail will be visible; if there is snow on the ground, there will probably be a multitude of tracks to follow. Stay on the west edge of the flats for a little less than 0.25 mile, then cross west over the ridgeline, now on climber's right (east) as you ascend. Stay at the bottom of the ridge's slope; no sidehilling is necessary.

Continue northeast while ascending gently through the trees, staying in the bottom of the gully that slowly becomes more and more pronounced. After about a mile, the trees begin to open up, and you'll have a view of Avalanche Gulch. When you hit the tree line, at roughly 7800 feet, Horse Camp is just off to climber's left in the trees. Looking up the mountain, your route should be clearly visible, framed in by Green Butte Ridge on climber's right and Casaval Ridge on climber's left.

From here, the top of the Red Banks may seem relatively close, but in reality it still sits more than 5000 vertical feet away. Now you have the option of going to climber's right or left of the massive moraine that splits the gulch from Horse Camp to Helen Lake. In my experience, the routes are relatively equal in distance, effort, and time, and either way will eventually get you up to Helen Lake (10,443 feet). Depending on snow conditions, it may be possible to climb on skins to Helen Lake or as high as

Hiking up the bottom of Avalanche Gulch shortly after sunrise

the Red Banks. Once skinning becomes a struggle, however, I am quick to switch to boot-packing and crampons both for safety and efficiency.

From Helen Lake, the route ascends more steeply toward the Red Banks, the aptly named diagonal reddish cliff band, and Thumb Rock. Generally people aim for a saddle slightly to climber's right, between Thumb Rock and the Red Banks. Be especially wary of falling rock and ice during this part of the climb because loose rime ice and rocks are prone to falling from the Red Banks as the day progresses and temperatures increase and there are likely to be others climbing above you. Climb one of the narrow chimneys and onto the top of the Red Banks. Continue along the ridge to a bench at the bottom of Misery Hill (13,200 feet).

Here you are about 1000 vertical feet from the summit; the top of the Trinity Chutes and the west face are just a short distance to the west, and the best skiing starts from here. As you climb Misery Hill, the top of the Konwokiton Glacier is to climber's right; take note, as you will descend this short portion of the Konwokiton on your way back down to the top of the Red Banks.

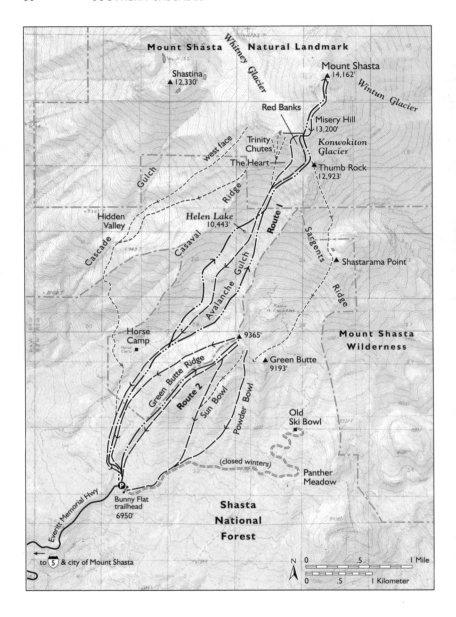

Once you crest the top of Misery Hill, a large, flat plateau that I like to call the Football Field leads to the final short push to the summit. Take in the views of the Whitney Glacier and Shastina to the northwest. Enjoy the relatively easy, flat walking on the plateau to the final scramble up to the summit of Mount Shasta. Be prepared for the smell of rotten eggs since an active fumarole emits its sulfurous gases just below the summit. The final push up onto the summit is on a mixture of rock and rime ice, and skiing off the true summit isn't recommended on this side of the mountain.

After snapping the mandatory summit photos, scramble back down to the plateau and cross it back to the top of Misery Hill. I recommend descending the top of the Konwokiton Glacier just to the skier's left of where you hiked up Misery Hill as there is usually better snow coverage; make sure to cross back over to the top of the Red Banks just a few hundred feet below. Most people typically drop into the Heart, between the Trinity Chutes and the Red Banks, since this is the most straightforward way back down the mountain. Be warned that the pitch from the top of the Red Banks to Helen Lake is sustained for 2500 vertical feet; a fall in this area could result in a very long uncontrollable slide.

Other descent options exist for savvy routefinders and experts, including the Trinity Chutes and the Hidden Valley (west face), or a more advanced descent linkup from the Thumb to Shastarama Point and Green Butte (Route 2). Ideally, if your timing and the weather cooperate, the snow will be a perfect blanket of velvet for the entire run back to the trailhead. Work the terrain to find the right aspect for the best snow conditions; the bottom of the gullies are typically the least smooth since most people hike and glissade in the path of least resistance. As the terrain begins to flatten out, pay close attention to retrace your route to the trailhead.

2 Green Butte

Starting Point	Bunny Flat trailhead, 6950 feet
High Point	9365 feet
Distance	3 miles
Elevation Gain	2400 feet
Time	1.5 hours
Difficulty Level	Moderate
Terrain Ratings	Green Butte Ridge 2; Sun and Powder bowls 3
Aspect	South-southwest-west
Seasons	Winter, spring, early summer
Maps	USGS McCloud; Mount Shasta

Mount Shasta is known for its huge vertical and long ski runs, but not every tour on the mountain needs to be an all-day sufferfest. There are a multitude of ways to get your feet wet on Mount Shasta without jumping all the way into a summit attempt. Many local and visiting skiers often spend their days lapping some of the lower, closer, and easier-access terrain located just above the Bunny Flat trailhead. One of these is Green Butte, at the bottom of the ridge that separates Avalanche Gulch from the Old Ski Bowl, and this ridge is a 2400-foot prominence that offers great skiing on numerous aspects. There are several descent options off of Green Butte: Powder Bowl, Sun Bowl, the Green Butte Ridge, and the west-facing slopes back down into

Skiing down Powder Bowl in silky smooth corn snow during late spring

Avy Gulch. The Everitt Memorial Highway is closed at the Bunny Flat trailhead during the winter, but the unplowed portion of the road makes for another obvious route out of this zone. Snowmobilers use this road to access the Old Ski Bowl, which closed in 1978 after an avalanche destroyed most of the lifts, and it is now the only part of the mountain above the tree line that allows motorized recreation.

GETTING THERE

From the central Mount Shasta exit off Interstate 5, turn northeast onto West Lake Boulevard (Everitt Memorial Highway, A-10). Follow this road through town and past the sports fields, then continue uphill for 11 miles and nearly 3000 vertical feet to the Bunny Flat trailhead.

THE ROUTE

The top of Green Butte is clearly visible from the Bunny Flat trailhead. Given decent snow coverage, the route up to the top couldn't be any easier. Simply head northeast through Bunny Flat and into the forest, ascending a moderate pitch along the Green Butte Ridge all the way to the top. About halfway up, you exit the forest, but the route remains moderately pitched to the top.

As you climb, you will have incredible views of Avalanche Gulch and Casaval Ridge to climber's left. Once at the top, you will get a view into the Old Ski Bowl to the southeast and the wealth of terrain that exists between the Green Butte Ridge and Shastarama Point.

The Green Butte Ridge that you just climbed offers the easiest and most straight-forward descent back to the trailhead. The west-facing slopes off of Green Butte Ridge have some great pitches that deposit you into Avalanche Gulch near Horse Camp. From here you follow Avalanche Gulch down, eventually wrapping around the bottom of the Green Butte Ridge back to Bunny Flat.

Sun Bowl is the first large bowl to the east of the Green Butte Ridge, and Powder Bowl is the next bowl to the east of that. Both of these south-facing bowls are relatively steep at the top but become progressively mellower as you descend. The far eastern edge of the ridgeline at the top of Powder Bowl is Green Butte proper (9193 feet), a large cliff above the Old Ski Bowl. After descending either Sun Bowl or Powder Bowl, continue downhill until you hit the snow-covered upper portion of Everitt Memorial Highway, then follow it west back to the trailhead.

3   Shastina: Cascade Gulch

Starting Point	Bunny Flat trailhead, 6950 feet
High Point	12,330 feet
Distance	10 miles
Elevation Gain	5490 feet
Time	6 hours to 2 days
Difficulty Level	Strenuous
Terrain Rating:	2
Aspect	South-southwest
Seasons	Spring, early summer
Map	USGS Mount Shasta

Shastina's location as a subpeak on Mount Shasta's northwest flank makes it an often-overlooked backcountry gem. While it is nearly 2000 vertical feet shorter than Mount Shasta, Shastina is actually the third-tallest Cascade volcano in the United States, and if it stood alone, it would likely draw more attention than it does. In fact, there is incredible terrain on all sides of Shastina, with year-round access from the Bunny Flat trailhead. The most easily accessible route on Shastina is Cascade Gulch, a large, moderately pitched southwest-facing gully formed where Shastina and Mount Shasta meet, rising for 2700 vertical feet above Hidden Valley. Overall the route is relatively simple, following Avalanche Gulch (Route 1) to Horse Camp, then contouring uphill around the bottom of Casaval Ridge and into Hidden Valley and following Cascade Gulch to a saddle just east of Shastina's summit crater. As a day trip, this route is quite long, with lots of vertical gain; however, the effort can be

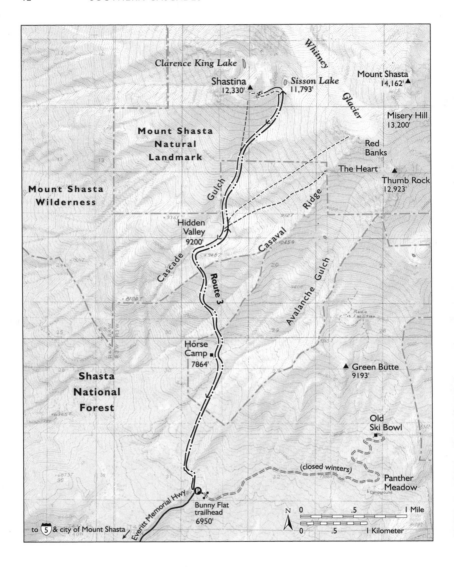

minimized by camping in Hidden Valley, a great option for those looking to spend some time exploring the wealth of possibilities on this side of the mountain.

GETTING THERE

From the central Mount Shasta exit off Interstate 5, turn northeast onto West Lake Boulevard (Everitt Memorial Highway, A-10). Follow this road through town and past the sports fields, then continue uphill for 11 miles and nearly 3000 vertical feet to the Bunny Flat trailhead.

THE ROUTE

Starting from the toilets and permit kiosk, head north along the western edge of the "bunny flat," following the Avalanche Gulch route (Route 1) to the tree line (roughly 7800 feet), with Horse Camp just off to climber's left in the trees. Horse Camp (7864 feet), which has a pit toilet and spring water, is often the first camp that groups use to climb the mountain on multiday trips.

From Horse Camp you leave Avalanche Gulch, and the hordes of people you are likely to see here, and head north for 1.25 miles and 1400 vertical feet, contouring the broad end of Casaval Ridge uphill and into Hidden Valley (9200 feet), below Shasta's west face and Cascade Gulch. Hidden Valley is a great spot to set up a base camp for overnight trips. From Hidden Valley, the large and moderately pitched Cascade Gulch rises above you to the northeast.

Head northeast and ascend this massive gully for 2700 vertical feet over 1.75 miles to the saddle at the top of the gulch by Sisson Lake (11,793 feet). From here the summit of Shastina sits a short 0.4 mile and 500 vertical feet to the west. Shastina's summit is part of a large volcanic crater that creates a rim above Clarence King Lake. There is fantastic skiing on all aspects of Shastina, so those with a great sense of direction, lots of energy, and a love for adventure may want to explore one of the other great pitches down the north or west sides of the mountain.

After hanging out on the summit, enjoy the long run back down Cascade Gulch to Hidden Valley, then return to Horse Camp and the trailhead by following your approach route in reverse.

Base camp in Hidden Valley at the bottom of Mount Shasta's west face (right) and Shastina (left) (Jon Rockwood)

4 Mount Shasta: Brewer Creek

Starting Point	Brewer Creek trailhead, 7285 feet
High Point	14,162 feet
Distance	11 miles
Elevation Gain	6900 feet
Time	6 hours to 2 days
Difficulty Level	Very strenuous
Terrain Rating	3
Aspect	East
Seasons	Late spring, early summer
Map	USGS Mount Shasta

Most people have given up on skiing or snowboarding for the season by the time the road to the Brewer Creek trailhead melts out. In late June and early July, while much of the rest of the state of California is in the grip of summer heat, 7000-foot runs are still ripe for the picking on the east side of Mount Shasta. With 4000 feet of uninterrupted fall-line skiing down the Wintun Glacier directly off the summit, this is bound to be one of the best runs you'll ever take in the month of June or July, a perfect way to cap off a backcountry season. As with the other side of the mountain, this route can take as few as six hours round-trip or be done more casually as an overnight. There are, however, no established camping areas on this side of the mountain, although a number of flat areas are suitable for those looking to spend the night.

GETTING THERE

From the City of Mount Shasta at Interstate 5, take CA 89 east to the town of McCloud. Just east of town, turn north onto Pilgrim Creek Road (Forest Road 13). After 7 miles, turn left on FR 19 and follow signs to Brewer Creek trailhead if there are any. Stay on FR 19 for 5.5 miles, then turn left toward Military Pass Road. After 1.5 miles you'll merge with Military Pass Road; continue on this for 2.6 miles, then turn left on Brewer Creek Road. Continue uphill on Brewer Creek Road as it begins to steepen; drive around a few switchbacks as you ascend. Hopefully, you'll make it all the way to the actual trailhead; otherwise, you may be blocked by snow farther down the road, adding some distance and vertical gain to your approach.

THE ROUTE

Get your permits at the trailhead, then begin your straightforward ascent of the east side of Mount Shasta. The terrain near the trailhead is sparsely tree covered, but you will have filtered views of the mountain between your car and tree line. If you're lucky and there is good snow coverage near the trailhead, get on your skins as soon as possible and take a direct route. If there isn't any snow at the trailhead, follow the

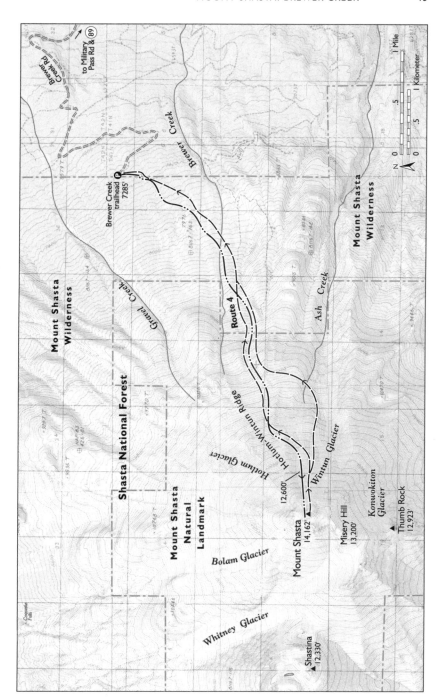

Making turns thousands of feet below Mount Shasta's eastern summit

summer trail. The trail is less direct than walking in a straight line on snow, but it is very easy to follow as it makes its way to the tree line and snow coverage.

From the trailhead you head west-southwest, and not far from the trailhead the trees begin to thin as you eventually hit tree line. From here you'll be able to see your route very clearly. Straight in front of you lies the Hotlum-Wintun Ridge, named for the glaciers that flank it on either side. Head directly toward this ridge and ascend climber's right side of its crest. The Hotlum-Wintun Ridge climbs steadily uphill, getting progressively steeper until cliffs block it at around 12,600 feet. At this point, traverse to climber's left onto the Wintun Glacier and into the bottom of the chute that you climb directly to the summit of Mount Shasta. It is typically necessary to switch to boot-packing and/or crampons in the steeper terrain on the upper part of this route.

Take in the panoramic summit views, snap some pics, then buckle down or strap in for the massive descent that awaits. If your timing is right (I usually aim for noonish), you'll have 6900 feet of perfect corn below you. You can ski nearly 4000 vertical feet of uninterrupted fall line down the Wintun Glacier directly from the summit. Stay just to skier's right of the Hotlum-Wintun Ridge once you exit the chute. The slope eventually benches out around 10,400 feet, where you traverse to skier's left and back to the route you ascended. You can also descend the chute from the summit to the same place where you crossed back to the ridge on the way up—cross to skier's left and follow the ascent route back to tree line.

Pay close attention as you get back down toward the tree line since the topography and terrain look very similar. Retrace your route to return to your starting location. If you use GPS, you may find it helpful to mark the trailhead to facilitate a more direct return to the car.

LASSEN VOLCANIC NATIONAL PARK

At 10,457 feet, cone-shaped Lassen Peak stands proudly as the centerpiece of Lassen Volcanic National Park, one of the least visited national parks in the country. The southernmost active volcano in the Cascade Range, Mount Lassen most recently erupted from 1914 to 1917, creating the Devastated Area—one of the finest descents on the mountain, via the northeast face. All aspects of Mount Lassen offer fine ski terrain in a spectacular spring and early summer skiing destination. With about half the vertical and effort of nearby Mount Shasta, California's smaller volcano still boasts 3000-foot-plus descents and skiing well into July in big snow years, as do the lower surrounding mountains such as Brokeoff Mountain and Mount Diller. The area around Lassen Peak remains geothermally active, with fumaroles and bubbling mud pots as some of the main attractions within the park.

Lassen Volcanic National Park is accessed from Interstate 5 at Redding by CA 44 and CA 89. The nearest towns are Old Station on CA 89 in the north and Chester on CA 36 in the south. Amenities are limited in these small towns, but gas and basic food supplies are available. Slightly farther from the park, the larger towns of Quincy to the south on CA 70/CA 89 and Susanville to the east on CA 44, or Redding and Red Bluff to the west on I-5, have everything you could ever need.

Spring and early summer are the best times to ski in Lassen Volcanic National Park, although in midwinter the southwest entrance station allows access to the terrain on Brokeoff Mountain and the variety of mellow bowls on the ridge of Mount Diller to Pilot Pinnacle.

The main park road, Lassen Peak Highway (CA 89), bisects the park from north to south and tops out at 8512 feet at the Summit trailhead and the Lassen Peak summer trail. CA 89 is closed between the north and south entrances to the park seasonally due to snow and reopens in the late spring or early summer as conditions allow. Deep drifts of snow on the upper reaches of the road may keep the road closed well into July. Portions of the road may reopen prior to the full opening of the road, allowing access to some of the backcountry bounty within the park; please see the park's website for the most current road conditions and information (see Resources). An entry fee good for seven days ($10 per vehicle) payable at either of the park entrances, or National Parks Pass, is required to enter or park within the park. The Devastated Area parking lot has pit toilets and trash and recycling service, and camping is permitted prior to the full opening of the road through the park.

5 Lassen Peak: Northeast Face via Devastated Area

Starting Point : Devastated Area parking lot (Emigrant Pass), 6450 feet
High Point : 10,457 feet
Distance : 7 miles
Elevation Gain : 4000 feet
Time : 3.5 hours
Difficulty Level : Strenuous
Terrain Rating : 3
Aspect : East-northeast-north
Seasons : Spring, early summer
Maps : USGS Lassen Peak; Reading Peak; West Prospect Peak

When Lassen Peak most recently erupted (1914–1917), it flattened the area at the base of the northeast face and created what is now known as the Devastated Area. While the peak has descent routes on all aspects, the northeast face to the Devastated Area is one of the best due to its sustained pitch, length, and wide-open slopes. This face serves as both the ascent and descent route, but getting to and from it is often the trickiest part. The 10-mile stretch of park road from the northwest entrance to the Devastated Area closure whisks skiers as close as you can get by car to the bottom of Lassen Peak's northeast face. While the park road is generally closed in winter, the Park Service typically opens this stretch of it weeks, sometimes months, before the road is opened all the way through the park, weather and snowpack conditions permitting. The required national park entry fee can be paid at either the north or south park entrance; sign in to the backcountry register at the Devastated Area trailhead. If your timing is right, the snow will be a perfect blanket of velvety-soft, smooth spring corn.

GETTING THERE

From Interstate 5 at Redding, take CA 44 east approximately 50 miles to reach the north park entrance; from CA 89 in the east, take CA 44 west from Old Station 13 miles. From I-5 at Red Bluff, take CA 36 east approximately 45 miles to CA 89, then go north 5.3 miles on CA 89 to reach the south park entrance; from the east on CA 36 at Chester, go west 25 miles to CA 89, then 5.3 miles north on CA 89. The park road (CA 89) is closed in winter and may reopen anytime from April to July based on snowpack depth. Park Service maintenance crews clear portions of the road in the spring and sometimes midwinter; check the park website for updated road conditions and closures (see Resources).

THE ROUTE

Until the park road opens all the way through the park, a descent of the northeast face typically begins at the road closure gate at the Devastated Area (a.k.a. Emigrant Pass) parking lot. The peak and its northeast face are clearly visible from here. Sign your group in to the backcountry register at the road closure gate, then walk past the gate and head southwest into the trees toward the peak.

The forest in the Devastated Area is primarily small conifers growing out of crumbled volcanic rock and pumicey dirt. Meander southwest through the trees as directly as possible toward the peak, making sure to stay just to climber's left (east) of the obvious drainage known as Lost Creek. There is no trail or marked route as you head south to the bottom of the face. After about 1.5 miles and 1000 vertical feet of gain, you exit the trees altogether and your route becomes more obvious.

There is no "best way" to the top of Lassen Peak, but the most prominent gully in the center of the face is generally my route of choice. Skin up the slope for as long as you can, to the top if possible, then switch to boot-packing when the skinning becomes too steep or difficult. Crampons and an ice axe may be helpful when the snow is very

Lassen Peak's northeast face in the late spring

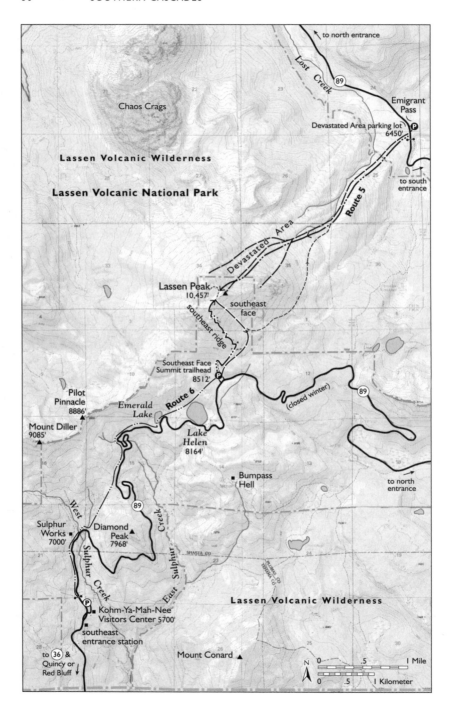

Chaos Crags

Lassen Volcanic Wilderness

Lassen Volcanic National Park

Lost Creek

89

Emigrant Pass

to north entrance

Devastated Area parking lot 6450'

to south entrance

Route 5

Devastated Area

Lassen Peak 10,457'

southeast face

southeast ridge

Southeast Face Summit trailhead 8512'

Pilot Pinnacle 8886'

Mount Diller 9085'

Emerald Lake

Route 6

Lake Helen 8164'

(closed winter)

89

to north entrance

Bumpass Hell

West Sulphur Creek

89

Sulphur Works 7000'

Diamond Peak 7968'

East Sulphur Creek

SHASTA CO

Kohm-Ya-Mah-Nee Visitors Center 5700'

southeast entrance station

to 36 & Quincy or Red Bluff

Lassen Volcanic Wilderness

Mount Conard

N

0   .5   1 Mile

0   .5   1 Kilometer

firm. The slope continually steepens as you climb, so match your ascent and descent with your ability.

The broad northeast face provides a large canvas for skiers to paint their tracks, and any of four or five ridges and gullies can be used for the descent, including the northeast face of the rocky prominence at the end of the east ridge. The northeast face holds its pitch for more than 2000 vertical feet before flattening out significantly. After that point, descend the way you came, being sure to stay east, skier's right, of Lost Creek on the way back down to the parking area. A GPS may be helpful for expediting your way back to the car, as the forest at the bottom of the Devastated Area all looks the same.

Option: From the summit, you can continue just slightly southwest along the ridge to the top of the southeast face and descend as you would for Route 6. After descending to the bench at the bottom of the face at 8800 feet, drop east, down into the large gully feature, for a few hundred vertical feet before traversing hard to the north to wrap back around to the Devastated Area. You may need to put skins back on if you get too low before traversing east and north, but it is possible to coast or sidestep around to return to the Devastated Area below the northeast face. Then retrace your approach route to return to the parking area as you would from the bottom of the northeast face for an 8-mile round-trip.

6   Lassen Peak: Southeast Face

Starting Points	Kohm-Ya-Ma-Nee Visitors Center, 5700 feet; summit trailhead, 8512 feet
High Point	10,457 feet
Distances	From visitors center, 12 miles; from summit trailhead, 3 miles
Elevation Gains	From visitors center, 4800 feet; from summit trailhead, 1900 feet
Times	From visitors center, 6–8 hours; from summit trailhead, 2.5 hours
Difficulty Level	From visitors center, strenuous; from summit trailhead, moderate
Terrain Rating	2
Aspect	Southeast
Seasons	Late spring, early summer
Maps	USGS Lassen Peak; Reading Peak; West Prospect Peak

Lassen Peak towers high above the surrounding mountains within the national park, its southeast face a broad, 2000-vertical-foot pitch that drops in from the summit plateau. The slope's exposure makes it prime terrain for growing that world-renowned California corn snow. Depending on the season's snowpack and whether or not the park road (CA 89) has been opened for the season, this route can be anything from

Dropping into Lassen Peak's southeast face (Oscar Havens)

a half- to full-day midwinter tour from the southwest entrance, which is accessible year-round, to a quick jaunt from the summit parking area when the park road is plowed later in the season (another option is ascending via Route 5 from the Devastated Area parking lot). The required national park entry fee can be paid at either the north or southwest park entrance. In big snow years, the flanks of Lassen Peak are often skiable into July.

GETTING THERE

From Interstate 5 at Redding, take CA 44 east approximately 50 miles to reach the north park entrance; from CA 89 in the east, take CA 44 west from Old Station 13 miles. From I-5 at Red Bluff, take CA 36 east approximately 45 miles to CA 89, then go north 5.3 miles on CA 89 to reach the south park entrance; from the east on CA 36 at Chester, go west 25 miles to CA 89, then 5.3 miles north on CA 89. The park road (CA 89) is plowed up to the Kohm-Ya-Mah-Nee Visitors Center at the park's southwest entrance year-round; the summit trailhead, 6.9 miles north of the southwest entrance, can be used once the park road reopens, anytime from April to July based on snowpack depth. Park Service maintenance crews clear portions of the road in the spring and sometimes midwinter; check the park website for updated road conditions and closures (see Resources).

THE ROUTE

From the visitors center: From the southwest entrance visitors center parking area, head north on the snow-covered park road as it climbs gently for 1 mile to the Sulphur Works. As the road begins to switchback to the south, just past the Sulphur Works, head northeast cross-country to climb the gully north of Diamond Peak and rejoin the park road at around 7800 feet. Follow the road east past Emerald Lake, then again head cross-country on a relatively flat approach past the north shore of Lake Helen (8164 feet) and up to the summit trailhead (8512 feet) at the base of Lassen Peak's southeast ridge about 4.5 miles (2800 feet elevation gain) from the southwest entrance parking area. From here follow the rest of the route described below to reach the summit and descend back to the summit trailhead. Then retrace your route to return to the southwest entrance parking area.

From the summit trailhead: When the park road has reopened for the summer, you can start this route from the summit trailhead at the base of the southeast ridge and follow the summer trail up Lassen Peak. From this parking area, the route up the southeast ridge to the summit plateau is a climb of just under 2000 vertical feet and 1.5 miles. If the ridge is clear of snow, the summer trail makes for a quick and easy ascent. As you ascend, you will be able to see the southeast face and choose a descent line based on the snow conditions.

Descend the southeast face to the bottom of the pitch, at roughly 8800 feet, where a hard traverse to the west brings you back around the southeast ridge to rejoin your ascent route back to the parking area. You can also do more laps from the 8800-foot level, since this route is relatively short: 3 miles round-trip, 1900 vertical feet.

One-way option: Once the park road has been cleared of snow and reopened through the park, a car shuttle can be done by parking one car at the Devastated Area parking lot and another at the summit trailhead, then hiking the switchbacks of the 1.5-mile summer trail from the summit trailhead to the summit and descending the northeast face 3.5 miles to the Devastated Area parking lot (Route 5), 5 miles one-way. By the time the road has opened through the park, the snow in the flats below the northeast face will generally have burned off, making for a longer dirt walk out to the Devastated Area parking lot.

7 Brokeoff Mountain

Starting Point	Brokeoff Mountain trailhead, 6635 feet
High Point	9235 feet
Distance	7 miles
Elevation Gain	2600 feet
Time	2.5 hours
Difficulty Level	Moderate
Terrain Rating	3
Aspect	South-southeast
Seasons	Winter, spring
Map	USGS Lassen Peak

The jagged, rocky summit of Brokeoff Mountain is the tallest remnant of the eroded crater of Mount Tehama and the second-highest peak within Lassen Volcanic National Park. The once-giant Mount Tehama was eroded by glaciers and hydrothermal activity over hundreds of thousands of years, leaving several craggy peaks, including nearby Mount Diller, Mount Conard, and Pilot Pinnacle as reminders of its former grandeur and fiery past. Brokeoff Mountain is located in Lassen Volcanic Wilderness within the national park, and its summit ridge extending above the sheer cliff walls of the mountain's north face affords an amazing view of Lassen Volcanic National Park, California's north-central valley, and Mount Shasta to the north. This moderate route is great for people with an aversion to steep terrain and is perfect for a short day of skiing with incredible views. This relatively mellow route has various more-advanced options, and this trailhead can be reached all winter long from near the park's south entrance. The required national park entry fee can be paid at either the north or southwest park entrance. The entrance stations are unmanned during the winter, so use self-pay envelopes during those months.

GETTING THERE

From Interstate 5 at Redding, take CA 44 east approximately 50 miles to reach the north park entrance; from CA 89 in the east, take CA 44 west from Old Station 13 miles. From I-5 at Red Bluff, take CA 36 east approximately 45 miles to CA 89, then go north 5.3 miles on CA 89 to reach the southwest park entrance; from the east on CA 36 at Chester, go west 25 miles to CA 89, then 5.3 miles north on CA 89 to the parking area for Brokeoff Mountain, a plowed pullout on the east side of CA 89 about 0.3 mile south of the southwest entrance and the Kohm-Ya-Mah-Nee Visitors Center. The Lassen Peak Highway through Lassen Volcanic National Park is closed in winter and reopens through the park anytime from late April to July,

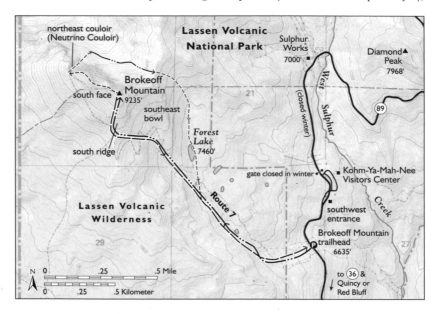

Standing atop Brokeoff Mountain's airy summit with a commanding view of Lassen Volcanic National Park and Lassen Peak

but the park road is plowed to the south entrance and visitors center year-round, so access to this trailhead is possible all winter. Check the park website for updated road conditions and closures (see Resources).

THE ROUTE

From the Brokeoff Mountain trailhead parking area on the east side of CA 89, cross the road and head west, following the path of the drainage. After you gain about 300 vertical feet, the drainage turns northwest and heads directly toward Forest Lake at the base of Brokeoff Mountain's impressive craggy south ridge. As you follow the path of the drainage, it gently gains elevation; the south ridge is above you to climber's left.

Follow the drainage for about 1.5 miles. Just before Forest Lake, begin to head west, climbing toward the south ridge. After 800 vertical feet or so, you reach the ridge that separates the southeast bowl from the south face of the mountain. From here, it is 800 vertical feet to the summit. I prefer to hike along the ridge for the views, but take whatever path looks easiest to you to reach the summit: the high point at the eastern end of the ridge.

On clear days the view from the summit of Brokeoff is truly amazing. If you know what to look for, you can see the other remaining parts of Mount Tehama's massive crater: Mount Diller and Pilot Pinnacle to the northeast, Mount Conard to the southeast. In fact, you can see nearly all of Lassen Volcanic National Park, including Lassen's south face, Sulphur Works, and Bumpass Hell. Look for Mount Shasta looming in the distance far to the north. Use caution along the summit ridge as large cornices may form here and it is a long drop down the sheer cliffs of the north face.

The descent route drops back down the south face to roughly the same point you crossed over the ridge on the ascent before heading east back down to the drainage you hiked up. Follow the drainage back to the trailhead. Those looking for a little more vertical can do a short lap or two in the southeast bowl or on the southeast ridge on their way out. In a big winter, some lines may even fill in from the summit down the southeast face, but that is not always common and you may need to evaluate when you're out there.

Option: There is also an expert descent down the north side of the peak called the Neutrino Couloir. This relatively short north-facing chute drops off the west end of the summit ridge and has a very steep and narrow entrance. This route requires a very high skill level, and anyone proficient enough to attempt it should be able to figure out the relatively straightforward route that wraps around the north side of the mountain back to the main descent route near Forest Lake and from there back to the trailhead.

Opposite: *Turns like this make the approach to Silver Peak well worth the effort.*

PART II
NORTHERN SIERRA

AS YOU MAKE YOUR WAY SOUTH from California's southern Cascades, the northernmost part of the Sierra Nevada are small in size but certainly not in natural beauty or skiing potential. While these mountains may not have the impressive vertical relief found in the southern end of the Sierra, the variety of fun terrain here can be accessed all winter and spring. For the purposes of this guidebook, the northern Sierra stretches south from rugged and scenic mountains like the Sierra Buttes in the Lost Sierra near historic Plumas-Eureka State Park to Castle Peak and the mountains in the Truckee area.

The Lost Sierra is a unique and less-traveled part of the range with fine descents when conditions allow and a wealth of ski routes near Truckee along or near the Pacific Crest. Of course, much more skiable terrain exists than is mentioned here, but long approaches, low starting elevations, and relative obscurity make many of those less desirable than the routes listed here.

The area between Graeagle on CA 89 and Truckee on Interstate 80 is largely undeveloped, but CA 89 and CA 49 easily connect these routes.

THE LOST SIERRA

The Sierra Buttes and Eureka Peak, the northernmost part of the Sierra Nevada, are in an area often referred to as the Lost Sierra. This unique region is home to some of the most rugged and picturesque mountains north of Lake Tahoe, with a rich mining history. Remnants of the mining days are visible all throughout these mountains, with relics of the bygone era scattered throughout.

The gold rush may have come and gone, but people can still find a recreational bounty in these hills. The jagged ridgeline of the Sierra Buttes is home to some of the steepest lines around, and the flanks of Eureka Peak offer a variety of excellent terrain above the historic town of Johnsville and Plumas-Eureka State Park. There are numerous other ski objectives in the area, including the north face of Mount Washington (just south of Eureka Peak) and Mount Elwell. The starting elevation in this area is relatively low, 5000 or so feet, so a good low-elevation snowpack is desirable for attempting these routes. That said, when the opportunity presents itself to ski in this area, it is a truly unusual experience that should not be missed.

To get to these routes, use CA 89 to reach the town of Graeagle or CA 49 about 25 miles south of Graeagle. About an hour north of Truckee, the sleepy little town of Graeagle is primarily a golf and retirement community, but it has a small market, a gas station, and a couple of restaurants.

8 Eureka Peak

Starting Point	Plumas-Eureka State Park headquarters and museum, 5190 feet
High Point	7447 feet
Distance	3.5 miles
Elevation Gain	2300 feet
Time	3 hours
Difficulty Level	Moderate
Terrain Rating	3
Aspects	Southeast-east, northeast
Season	Winter
Maps	USGS Johnsville; Gold Lake

Nestled in the heart of the northern Sierra, the tiny little town of Johnsville is home to Plumas-Eureka State Park, the location of a once-booming gold mine that now features a museum and park highlighting the area's rich mining history. Gold was

Dropping into Eureka Peak's expansive south-facing terrain

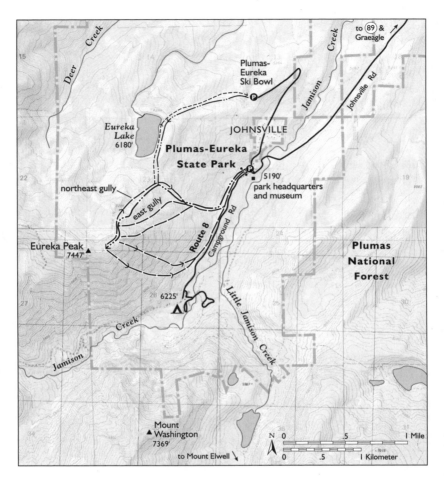

discovered in 1851 on what was then known as Gold Mountain, now Eureka Peak, and by the end of the mining heyday, 30 miles of mine shafts had been dug inside of the mountain. As early as the 1860s, miners began skiing to pass the time in the winter, and the Plumas-Eureka Ski Bowl became one of the first places in the country for recreational skiing. "Longboard" races are still held annually, when conditions permit, on gear from that era to celebrate this rich and historic skiing legacy. Due to the mining history of this area, be on the lookout for various hazards and obstacles while skiing, such as old cables, mine shafts, or scraps of wood and metal. This area is certainly off the radar for most backcountry skiers, although a handful of local Graeagle and Johnsville residents ski here regularly. This is a special place to take a few runs, so be sure to pounce on the opportunity when low-elevation snow allows. The mountain holds a wealth of great terrain on a variety of aspects, and when coverage and conditions are right, this is some of the best and easiest accessed backcountry in the Lost Sierra. Above Eureka Lake are a couple of northeast- and east-facing gullies, and the southeast face offers some of the longest consistent pitches you can find in the area. There is currently no chairlift operating at the Plumas-Eureka Ski Bowl, but a community movement is afoot to put in a working lift.

GETTING THERE

From Truckee, follow CA 89 north for 49 miles to the town of Graeagle. Just past the "downtown" area of Graeagle, turn left on Johnsville Road and follow it 5.1 miles to the Plumas-Eureka State Park headquarters and museum parking area in the small town of Johnsville. To start from the Plumas-Eureka Ski Bowl, turn right to continue on Johnsville Road another 1.4 miles to the parking area.

THE ROUTE

There are various ways to approach Eureka Peak, but if there is snow to the valley bottom (5190 feet), starting from the park headquarters and museum parking area provides the most bang for your hiking buck as well as a longer run. From the parking area, head southwest along the snow-covered road that leads to the summer campground. After approximately 0.5 mile, turn west and begin to ascend the prominent gully that leads to the bottom of the steeper east gully. After roughly 800 feet of ascent, you reach the bottom of this east-facing gully. Continue climbing to the west and onto the ridge that separates this gully from the next—the northeast gully. (This is where the optional route from the ski bowl joins the main route.)

As you ascend this mellow ridge to the southwest, look around at all of the descent options on both sides of you. The terrain is slightly steeper to skier's right and slightly mellower to skier's left. Once you top out on the ridge at 7200 feet, head south to reach Eureka Peak's summit. Take in the amazing view of the Lost Sierra from here, including the Sierra Buttes (Route 9) in the distance and the amazing north-facing terrain of Mount Washington and Mount Elwell across the Jamison Creek drainage.

From the summit, head back down the ridge the way you came to return to the east or northeast gully—or, if corn skiing is what you are after, drop into one of the several south-southeast-facing lines that run an impressive 2200 feet down to Jamison Creek. These amazing runs do require good snow coverage, something that is often lacking on south faces below 6000 feet. You can see to the bottom from the top, so coverage shouldn't be a mystery. Once at the bottom of the south face, return to the parking area by heading northeast for roughly a mile along the path of the campground road that you started on.

Options: You can also start from the parking area of the Plumas-Eureka Ski Bowl and hike up the ski slopes to Eureka Lake. Hike across Eureka Lake and join the main route on the ridge that separates the east and northeast gullies. The ski bowl approach shaves off a few hundred feet of ascent and is more gradual, and it also provides for more mellow terrain for the descent back to the parking area. You could also ascend on the main route and descend on the ski bowl route—or vice versa—for a loop.

9 Sierra Buttes: Violet Couloir

Starting Point	CA 49 pullout, 5000 feet
High Point	8150 feet
Distance	4 miles
Elevation Gain	3200 feet
Time	3 hours
Difficulty Level	Moderate
Terrain Rating	5
Aspect	North-northeast
Season	Winter
Maps	USGS Gold Lake; Sierra City; HayPress Valley; Clio

The Sierra Buttes are among the most impressive mountains to look at in the northern Sierra. The jagged summit ridgeline is a sight to behold, home to a number of chutes and gullies on a variety of aspects. The impressively steep Violet Couloir, the steepest of these chutes, is often the goal of backcountry skiers in this zone. Violet Couloir requires a good low-elevation snowpack, and often the lowest several hundred feet of this area may be patchy or lacking snow completely. It is important to attempt this route when conditions are right, typically midwinter with a decent low-elevation snowpack. If really steep skiing isn't your thing, there is an abundance of more moderate options. From the playful rolling terrain around and below the Violet Couloir to the massive north-facing gullies above the Sardine Lakes, there is something for everyone here. The Violet Couloir zone is separated from the Sardine Lakes side of the mountain by a ridge, so if you choose the Sardine Lakes option, you'll use a different approach. The Sierra Buttes area was the site of serious mining operations in the past, so don't be surprised to see remnants of this scattered about the mountain.

GETTING THERE

Follow CA 89 to Sierraville, about 25 miles south of Graeagle and 23 miles north of Truckee. In Sierraville, continue northbound on CA 89 north, which is now also CA 49 south for a few miles. When CA 89 continues north, stay left on CA 49 south (actually heading west here) up and over Yuba Pass. Continue south on CA 49, following it 22 miles from CA 89, to a pullout on the north side of the road at a "5000-FOOT-ELEVATION" sign.

THE ROUTE

From the "5000-FOOT-ELEVATION"-signed pullout, head to the south end of the pullout and follow an old dirt road south for a few hundred feet. Head west up the boulder-strewn and somewhat open area of the otherwise densely forested slope. Climb this open slope, which is much more sparsely treed than the surrounding forest,

The jagged and beautiful ridgeline of the Sierra Buttes

for approximately 800 vertical feet, then begin to contour south around the ridge until it opens up as you enter the Flume Creek drainage (around 5800–6000 feet).

Once in the creek drainage, you have an impressive view of the rugged terrain that lies above. A rocky buttress separates the two main gullies that you can ascend to the base of the Violet Couloir. Climber's left is somewhat steeper and more direct, while climber's right follows the path of Flume Creek and is slightly longer and more moderate.

From Flume Creek at 6000 feet, climb your chosen ascent route to the base of the Violet Couloir (7400 feet). Boot-packing is generally the only way to make it to the top of the couloir, and crampons and an ice axe may be useful on most days.

The top of the Violet Couloir is very steep, but there are many options for excellent skiing up here, so look around and find something that suits your ability level and the snow conditions. Drop in for some steep turns, followed by fun, playful terrain back down to Flume Creek. Then return to the parking area the way you came. One of the alternate gullies takes you east of the ascent route to rejoin the main route where it exits the creek drainage.

Sardine Lakes option: This tour is longer than the Violet Couloir, 9 miles round-trip, but with the same elevation gain and a wealth of terrain above the lakes worthy of exploration. On CA 49, 12.9 miles from CA 89, there is ample parking near the road closure just north of the intersection with the Gold Lakes Highway in Bassetts. From this parking area, head west along the snow-covered Gold Lakes Highway. This road, which is generally closed for the winter at the intersection with CA 49, is often used by snowmobilers to access the area (if you have a snowmobile, you can use it to cover

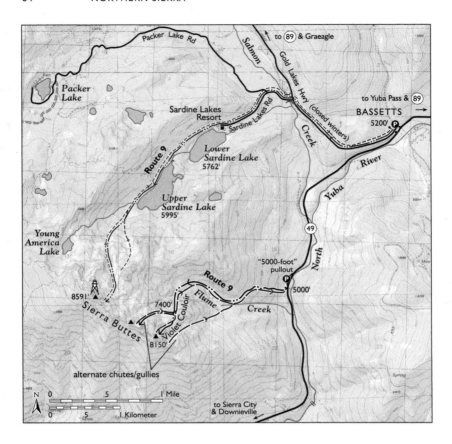

the relatively flat approach into the Sardine Lakes). Follow the Gold Lakes Highway for approximately 1.5 miles, then turn left onto Sardine Lakes Road. Cross the bridge over Salmon Creek and follow the road west past Packer Lake Road for 0.5 mile to the Sardine Lakes Resort and Lower Sardine Lake (5762 feet). Continue along the rocky summer road that skirts north of and above Lower Sardine Lake up to the dam at the northeast end of Upper Sardine Lake (5995 feet).

From here you should have a great view of the several large, moderately pitched north-facing gullies on the Sierra Buttes. These all get relatively steep or end in sheer cliff walls the closer you get to the ridge. If the lake is frozen, the flat surface is the quickest way over to the base of these gullies. If the lake is not frozen, hike around its north side until you reach the base of the gully you would like to ski. No matter what line you choose back here, it is difficult to reach the true summit and fire lookout (8591 feet) in winter unless you take a circuitous route around to the back side of the peak. Skin up as far as you can, then switch to boot-packing when it gets too steep if you want to make it to the ridge. Ski the gully of your choice and retrace your route to return to the parking area.

THE TRUCKEE AREA

The northern Sierra town of Truckee lies north of Lake Tahoe just east of the Sierra crest and Donner Summit. A large population of outdoor enthusiasts live in Truckee for its myriad recreational opportunities. A number of fine backcountry zones are in close proximity to town, and Truckee is ideally situated to access locales on the north and west shores of Lake Tahoe just 15 miles south (see Part III, Lake Tahoe Area). Historically, Truckee is known for the tragic plight of the Donner Party in 1846–1847 and the route of the first transcontinental railroad through town and over Donner Summit, completed in 1869.

Conveniently located on Interstate 80 at the junction with CA 89, Truckee is a growing town of more than 16,000 year-round residents. It has all types of restaurant and lodging options. Numerous local outdoor gear shops specialize in backcountry equipment and some even offer rental packages.

Atop Donner Summit, Sugar Bowl Resort operates the Backcountry Adventure Center and offers guided backcountry tours and skills clinics in cooperation with Alpine Skills International (ASI). Locally operated ASI and other groups also offer avalanche courses, backcountry skiing courses, and guided tours throughout the winter. The Sierra Avalanche Center provides a regular avalanche advisory for the area. See Resources for all these organizations.

Three Sierra Club huts are located near Truckee. The Peter Grubb Hut sits just west of Castle Peak in Round Valley, the Benson Hut is perched just north of Anderson Peak on the Pacific Crest, and the Bradley Hut lies up Pole Creek near both Silver Peak and Deep Creek. These huts, a great way to spend a night or two in the backcountry, are available by reservation through the Clair Tappaan Lodge (see Resources).

10   Castle Peak: North Gullies

Starting Point	Donner Summit rest stop, 7250 feet
High Point	8800 feet
Distance	4 miles
Elevation Gain	2300 feet
Time	3 hours
Difficulty Level	Moderate
Terrain Rating	3
Aspects	North, south-southwest
Seasons	Winter, spring
Map	USGS Norden

Castle Peak sits regally atop Donner Summit, just north of Interstate 80, across from the Boreal Mountain Resort ski area. When viewed from the south, the peak's summit

Heading up for another lap on the north gullies of Castle Peak

ridge and cliffy walls resemble a fortified medieval castle, and much like its namesake, Castle Peak holds a treasure of terrain on both its north and south sides. The peak's ridge extends east-west more than a mile, with skiing options on both the east and west sides of the summit. The chutes and gullies of Castle Peak's north side remain sheltered from the sun and offer a variety of fun short lines that are quick and easy to lap. The mellow south face is a great option for short laps to harvest corn snow, and it is also good introductory backcountry skiing terrain via Castle Valley. The relatively high starting elevation also makes both approaches to this area great for early- and late-season skiing when lower-elevation routes may not have adequate snow.

GETTING THERE

From Truckee, head westbound on Interstate 80 for 8 miles. At the top of Donner Summit, turn into the rest stop and park at the east end of the parking area. This parking area can be approached only from the east on I-80.

THE ROUTE

From the east end of the rest-stop parking area, head due north toward Castle Peak. After a few hundred feet, you emerge from the trees and onto the rolling, boulder-strewn terrain that makes up the lowest slopes on this side of the mountain. You'll be able to see the south face and your route clearly from here. The easiest way up to the

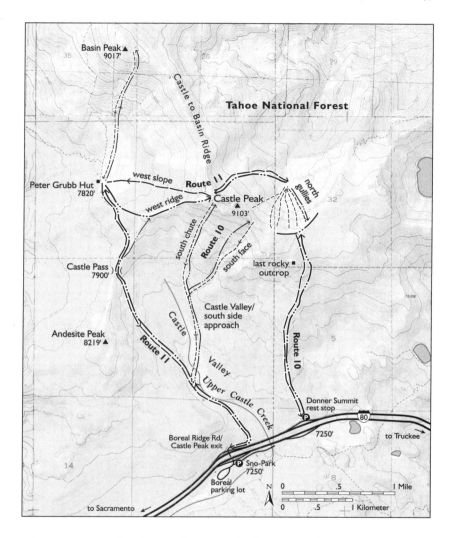

Basin Peak ▲
9017'

35   36

Castle to Basin Ridge

Tahoe National Forest

west slope   **Route 11**
Peter Grubb Hut ■
7820'   north gullies
west ridge   → Castle Peak
▲
9103'   32

south chute   Route 10
south face
Castle Pass)(last rocky ■
7900'   outcrop

Castle Valley/
south side
approach

Andesite Peak
8219' ▲   Route 11   Route 10   5
Castle

Valley

Upper Castle Creek

Donner Summit
rest stop
7250'   80
Boreal Ridge Rd/   to Truckee
Castle Peak exit

14   P Sno-Park
7250'
Boreal
parking lot   N   0   .5   1 Mile

to Sacramento ←   0   .5   1 Kilometer

ridge is to continue heading north, aiming for the open southeast-facing slope that rises just to climber's right (east) of the last rocky outcropping on the south side of the peak.

As you climb toward the open slope, stay along the crest of the prominent lower ridge that leads you directly to the base of the upper slope. After about 0.75 mile and 700 feet or so of climbing, you begin to ascend slightly more steeply up the open south-facing slope, just on the east side of the rock outcrop. At the top of the slope, follow the natural contours of the mountain generally north, continuing into the trees and across the relatively flat plateau of the ridge. After about 0.25 mile you hit the ridge at the top of the north-facing gullies of Castle Peak.

There are myriad descent options off the north side of the peak. The closer to the summit (west) you get, the steeper and more advanced the runs get. The farther east you go down the ridge, the less steep the runs become. For the most part, you can see from the top to the bottom of all these runs, which vary from 600 to 800 vertical feet. From the bottom of a run, take a good look at the zone while you scout your next descent line.

After you've skied down the north side, skin back up one of the mellower gullies at the eastern end of the ridge to return to the top of your approach track. When you've skied enough laps down the north side, follow your track back over to the south slopes and descend the way you came, back to the parking area.

Castle Valley option: From the Donner Summit rest stop on I-80, continue westbound 0.2 mile to the next exit, exit 176 for Boreal Ridge Road and Castle Peak. Turn left and park on the south side of I-80 in the Castle Valley Sno-Park, near the Boreal Inn and ski area parking lot. From the Sno-Park, walk back under the interstate and head up the road to the north, following as it wraps around the south end of Andesite Ridge and into the Upper Castle Creek drainage, known as Castle Valley. Follow the road as it parallels the creek heading north-northwest, and after about 0.75 mile, bear right off the road and follow the drainage north to the base of the south face of Castle Peak. This broad face has numerous moderately pitched gullies as well as the south chute, a steeper option that splits the upper cliff band and tops out on the summit ridge (9103 feet). Climb along the face to the descent route of your choosing, then ski down and retrace your route to return to the Sno-Park.

You can also access the north gullies from this approach by heading east along the summit ridge to join the main approach described above. Retrace your route to return to the parking area.

II   Castle Peak: Castle Pass and Peter Grubb Hut

Starting Point	Castle Valley Sno-Park, 7250 feet
High Points	9103 feet; Basin Peak, 9017 feet
Distances	5.5 miles; Basin Peak, 7 miles
Elevation Gains	1950 feet; Basin Peak, 1850 feet
Time	3 hours
Difficulty Level	Moderate
Terrain:	2
Aspects	All
Seasons	Winter, spring
Map	USGS Norden

A group prepares to leave an almost completely buried Peter Grubb Hut.

The Peter Grubb Hut sits at the southern end of Round Valley, just west of Castle Peak. This small Sierra Club hut is a wonderful place to spend a few nights with friends while exploring the nearby terrain of Castle Peak (see Resources). Round Valley is flanked by a ridge that connects between Castle Peak and Basin Peak, with moderate terrain that ranges from west- to southwest-facing. It's also just a short distance up Castle Peak's west ridge to reach the summit and drop onto the peak's north or south side (Route 10). Spending a night or two at the Peter Grubb Hut (like the other Sierra Club huts in the area) is a novel experience and a great way to get out and enjoy the Castle Peak area via Castle Creek and Castle Pass.

GETTING THERE

From Truckee, head westbound on Interstate 80 for 8.2 miles to exit 176 for Boreal Ridge Road and Castle Peak, the first exit west of the Donner Summit rest stop. Turn left and park on the south side of I-80 in the Castle Valley Sno-Park near the Boreal Inn and ski area parking lot.

THE ROUTE

From the Sno-Park, walk back under the interstate and head up the road to the north, following as it wraps around the south end of Andesite Ridge and into the Upper Castle Creek drainage, known as Castle Valley. Follow the path of the fire road as it parallels the creek heading north-northwest. Instead of heading toward Castle Peak's south face, stay on the path of the road just below Andesite Ridge and continue heading northwest for nearly 2 miles as you make your way to the head of Castle Valley and up to the saddle between Andesite Peak and Castle Peak, known as Castle Pass (7900 feet). Continue north, contouring the slope below Castle Peak's west ridge for another 0.75 mile until you reach Round Valley. The Peter Grubb Hut sits at the edge of the huge meadow in the trees on the southwest end of Round Valley to the west of Castle Peak at 7820 feet.

Visitors to the Peter Grubb Hut often approach the north side of Castle Peak by hiking along its west ridge up to the summit. From here you can drop into the northeast slope, just north of the summit, which leads down to the basin below the north gullies (Route 10). This sets you up to do laps on the north gullies or the northeast face, eventually returning to Round Valley and the hut via the west slope. Of course, the variety of south-facing terrain above Castle Valley is also in striking distance from the summit on the other side of the west ridge.

No matter your ski objectives from the hut, the return route from Round Valley is the same as the way in. Head south over Castle Pass and continue southeast down Castle Valley to return to the Sno-Park.

Basin Peak option: The most obvious ski objective from the Peter Grubb Hut is the terrain that rises directly above Round Valley on the ridge that extends over a mile from Castle Peak (9103 feet) north to Basin Peak (9017 feet). The ridge has moderately pitched runs dropping back down to Round Valley up to 1200 vertical feet that range from northwest- to south-facing. The direct route to Basin Peak gains 1200 feet of elevation over about a mile.

12   Mount Judah: Lake Run

Starting Points	Top of chairlift, 8180 feet; Donner Summit, 7056 feet
High Point	8180 feet
Distances	From chairlift, 1.75 miles; from Donner Summit, 2.8 miles
Elevation Gains	From chairlift, 0 feet; from Donner Summit, 1100 feet
Times	From chairlift, 1.5 hours; from Donner Summit, 2.5 hours
Difficulty Level	Easy
Terrain Ratings	2–3
Aspect	East-northeast
Seasons	Winter, spring
Map	USGS Norden

Dropping into one of the variations of the Lake Run on a late-season powder day

From the Donner Party to the transcontinental Central Pacific Railroad, the Donner Pass area is steeped in history. The same terrain and snowfall that caused such hardship for these people ages ago is an easy-access backcountry playground for skiers today. Mount Judah, the starting point of the Lake Run, is located on the south side of Donner Pass Road (Old Highway 40) and conveniently off the back side of Sugar Bowl Resort, so it is often accessed from the resort, thanks to their open-boundary policy. Mount Judah is also reached from Donner Pass for those without a Sugar Bowl ticket. Judah Ridge extends south for nearly a half mile to the true summit of Mount Judah; Donner Peak lies a short distance northeast of Judah Ridge across a small saddle. The Lake Run drops 2300 vertical feet down fun, moderate terrain from the top of Judah Ridge to the west end of Donner Lake—hence the route's name. In the neighborhood at the west end of the lake, a small parking area facilitates the car shuttle back to your starting point. (Otherwise, arrange for a pickup at the end of the run or jump in with someone else's car shuttle.) There is a wealth of other outrageous ski opportunities in the immediate area, especially for experts looking to push their limits in the complex terrain on the northeast face of Donner Peak.

GETTING THERE

Donner Lake car shuttle: From Interstate 80, take exit 184 just west of downtown Truckee and drive west on Donner Pass Road (Old Highway 40) 5.9 miles to South Shore Drive at the west end of Donner Lake. Turn south onto South Shore Drive and take the sixth right, onto Pine Street, then the third left, onto Tinker Court. Park a shuttle car in the small parking area at the end of Tinker Court, then return to Donner Pass Road and turn left to drive to your chosen starting point.

Donner Summit approach: From exit 184 off I-80, drive west on Donner Pass Road 6.7 miles, past South Shore Drive, to the top of Donner Summit. Park as close to the Sugar Bowl Academy building and as far off the road as possible.

Chairlift approach: Continue west on Donner Pass Road 0.2 mile and turn south onto Sugar Bowl Road. Park near Judah Lodge and purchase a lift ticket at Sugar Bowl Resort.

THE ROUTE

Chairlift approach: From Sugar Bowl Resort, take the Mount Judah Express up to the Summit chairlift and ride that to Mount Judah ridge.

Donner Summit approach: From Donner Pass, hike south across the flats and start the ascent just east of Lake Mary. Wrap around the west end of the broad ridge that extends northwest from Mount Judah's summit ridge and gradually ascend toward the southeast, staying north of the Sugar Bowl Resort boundary up to the north end of the ridge near the top of the Mount Judah Express. Climb up through the north-facing trees to the top of the ridge by the distinctive radio reflectors and the Summit chairlift.

From Judah Ridge at the top of the Summit chairlift, the Lake Run drops northeast toward the saddle between Mount Judah and Donner Peak, then heads east and stays high, contouring slightly north, which puts you atop the broad east-northeast-facing slope of Donner Peak. Ride this face for 900 vertical feet down into the gully that leads to the old train tracks between Donner and Trestle peaks.

When you reach the old railroad bed, follow it northeast. The route now enters the train tunnel, so it is helpful to bring a headlamp or flashlight for this dark and generally icy walk underground. Head northeast through the tunnel, and as it turns to the east you can emerge through one of several openings in the snowshed wall. Now you are atop another 800 vertical feet of fun, playful, north-facing terrain down to the west Donner Lake neighborhood. This slope is quite wide, so spread out and get some freshies, then make your way to your waiting vehicle at the end of Tinker Court.

Judah Ridge options: Among the other ways you can extend the tour in this area, you could spend a whole day doing laps on Judah Ridge alone. This broad east face extends from the top of the Summit chairlift south for almost a half mile to Mount Judah's summit with excellent, albeit short, runs along the way. Where the east face of Judah flattens out, simply hike northwest up to the saddle between Judah and Donner to rejoin the Lake Run route or continue to ascend southwest up the ridge back to Judah's summit ridge to do laps.

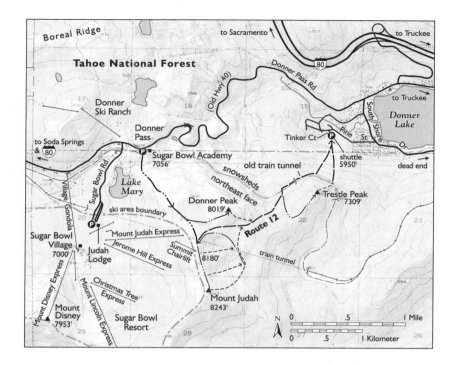

Trestle Peak option: Those looking to add a little extra work to their Lake Run can detour above the train tunnel and hike 400 feet to the top of Trestle Peak (7309 feet) for some quality turns back to the snowshed. Head down the northeast ridge to avoid the train tunnel completely, unless you would like to jump 20- to 30-foot cliffs off the train tunnel.

Donner Peak options: The Lake Run can also be started from the top of Donner Peak by heading due east from the main approach route to the top of Donner, then off it to the southeast, joining the main route after just a few hundred vertical feet. The northeast face of Donner Peak is home to some of the most extreme terrain in the entire Tahoe region. Lines like the Rollover, the Heart, and the Bubbles have beckoned expert skiers and snowboarders for decades. With significantly more avalanche hazard and exposure, these lines are not to be taken lightly, and those attempting to ski in this area should be highly skilled in scouting lines and routefinding in very steep and cliffy terrain. These descents are serious enough that they are not described in detail here. If you're good enough to attempt these extreme routes, you should be able to figure them out for yourself. This terrain is all clearly visible from Donner Pass Road and can easily be scouted from there.

13 Anderson Peak and Benson Hut

Starting Points : Top of chairlift, 8380 feet; Donner Summit, 7056 feet
High Point : 8683 feet
Distances : From chairlift, 6 miles; from Donner Summit, 11 miles
Elevation Gains : From chairlift, 1600 feet; from Donner Summit, 3300 feet
Time : 4 hours to 2 days
Difficulty Level : From chairlift, moderate; from Donner Summit, strenuous
Terrain Ratings : 2–3
Aspects : East-northeast-north, northwest
Seasons : Winter, spring
Map : USGS Norden

Anderson Peak sits on the Pacific Crest 3 miles southeast of the summit of Mount Lincoln at the Sugar Bowl Resort. There are a couple of ways to approach Anderson Peak: ride the chairlift to the top of Mount Lincoln (lift ticket or season pass required) or start from Donner Summit and hike and ski to the top of Mount Lincoln.

Looking south along the route from Sugar Bowl Resort to Anderson Peak

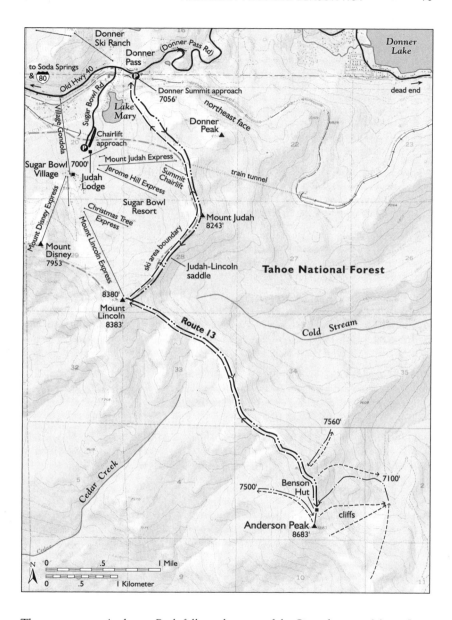

The route out to Anderson Peak follows the crest of the Sierra between Mount Lincoln and Anderson Peak, with excellent short, steep ski terrain dropping off the east side of the ridge the entire way. Anderson Peak's western slope is the headwaters of the North Fork of the American River, while the eastern slopes drain into Cold Stream Canyon and the Truckee River. Anderson Peak itself offers a variety of fun short bowls, steeps, and tree skiing on its eastern and northwestern slopes. The Benson Hut, nestled in the trees on the ridgeline just north of Anderson Peak, has sleeping quarters upstairs and a kitchen, table, and woodstove on the ground floor. This two-story structure is an excellent place to spend a night or two while exploring the surrounding terrain after the otherwise long approach.

GETTING THERE

Donner Summit approach: From Interstate 80, exit into downtown Truckee and drive west on Donner Pass Road (Old Highway 40) for approximately 8 miles to the top of Donner Summit. Park as close to the Sugar Bowl Academy building and as far off the road as possible.

Chairlift approach: Continue west on Donner Pass Road 0.2 mile and turn south onto Sugar Bowl Road. Park at Judah Lodge, purchase a lift ticket at Sugar Bowl Resort, ride the Jerome Hill Express to the Mount Lincoln Express, then ride the Mount Lincoln Express to the top of Mount Lincoln.

THE ROUTE

Donner Summit approach: From Donner Summit, skirt the ski area boundary up and over Mount Judah (Route 12), follow the ridge south and then southwest as you ski down to the Judah-Lincoln saddle, then ascend the ridge to the top of Mount Lincoln.

Chairlift approach: From the top of Mount Lincoln, the Pacific Crest and your route out to Anderson Peak are clearly visible. Exit the ski area through the boundary gate and descend the ridge southeast. This ridge is your route the entire way out to Anderson Peak. After the initial descent, the ridge walk is rolling but mostly a very gentle climb to the southeast for the first couple miles. Beware of cornices that form on the east side of the ridge. As you get closer to Anderson Peak, the route does a sidehill traverse along the west side of the ridge before arriving at the saddle just north of Anderson Peak. As you continue toward the peak, be on the lookout for the Benson Hut; it is generally hard to miss, but in big snow years it can sometimes be almost completely buried.

The easiest way to the summit of Anderson Peak is up the northwest slope since the east side of the peak is a large cliff face. Immediately below this cliff face is a moderately pitched bowl, but below that lies a very steep rollover littered with complex cliffy terrain. This terrain has a variety of ways through, but scout this zone before attempting it. Slightly to the north and the south of this rollover is more moderate terrain with easier ways through. The northwest face of Anderson Peak also offers some good skiing down the open slopes and into the forested gully below. Skiing on either side of Anderson Peak requires climbing back up to the ridge.

If you venture out to Anderson Peak, I highly recommend spending the night at the Benson Hut; it is the best way to experience the terrain out in this area. Whether you do a day trip or an overnight, reverse your route north along the ridge back to the top of Mount Lincoln. To return to your car, either descend to the Judah Lodge parking area or retrace the route back to Donner Summit.

14   Billys Peak: Deep Creek

Starting Point : Deep Creek pullout, 6000 feet
High Point : 8560 feet
Distance : 7.5 miles
Elevation Gain : 2600 feet
Time : 3 hours
Difficulty Level : Moderate
Terrain Rating : 2
Aspect : North
Season : Winter
Maps : USGS Truckee; Tahoe City; Granite Chief; Norden

Between Truckee and Tahoe City, four major creek drainages spill down from the Sierra crest to feed the Truckee River. Two of these are home to the world-class ski resorts of Squaw Valley and Alpine Meadows. The other two provide some of the closest ski touring to Truckee—Deep Creek is only 5 miles from town, a great spot to find powder snow in the north-facing trees that line the ridge between CA 89 and Billys Peak. Varying in length from 1200 to 1500 vertical feet, these runs are quick to lap once you're back in here, and a slightly longer approach (relative to other routes in the area) helps thin the crowds slightly. The sheltered north-facing aspect hides the snow from the effects of wind and sun, keeping the snow powdery for longer. The entire ridge has great ski terrain, although the runs get progressively shorter and the trees somewhat tighter the farther east you are. This zone is sometimes approached

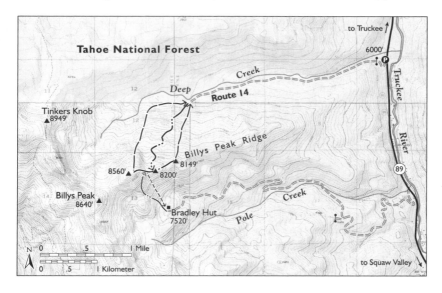

Slashing turns in the cold, sheltered powder in the north-facing trees in Deep Creek

from the south by people staying at the Bradley Hut (Route 15), which lies on the south side of the Billys Peak ridge in the Pole Creek drainage.

GETTING THERE

From Donner Pass Road (Old Highway 40) in Truckee, take CA 89 south 4.8 miles to where the highway crosses Deep Creek (9 miles north of Tahoe City), just south of Goose Meadows campground. Park off the road on either side of the highway wherever you can but do not block the driveway that drops from the highway down to the homes on the Truckee River.

THE ROUTE

From the west side of CA 89, look for the very obvious Forest Service road on the south side of Deep Creek. Follow this road uphill as it wraps around the end of the ridge extending east from Billys Peak and then continues west in the Deep Creek drainage. The first couple miles follow this road until you reach the moderate tree runs farther back in the drainage.

Over the course of 2.5 miles, you gain approximately 1100 vertical feet, and at that point you leave the road to head southwest and begin ascending the trees on the moderately pitched north-facing ridge that separates Deep Creek and Pole Creek. A large area of widely spaced north-facing trees back in this area has runs ranging from 1200 to 1500 vertical feet; the farther west you go, the longer the runs are, from the top of the ridge back down to the creek floor.

From the top of the far western end of this ridge—not quite to Billys Peak—you'll have a great view of the Pacific Crest, from Tinkers Knob (just south of Anderson Peak) to Squaw Valley, Silver Peak to the south, and down into both the Deep Creek and Pole Creek drainages. Pick a zone and put in a skin track, do a lap or two, or spend the whole day skiing here.

When you've had enough fun, head back the way you came down the Forest Service road to return to the parking area on CA 89.

15 Silver Peak

Starting Point	Pole Creek pullout, 6024 feet
High Point	8424 feet
Distances	6 miles
Elevation Gain	2400 feet
Times	Silver Peak, 2.5 hours
Difficulty Level	Moderate
Terrain Rating	2
Aspects	Northwest
Season	Winter
Maps	USGS Tahoe City; Granite Chief

Located just north of Tahoe's most iconic expert ski resort, Squaw Valley, Silver Peak offers a wealth of moderate ski terrain hidden just out of sight from the masses riding the chairs next door. This route's relatively long approach follows a fire road before climbing a moderate ridge to the top. Silver Peak, part of the ridgeline that separates Squaw and Pole creeks, offers excellent skiing on its east and north flanks. Despite having generally moderate terrain, Silver Peak is subject to high winds during storms, and the wind-loaded ridgetops are frequent avalanche performers that should be approached with caution following new snow and wind events. The Pole Creek

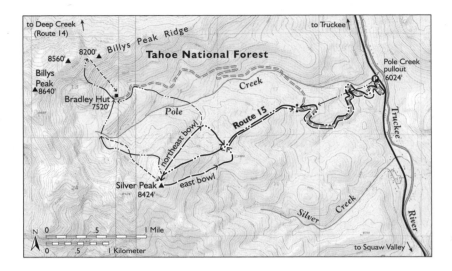

trailhead is popular with backcountry skiers, cross-country skiers, and snowshoers who use it to access Silver Peak as well as the Bradley Hut. One of the Sierra Club huts in the Tahoe area, Bradley Hut sits near the head of the Pole Creek drainage and makes a fun side trip to spend a night or two while exploring this area.

GETTING THERE
From Truckee take CA 89 south 6.3 miles to Pole Creek Road (7.5 miles north of Tahoe City). Park in the plowed pullout on the west side of the road near a locked Forest Service gate.

THE ROUTE
From the parking area, the route begins a very gradual ascent along the fire road. Although following it is very straightforward and easy, this road does take a circuitous route up the slope, and it is often much more efficient to walk in a straighter line and cut off the switchbacks as you ascend to the west. By staying on the high part of the ridge and keeping Pole Creek to your north, you can save a lot of distance. After about a mile and 600 or so vertical feet of gain, you rejoin the fire road just before it splits. If snow coverage is poor, simply follow the road to this point.

At the split in the fire road, for the main route to Silver Peak head straight (west) past the gate, which may or may not be buried in snow (the road to the right leads to the Bradley Hut; see below). Once past the gate, you leave the road and continue west up the moderate forested slope. Stay along the high point of this ridge as it begins to head southwest toward Silver Peak. After about a mile, you reach 7400 feet and the base of the steeper but still relatively moderate ridge, which you ascend to the top of Silver Peak.

Topping out on the ridge above the Bradley Hut with Silver Peak and Lake Tahoe in the background

Now you must choose whether to descend the northeastern or eastern slopes of Silver Peak; either way, you will find about 1300 vertical feet or so of continuous pitch. The eastern slopes draw you into the Silver Creek drainage, while the northern slopes deposit you in the Pole Creek drainage. From the bottom of either pitch, traverse hard to return to the ascent route. In deeper snow, it will probably require putting skins back on, especially if the skiing is good and you do more laps.

For the easiest return to the parking area, retrace your path on the fire road. This is somewhat convoluted terrain, so reversing your approach is generally the most straightforward way to exit this area.

Bradley Hut option: Where the fire road splits, the north branch goes down to Pole Creek and toward the Bradley Hut, a great spot to spend a couple of nights with friends. Most people staying at the Bradley Hut stop there first to drop their overnight gear before heading out to ski. To reach the hut, from the main ascent route take the right fork before the gate and follow this road as it drops down and crosses Pole Creek. It then contours west up the south side of the drainage to the hut at the head of the Pole Creek drainage, 2.8 miles from the split in the fire road. Silver Peak is generally accessed from the hut by heading south and then contouring east around the head of Pole Creek before ascending Silver Peak's north ridge. The northwest face of Silver Peak offers the easiest return to the hut, though it is likely you will need to put skins back on for a bit to get back to the hut after crossing Pole Creek. Also, from the northeast bowl you can simply follow the contours of the mountain down to Pole Creek, then cross the creek and ascend west-northwest to rejoin the snow-covered approach road.

Immediately north-northwest of the hut are some short pitches of easily accessible southeast-facing terrain; the top of this ridge is also the top of the north-facing tree-skiing terrain in Deep Creek (Route 14).

Opposite: *Dropping a knee in some prime corn snow in Mount Tallac's Cathedral Bowl*

PART III
LAKE TAHOE AREA

LAKE TAHOE IS THE LARGEST ALPINE LAKE in North America and, at a depth of 1645 feet, is the second-deepest lake in the United States. The Lake of the Sky sits at an elevation of 6225 feet, ringed by picturesque mountains that rise from its 72 miles of shoreline on all sides. The lake, 22 miles long and 12 miles wide, straddles the California–Nevada state line.

In addition to stunning natural beauty, the Tahoe area is home to plenty of fine backcountry skiing and snowboarding in the mountains that rise dramatically from its shores. Tahoe is also home to numerous world-class ski areas, including Squaw Valley–Alpine Meadows, Northstar-at-Tahoe, Heavenly Mountain Resort, and Kirkwood Mountain Resort as well as a number of smaller resorts.

Lake Tahoe is a year-round tourist and recreation destination, with easy access via Interstate 80 at Truckee in North Lake Tahoe, CA 50 in South Lake Tahoe, and the Reno-Tahoe International Airport nearby in Reno, Nevada. For the purposes of this guidebook, the Lake Tahoe area is divided into two regions, north and south, with the dividing line at Emerald Bay. Not only do North and South Lake Tahoe have distinctly different characteristics, but CA 89 through Emerald Bay is subject to closure during and after winter storms, often making travel between the regions more difficult.

NORTH LAKE TAHOE AND WEST SHORE

North Lake Tahoe includes the towns of Tahoe City and Kings Beach, California, and Incline Village, Nevada. This guidebook includes in the North Lake Tahoe region the west shore of Lake Tahoe down to Emerald Bay plus a couple routes in Nevada on the lake's northeast shore. Excellent winter and spring backcountry routes exist throughout this area, with breathtaking scenery and a variety of terrain.

From Interstate 80 in Truckee, CA 89 heads to the north shore of Lake Tahoe in Tahoe City and extends south down the west shore to Emerald Bay. CA 89 through Emerald Bay is subject to closure during and after storms for avalanche safety and snow removal, possibly affecting route selection and travel in that area. CA 28 stretches along the north shore of the lake to Incline Village and NV 431 to access the routes on Mount Rose and the east shore. Backcountry skiing and snowboarding are popular with both locals and visitors in this area, and parking is somewhat limited in places, so please leave as much space as possible for others to park and always park completely off the roadway.

Dining and lodging options abound among the towns of North Lake Tahoe, with gas, groceries, and numerous outdoor shops specializing in backcountry gear. The west shore of Lake Tahoe is less developed, and there is no gas available between Tahoe City and South Lake Tahoe, although there are a number of small restaurants and markets.

The Sierra Avalanche Center provides a regular avalanche advisory for the mountains in this area (see Resources).

16   Tamarack Peak

Starting Point : Pullout north of Mount Rose summit, 8650 feet
High Point : 9897 feet
Distance : 2 miles
Elevation Gain : 1250 feet
Time : 2 hours
Difficulty Level : Easy
Terrain Rating : 2
Aspects : North, northeast, east
Seasons : Winter, spring
Map : USGS Mount Rose

While it is technically located in the state of Nevada, the Mount Rose area of North Lake Tahoe is generally lumped in with the state of California as far as backcountry skiing is concerned. Situated only a few miles east as the crow flies from the state line, Mount Rose draws skiers from both Reno and the California side of the lake to its variety of high-elevation bowls. The short approach to Tamarack Peak is great for a quick lap before work, and the high starting point is beneficial when warmer storms may bring rain to lower elevations. With several bowls dropping off Tamarack's ridge and good skiing on the nearby slopes of Relay Peak, Mount Houghton, and Mount Rose,

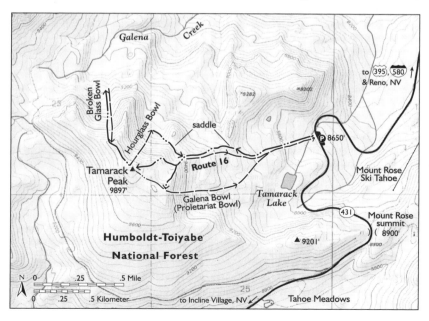

this is also a great spot for an extended tour with multiple runs. All the terrain in the Tamarack Peak area is relatively short but easily linked together to create longer tours.

GETTING THERE

From Incline Village, Nevada, on NV 28, head north toward Reno on the Mount Rose Highway (NV 431) for 9 miles. The best parking area is a plowed pullout on the right (east) side of NV 431, approximately 0.9 mile north of the Mount Rose summit. From South Reno on US Highway 395, drive 15.3 miles south on NV 431 toward Incline Village; the pullout is on the left approximately 0.9 mile before the Mount Rose summit.

THE ROUTE

From the parking area, get on your skis directly across the highway and head west. Walk past the "NONMOTORIZED RECREATION" sign and continue slightly southwest along the flats about 0.25 mile, then make a couple switchbacks up about 150 vertical feet onto a flat bench. Once you crest the top of this short slope, continue generally west through the sparse trees in the gently rolling terrain, going with the natural contours of the mountain. After another 0.25 mile or so, you pass through a small saddle. From here, head northwest for a couple hundred feet and up onto the ridge that continues west.

Hike west along the crest of this ridge for 0.25 mile, up to where it meets the ridge that drops north from the top of Galena Bowl. Head southwest up this ridge for a couple hundred vertical feet, then contour west across the bottom of the large, mellow bowl that separates Tamarack Peak's summit from the top of Galena Bowl. Gain the ridge that forms the eastern edge of the Hourglass Bowl and follow it west to the top of Tamarack Peak.

From Tamarack Peak, you'll have a great view of the windswept slopes and gullies of Mount Rose to the north, Mount Rose Ski Tahoe to the east, and the popular snowmobiling zone of Relay Peak to the west.

Directly off the top of Tamarack Peak, the primarily northeast-facing Hourglass Bowl drops for about 600 vertical feet. The main gut of this bowl funnels down through a narrow choke and looks like an hourglass when viewed from a distance. Hourglass Bowl is quite broad, and the treed slopes on either side of the main gully offer fun short runs as well. From the bottom of the Hourglass Bowl, put your skins back on and hike southeast for 150 vertical feet or so, up to the low saddle at the base of the east ridge of the bowl. Make your way back to your original ascent skin track for more laps or follow it back down to the parking area.

The next bowl northwest of the Hourglass is another short, mellow, primarily north-facing bowl, known as Broken Glass. From the top of Tamarack Peak, follow the ridge northwest, across the top of the Hourglass, and cut through the short trees at the end of the ridge and into the top of another large north-facing bowl. Ski it until it flattens out, then skin back up the way you descended to return to the top of the Hourglass Bowl.

The inviting east face of Galena Bowl (a.k.a. Proletariat Bowl) is another great option for turns on the way back to the car. From the top of Tamarack Peak, the top

Hiking up for another lap on Tamarack Peak

of Galena Bowl is about 0.25 mile southeast, a quick traverse or hike away, or a short detour while hiking back up your original ascent route from an Hourglass lap. Instead of contouring over to the top of Tamarack Peak and the Hourglass, continue up the north ridge of Galena Bowl to the top. Like the other descents in this area, Galena Bowl is only about 500–600 vertical feet, but it is slightly steeper than either the Hourglass or Broken Glass. Once it flattens out at the bottom, head northeast to return to your original ascending skin track, or continue east, bearing slightly skier's left, to return to the highway and parking area.

17 Herlan Peak: Bear Scratch

Starting Point	Pullout south of Incline Village on NV 28, 6260 feet
High Point	8775 feet
Distance	3 miles
Elevation Gain	2515 feet
Time	3 hours
Difficulty Level	Moderate
Terrain Rating	3
Aspects	West, northwest
Season	Winter
Map	USGS Marlette Lake

The chutes and glades of Herlan Peak are one of the few ski objectives on the east shore of Lake Tahoe. Towering high in Lake Tahoe Nevada State Park, above Sand Harbor State Park and the crystal-clear boulder-strewn waters of the lake, this is truly a breathtaking and scenic place to ski. The most sought-after descent on Herlan Peak is the Bear Scratch, or Bear Claw (a.k.a. Sand Harbor Chute), named for the several parallel gullies that, viewed from a distance, resemble the scratch marks of a bear's claws. The main Bear Scratch Chute drops an impressive uninterrupted 2000-plus vertical feet, some of the best consistent vertical around the lake. There is a great pitch of northwest-facing trees along the ascent route that also makes for an excellent descent. In an average or better winter, this zone is best skied during the colder months of December, January, and February when the low-elevation snow coverage is good. This location on the lake's east shore typically means that it receives approximately half the snow of the peaks on the west side. Additionally, this area's western exposure lends itself to lots of warm afternoon sun, making it prone to melting out more quickly than other spots around the lake, and even when the coverage is "good," it is likely that the lowest couple hundred vertical feet may be thinly covered and full of obstacles. That said, when conditions allow, Herlan Peak offers some amazing skiing that should definitely be on your list.

GETTING THERE
From Incline Village, Nevada, head south on NV 28 for 4 miles to a large, scenic pull-out (restrooms) on the west side of the highway just north of Sand Harbor State Park.

THE ROUTE
From the parking area, head south a hundred yards or so and cross the road. Head up onto the slope, and don't be discouraged if the coverage here is poor—it usually is, but it gets better as you climb higher into the protection of the trees. Head east

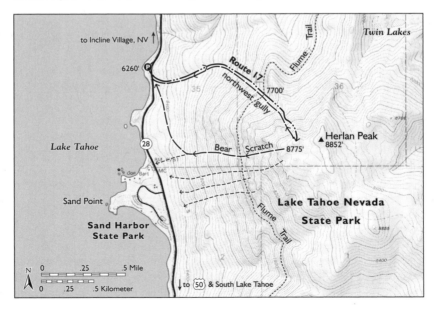

Skiing powder on Lake Tahoe's east shore in the Bear Scratch on Herlan Peak
(Adam Ryan)

and after a couple hundred vertical feet or so of ascent, head into the obvious gully. The lower reaches of this gully on the northwest side of Herlan Peak are thickly tree covered, and travel through them is usually a little convoluted. After another couple hundred vertical feet or so of ascent, the gully begins to turn southeast and opens up with more widely spaced trees.

Switchback up this obvious gully for about 800 vertical feet; it gets progressively steeper until you cross over the historic Flume Trail (7700 feet). In summer, the iconic Flume Trail is among the most popular and scenic mountain-bike rides in the Tahoe Basin, but you won't even notice it in the winter except for the fact that the steepness of the pitch slackens a bit. As you continue climbing southeast, the gully widens and the trees become larger and more spread out. Now the route gets progressively steeper until you top out on the high point just west of Herlan Peak proper (8852 feet). The top of the Bear Scratch offers one of the most amazing panoramic vistas of Lake Tahoe anywhere, so factor in some time to stare in wonder at the view.

The top of the Bear Scratch is quite obvious, and when you are standing at the top of it you can see straight down all the way to the bottom of the run. The top of this line can often be a bit wind scoured, and entering sometimes involves negotiating some peppery rocks. Once you're in the chute, however, it is a very straightforward fall-line descent. When the pitch really begins to flatten out about 400 feet from the bottom, I recommend a traverse hard right to return to the parking area on a gently descending line that may require some pushing through the flats, or you could continue straight down to the road and return to the parking area with a short walk along the road (watch out for traffic).

Options: From the top of this route, numerous Bear Scratch claw marks are to skier's left (south) along the face, and each offers some great skiing, although they are more difficult to enter from the top than the primary one described above. The other option from the top of Herlan Peak is to descend the gladed slopes roughly the same way you came up. This descent is slightly more moderate in pitch and definitely more protected from the winds that often damage the more exposed Bear Scratch. The uppermost part of this pitch has a large rock outcrop to skier's left of the ascent route. Nicely spaced, steep tree skiing lies on the fall line from here and funnels you back down into the gully you came up. Lower down, be sure to return to the gully you ascended and follow it back down the way you came to return to the parking area.

18   Twin Peaks

Starting Points	Chairlift approach, 8637 feet;
	Grouse Ridge approach, 7200 feet
High Point	8878 feet
Distance	6.5 miles for either approach
Elevation Gains	Chairlift approach, 1300 feet;
	Grouse Ridge approach, 2500 feet
Times	Chairlift approach, 3.5 hours;
	Grouse Ridge approach, 4 hours
Difficulty Level	Moderate
Terrain Rating	3
Aspect	Northeast
Seasons	Winter, spring
Map	USGS Tahoe City, Homewood

Twin Peaks is named for its jagged, rocky twin summits that give the mountain an imposing look when viewed from afar. Located just south of Alpine Meadows ski area, Twin Peaks stands proudly at the head of Ward Canyon. The northeast-facing slope beckons skiers to make the hike out from the ski area's summit chairlift (day ticket or season pass required) or from the end of Courchevel Road via Grouse Ridge. From either starting point, both approaches intersect at Grouse Rock. Getting there involves a beautiful ridgeline tour with incredible views the entire way. From the notch in Twin Peaks, two separate steep entrances lead down into a large northeast-facing apron. At the bottom of the pitch, mellow sidehill skinning leads from Ward Creek around the bottom of Grouse Ridge to return to a chairlift back to the ski area or to a vehicle parked nearby. Numerous options exist for extending this tour and doing more skiing on nearby slopes out in Ward Canyon.

GETTING THERE

Chairlift approach: From Tahoe City, take CA 89 north 3.7 miles to Alpine Meadows Road and follow it to Alpine Meadows ski area parking.

    Grouse Ridge approach: From Tahoe City, take CA 89 south 2 miles and turn right (west) onto Pineland Drive. Follow Pineland Drive west to the first intersection, bearing left onto Twin Peaks Road; this quickly turns into Ward Creek Boulevard as the road bears right. About halfway up the hill, Ward Creek Boulevard turns into Courchevel Road. Three miles from CA 89, at the top of the hill, you'll see the base of Sherwood chairlift on the back side of Alpine Meadows ski area. Parking is tricky in this area. A small lot exists for members of the Alpine Peaks Homeowners Association, but any other parking is extremely limited. Parking on the roadway is not permitted in winter—you will get a ticket—so you must park your entire vehicle off the road; please do not park in anyone's driveway. There is generally a plowed spot or two, but they may be a short distance away from the very top of the road.

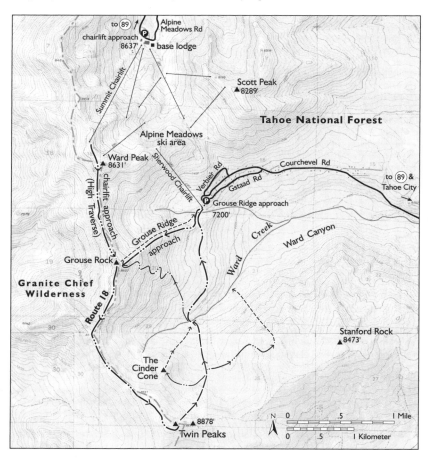

Breaking trail on the approach to Twin Peaks

THE ROUTE

Chairlift approach: From the Alpine Meadows ski area parking lot, take the Summit chairlift to the top, then head south along the ridge known as the High Traverse. Just west of Ward Peak, the route roughly joins the path of the Pacific Crest National Scenic Trail, which runs along the west side of the ridge. Follow the contours of this ridge as it dips and dives for about a mile until you reach the prominent rock outcropping known as Grouse Rock.

Grouse Ridge approach: From the end of Courchevel Road, walk behind the bottom terminal of Sherwood chairlift and head south toward the base of the ridge that extends east down from Grouse Rock. Cross the creek and skin up onto the ridge. Continue up the crest of this southwest-trending ridge, the most direct way up to Grouse Rock. This approach gains 1400 vertical feet over a little more than 1 mile.

Both approach routes come together here at Grouse Rock. Skirt around Grouse Rock to its south side, staying as high as you can, and regain the ridge. From here you will get a view of your destination as well as your route out to Twin Peaks, which is still a couple of miles away. Stay on the ridge, following it as it wraps southwest, then southeast, and gently climbs to the shoulder of Twin Peaks. As you hike the ridge, be aware that large cornices often form here; in places you may want to stay as far as 30 feet back from the edge.

As you get close to Twin Peaks, you actually skirt around the west side of the north peak. The snow is often burned off on the back side here, and you may need to take your skis off to walk up to the notch between the twin summits and the prominent rock that separates the two entrances to the northeast face of Twin Peaks.

Both entrances are quite steep right off the top. The entrance to skier's right is slightly steeper and often guarded by a small cornice. The entrance to skier's left is more straightforward, but still surprisingly steep for the first 200 vertical feet or so. As you descend, the pitch gradually slackens until it flattens out completely around 7400 feet. Here is a great point for savvy backcountry skiers to extend their tour (see Options, below).

The main route continues downhill but bear left (north) toward the bottom of the south-facing slopes extending down from Grouse Rock. You'll need to transition back over to skins to exit the valley, but you have options. You can stay low and sidehill-skin along the bottom of the south-facing slopes of Grouse Ridge, the easiest way, eventually wrapping around the end of the ridge and back to the bottom of Sherwood chairlift where the Grouse Ridge approach started. If you started from the chairlift approach on the front side of Alpine Meadows, ride Sherwood chairlift back up and ski around and down back to the main lodge parking area.

Options: Those with energy to burn can depart the main descent route at around 7400 feet. To the east are the nearby northwest-facing slopes of Stanford Rock, where a descent of the trees and gullies takes you down to Ward Creek, about a half mile northeast of the main descent route. To the west are the steep northeast-facing gullies of the Cinder Cone, where your descent rejoins the main descent route at Ward Creek. Or from the main descent route at Ward Creek, climb up the south-facing slopes of Grouse Ridge, regaining the ridgetop just east of Grouse Rock. From here you can ski the rolling, treed north-facing terrain of Grouse Ridge down to the bottom of Sherwood chairlift.

19   Blackwood Canyon Cliffs: Fourth of July Chutes

Starting Point	Ellis Peak trailhead, 7790 feet
High Point	8514 feet
Distance	2 miles
Elevation Gain	750 feet
Time	1.5 hours
Difficulty Level	Easy
Terrain Rating	3
Aspect	North
Seasons	Late spring, early summer
Map	USGS Homewood

Sitting atop Barker Pass at the top of Blackwood Canyon, one of several deep valleys on the west shore of Lake Tahoe, are the Fourth of July Chutes. These short, steep, north-facing chutes cut white lines down a sheer cliff face that lies directly on the

Pacific Crest. This area's location, elevation, and aspect lead to some serious wind loading throughout the winter, which results in a deep snowpack that often lasts well into summer. Named for the fact that these chutes are sometimes skiable as late as the Fourth of July, this is often the last skiing of the year for many in the Tahoe area. It depends on the season, but more often than not these chutes are accessible earlier than the Fourth of July, generally late May to early June in an average year. When Barker Pass Road is closed in winter, it has one of the few Sno-Parks in the Tahoe area, and the Blackwood Canyon area is one of the lake's primary snowmobile-accessible zones. As summer approaches and the snows recede, however, the pavement of Barker Pass Road makes for a quick and easy approach once the road opens. Prior to the opening of the road for the summer, adventurous skiers and snowboarders often ride their bicycles past the locked gates for several miles up to the snow line before hiking the rest of the way to the Ellis Peak trailhead.

GETTING THERE

From the Y in Tahoe City, at the junction of CA 89 and CA 28, follow CA 89 south 4.2 miles to the Sno-Park at the mouth of Blackwood Canyon (23 miles north of the South Lake Tahoe Y at the junction of CA 89 and US Highway 50, just north of Homewood). In winter the Forest Service gate just a couple hundred yards west

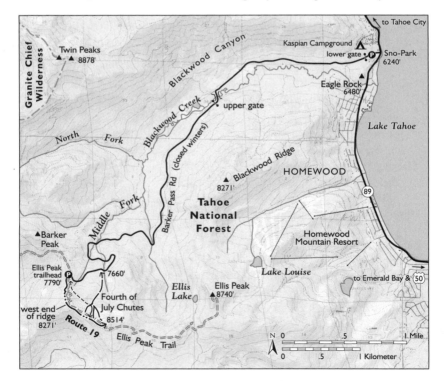

A skier makes his way down one of the Fourth of July Chutes.

up Barker Pass Road from CA 89 is closed. You can ski all the way in from this gate, but when there is enough snow coverage here for skiing in, you are better off skiing bigger and better terrain around the lake. When the road is open, drive paved Barker Pass Road as it parallels Blackwood Creek for 2.1 miles. Continue on the road as it turns left and crosses Blackwood Creek on a bridge, then turns right and starts to climb the south side of the canyon. If the second Forest Service gate at 2.4 miles is open, continue uphill for 4.6 more miles to the top of Barker Pass Road, where the pavement ends and the road begins to descend the western slope; here, you can look south to glimpse the chutes a short distance above. Park in the dirt parking area on the left side of the road, the Ellis Peak trailhead (7 miles from CA 89). Occasionally, when the upper road hasn't been cleared of snow or debris, the road will be closed at this second gate. If you ride a bike past either of the gates, follow the paved road to the top of the pass, the same spot you would park if you drove.

THE ROUTE

From the Ellis Peak trailhead, follow the Ellis Peak Trail south as it begins to climb the treed slope leading up to the ridge. The summer trail makes a number of switchbacks up this steep slope, but hopefully if you're here to ski it will still be snow-covered. The fastest way to the top is boot-packing in a straight line to the high point above. This is a relatively short hike, about 0.5 mile and 500 vertical feet to this high point (8271 feet) at the west end of the Fourth of July Chutes ridge.

From here, you should be able to see the precipitous cliff face and your route along the ridge on the summer trail to access this terrain. As you head southeast along this ridge, you gain some more vertical as you begin to pass the ski lines. In a good year, there are as many as five separate short, steep chutes that drop though these cliff walls. The first chute you come to is the shortest but also the steepest. Farther east, near the ridge's high point (8514 feet), are the rest of the chutes, each dropping about 300 or so vertical feet before they open up into the apron below.

Choose a chute and make a run—but once you're up in this area, you might as well do a few laps. There often is a boot-pack up one of the chutes back to the ridgetop, but if there isn't, it is easy enough to put one in.

When you're done making late-season laps, traverse hard left (northwest) back to the road near the trailhead at the top of the pass. You can also descend due north through the forest below the face to eventually be funneled into a drainage that leads down to the road a little farther downhill. Either way is usually slow going through dense forest with thin late-season coverage, so use caution. From the road, travel on the road back to wherever you left your bike or car.

20   Rubicon Peak

Starting Points	Highland Drive, 6900 feet; pullouts on CA 89, 6350 feet
High Point	9183 feet
Distance	4 miles for either approach
Elevation Gains	From Highland Drive, 2300 feet; from CA 89 pullouts, 2800 feet
Times	From Highland Drive, 2 hours; from CA 89 pullouts, 2.5 hours
Difficulty Level	Moderate
Terrain Rating	2
Aspects	North-northeast, east
Seasons	Winter, spring
Maps	USGS Rockbound Valley; Meeks Bay; Homewood

Rubicon Peak stands just on the edge of the Desolation Wilderness above Rubicon Bay at the northern end of the Jakes-Rubicon ridge that dominates Lake Tahoe's west shore skyline. There are five distinct high points on the Jakes-Rubicon ridgeline,

Blowing up a massive powder cloud on Rubicon Peak

but picturesque Rubicon Peak is easily distinguishable from its neighbors due to the pointy rock nipple that forms its summit. Rubicon's moderately pitched north- and east-facing slopes are covered with widely spaced old- and new-growth conifers, which are perfect for those who prefer mellower slopes or those just getting into backcountry skiing. Rubicon is less prone to instability than other zones in the area, making this a popular area during and immediately after storms. There are a couple different spots to start a tour on Rubicon Peak, but parking in this area continues to be an issue; you may get a warning or ticket no matter where you start this tour. That said, this is an ideal spot for a quick morning hit or a full day doing laps, and there is plenty of fine skiing to be done on this broad face above Tahoe's crystal-clear waters. It is well worth exploring the various other pitches of this sheltered, tree-covered slope, including Hidden and Jakes peaks (Routes 21–22).

GETTING THERE

Highland Drive: From Tahoe City, take CA 89 south 13.5 miles (or 13.9 miles north of the Y in South Lake Tahoe) and turn uphill on Scenic Drive; immediately take your first right, on Woodland Drive. Then take the second right, on Brook Road, then a left on Crest Drive, a right on Forestview Drive, a left on Highview Drive, and finally a right on Highland Drive. Continue to where Highland Drive dead-ends at a locked gate with a water tank just up the hill. This is the most convenient place to park—*however,* parking on the roadway is not permitted during the winter. You can

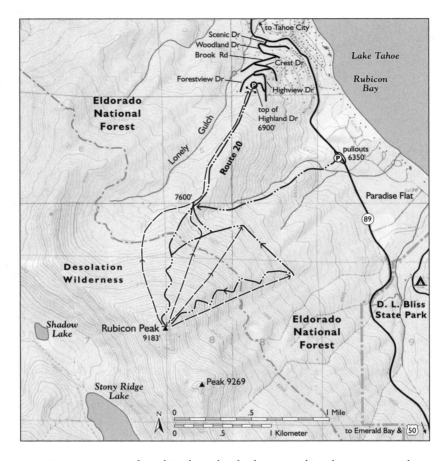

sometimes get away with parking here, but backcountry skiers have gotten tickets, especially during snow-removal periods. It remains a roll of the dice. Park completely off the roadway if possible, but please do not park in anyone's driveway. The dead end of Forestview Drive, one road below, may be a good alternative.

CA 89 pullouts: From the turnoff onto Scenic Drive, continue 1 mile farther south on CA 89 to a pair of pullouts on both sides of the road, which are also used for the approach to Rubicon Peak, with less risk of a parking ticket. This starting point is roughly the same distance but adds about 500 vertical feet to the climb.

THE ROUTE

From Highland Drive: From the end of Highland Drive, head southwest past the locked gate and follow the path of the summer hiking trail to gain the top of the prominent ridgeline that extends from the north side of Rubicon Peak. Skin along the north side of this ridge, just below the ridgetop, to the base of the steeper north-facing slopes at about 7600 feet.

From CA 89: From the pullouts on CA 89, follow the main drainage due west, then southwest, for about 1200 vertical feet up to the base of the steeper north-facing slopes at about 7600 feet, to join the main route.

From here, the main route turns south and switchbacks up through the trees for 1400 vertical feet before topping out on the north side of Rubicon's cliffy summit. It is possible to scramble up onto the rocky summit of Rubicon Peak from the west side, but it can be tricky. Some tough moves are made even more difficult in ski boots. Be aware that the summit is small, and there is a 100-plus-foot cliff off the east side.

Take in the panoramic view of Lake Tahoe, Stony Ridge Lake, Crag and Phipps peaks immediately to your west, and the Crystal Range in the distance behind that. You've got numerous descent options from here: the north-facing trees on either side of the skin track, the northeast-facing trees, or the east-facing slope.

The north and northeast trees hold cold snow the longest, and the north slope affords the easiest return to the ascent's skin track. Just remember where you are in relation to your uptrack: it is somewhat easy to ski below the level of the ridge that you hiked in on, so you may need to climb just slightly to return to it. From the bottom of the northeast descent, you'll need to put skins back on to climb west back up to the ascent route.

For a longer run, traverse under the summit cliff and ski the east-facing trees; they hold a consistent moderate pitch for around 2000 vertical feet. Returning to the skin track from here, however, requires a bit more effort and typically involves cutting a new skin track to return up the east ridge to the summit or wrapping back around to the ascent route on the north side of the mountain.

From whatever point your descent rejoins your ascent route, retrace your uptrack back to where you parked.

21 Hidden Peak

Starting Point	Pullout north of Lester Beach Road, 6500 feet
High Point	9180 feet
Distance	3 miles
Elevation Gain	2680 feet
Time	2 hours
Difficulty Level	Moderate
Terrain Rating	2
Aspect	Northeast
Seasons	Winter, spring
Maps	USGS Rockbound Valley; Emerald Bay

Sitting in the middle of the ridgeline from Rubicon Peak to Jakes Peak on the west shore of Lake Tahoe above D. L. Bliss State Park, Hidden Peak is prime easy-access tree-skiing terrain right above the lake. Despite its name, Hidden Peak isn't all that

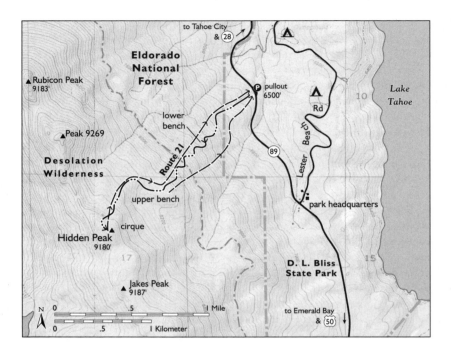

hidden, and it often sees as much traffic as its very popular neighbors, all of which are just inside the Desolation Wilderness. That said, there is plenty of room to spread out in the beautifully spaced northeast-facing trees to find fresh snow even days after a storm. Hidden Peak's lower flanks offer great tree skiing from a bench at 8300 feet down to the parking area on CA 89. Above this bench are a gorgeous but extremely steep and barely skiable cirque sitting just below the summit and a mellow north-facing pitch of mountain hemlocks leading from the summit around the cirque to the bench. Hidden Peak is another of many amazing places to ski on the west shore of Lake Tahoe, certainly one worth checking out.

GETTING THERE

From Tahoe City, head south on CA 89 for 15.6 miles to a pullout on the east side of the highway 0.8 mile north of the entrance and park headquarters for D. L. Bliss State Park, at Lester Beach Road. This pullout, which accommodates roughly ten vehicles, often fills up on weekends. From the Y at South Lake Tahoe, head north on CA 89 for 11.6 miles to this pullout.

THE ROUTE

From the uphill end of the pullout, cross CA 89. This is a relatively popular back-country skiing destination on the west shore, so it is likely that there will already be a skin track to follow whenever you arrive. Head into the forest in a southwesterly direction. The pitch starts out very gradually and gets progressively steeper as you go. After about 800 vertical feet, you reach a small but noticeable bench. The terrain below you is fun on the way out of this area, but the best skiing lies in the trees just above you up to the upper bench. Continue southwest, switchbacking up the slope. Take note of the terrain all around you, as this is all excellent gladed ski terrain.

After another 900 vertical feet or so, you arrive at the larger upper bench. The best skiing on Hidden Peak lies below you on either side of the skin track. Looking southwest toward the peak's summit, you will see the steep and craggy east-facing cirque. There are skiable lines down through this face, although they are very exposed and committing and should only be attempted by those with the routefinding and skiing skills necessary to tackle this kind of complex terrain.

The route to the summit climbs up through the forest just north of this cirque. Head west from the bench and begin to climb the forested slope. Ascend through the hemlock forest and eventually turn south toward the summit of Hidden Peak. It is roughly 800 vertical feet from the upper bench to the top.

Enjoying a sunny powder day on Hidden Peak

Head back down the way you came to return to the bench, then pick a nice lane from the upper bench back down to the parking area. Take note of which side of the skin track you are on, and as the pitch flattens out near the bottom, cut back to the skin track for the easiest return back down to the parking area on CA 89.

22   Jakes Peak: Northeast Side

Starting Point	Pullout south of Lester Beach Road, 6850 feet
High Point	9187 feet
Distance	3 miles
Elevation Gain	2300 feet
Time	2 hours
Difficulty Level	Moderate
Terrain Ratings	2–3
Aspect	Northeast-east
Seasons	Winter, spring
Map	USGS Emerald Bay

You've got to get up really early to beat the dawn patrollers to the northeast side of Jakes Peak on a powder day. The same handful of people put in this skin track virtually every time it snows. If you don't like to hike in the dark, don't worry: you're guaranteed to have a track put in by the time you get there. The steep trees and open gullies that flank the northeast and east sides of Jakes Peak make this zone one of the most popular among backcountry skiers in the entire Lake Tahoe Basin. Named in honor of Jeffery James (Jake) Smith, a ski patroller who died in an avalanche at Alpine Meadows ski area in 1982, Jakes Peak is a Tahoe classic. Perched above D. L. Bliss State Park on Emerald Bay on Tahoe's west shore and just inside the Desolation Wilderness, Jakes is also among the more beautiful places to ski in the world—not to be missed.

GETTING THERE
From Tahoe City, follow CA 89 south 16.4 miles to Lester Beach Road and the entrance to D. L. Bliss State Park. Continue approximately 0.25 mile south to a pullout on the east side of CA 89. From the Y in South Lake Tahoe, drive 10.6 miles north on CA 89 to this pullout. Park here, but this is a popular backcountry skiing destination, so leave as much room as possible for others. If this parking area is full, park at the pullout a little farther south on the west side of CA 89.

THE ROUTE
The route starts on the west side of CA 89, directly across from the pullout. There generally is a skin track here—a very steep one—by the time you or anyone else arrives. Head directly west on it, gradually ascending for about 0.25 mile to the base of the

Fresh powder and great views on Jakes Peak

steep, tree-covered slope at the bottom of Jakes. Continue west, switchbacking up this slope through a beautiful old-growth conifer forest for about 900 vertical feet, where you crest up onto a large and relatively flat bench that breaks up the upper and lower pitches on this side of the mountain. Follow the bench west as it gradually climbs to the base of the upper slope and the broad northeast ridge you will ascend to the summit.

Continue switchbacking up this ridge, taking in the outrageous panoramic views of Lake Tahoe, Emerald Bay, and the mountains along the west shore. The wide-open gullies that descend the east flank of the mountain should be visible, as should the steep and more confined gullies and trees that drop down the peak's northeast side. The higher you get on Jakes, the greater the potential for wind loading and snowpack instability, and although this zone is tree covered and people are comfortable skiing here during storms, that doesn't mean that avalanches can't happen here. In fact, the east slope is often referred to as the Avy Path and is prone to slides.

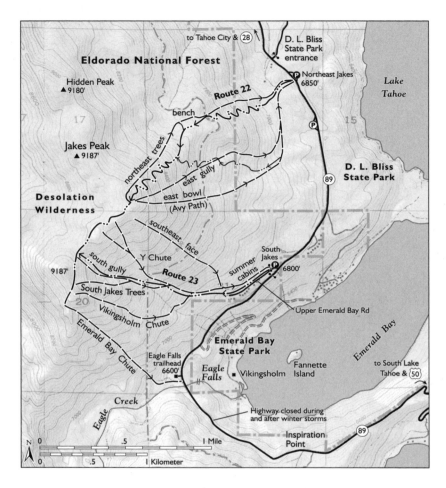

The true summit of Jakes sits along the ridge a short distance northwest, but the primary skiing terrain is accessed from the high point here on the top of Jakes' southeast shoulder. The numerous descent options include the east gully, the east bowl (Avy Path), and the northeast trees. The descent options drop for nearly 2000 vertical feet before they lose their pitch among the manzanita and willow bushes at the base of the slope; in big snow years these bushes may be completely covered, but you must often deal with them at the bottom of these runs. Stay to skier's left while you filter back down to the skin track or continue down to the road for a short walk back to the parking area.

If you want more laps, though, before traversing left back toward the highway, instead bust a skin track to the west, back up to join the one you ascended earlier above the bench, and climb back to the top. From here you can do more laps on the east bowl or drop into the trees and gullies to skier's left (north) of the ridge you climbed. The trees of the upper northeast face have really nice spacing and the pitch holds for around 1300 vertical feet before you hit the bench. From the bench, return to the skin track for more laps on the upper half or follow the skin track down the bench to the lower slope and slalom your way through the widely spaced tree trunks back to the parking area.

23 Jakes Peak: South Side

Starting Point	Gate on CA 89, 6800 feet
High Point	9187 feet
Distance	3 miles
Elevation Gain	2300 feet
Time	2 hours
Difficulty Level	Moderate
Terrain Rating	3
Aspect	East-southeast-south
Seasons	Winter, spring
Map	USGS Emerald Bay

Jakes Peak is one of the most popular backcountry skiing locations in Lake Tahoe, for obvious reasons. Situated on the north side of Emerald Bay, with skiable flanks that rise straight from the lake's west shore, Jakes is among the most beautiful places to go skiing in the entire world. Just a 20-minute drive from either Tahoe City or South Lake Tahoe, Jakes is centrally located for backcountry skiers coming from either end of the lake. With slopes that range in aspect from south to east just inside the Desolation Wilderness, the south side of Jakes Peak is a great spot to find spring conditions or cold midwinter powder when the stars align. South Jakes' southern exposure lends itself to great corn snow conditions, but for that same reason it is prone to burning off early in the season, so check the coverage in this area before attempting these routes. Be mindful of the corn cycle, and try to time your descents for optimal ski conditions. Typically the corn is ripest between 11:00 AM and 1:00 PM on slopes of this aspect. Skiing later in the day may leave trenches, essentially ruining the corn, so do yourself and everyone else a favor and pay attention to your timing and the softness of the snow. Due to the popularity of this zone, parking can often be an issue, especially on sunny spring weekends; please be considerate of others.

GETTING THERE

From Tahoe City, take CA 89 south approximately 18 miles to Upper Emerald Bay Road, a short Forest Service road littered with a number of summer cabins. This is also the location of a pullout on the west side of CA 89 by the northern Emerald Bay closure gate. From the Y in South Lake Tahoe, take CA 89 north 9.4 miles to this pullout. If the Emerald Bay gate is closed, do not block it; also be sure to allow enough room for snowplows to turn around in the pullout.

Heading up at sunrise to ski south-facing powder above Emerald Bay and Lake Tahoe (Oscar Havens)

THE ROUTE

Upper Emerald Bay Road, which is closed in winter, is the beginning of your ascent route. Follow this road west, behind the summer cabins, until it ends at the bottom of the prominent gully on the south side of the mountain. The bottom of the gully is covered in sparse trees and bushes, but you quickly exit them and have a clear view of your ascent route up the main south gully. Although the climb starts gradually, this gully steadily increases in pitch over its 2200-vertical-foot rise. Keep your eyes peeled as you ascend because the primary descent routes will be visible to you at some point during the climb.

The steep pitch of the upper gully eventually slackens just before you top out on the ridge south of Jakes Peak. From here you can drop in and descend the way you came for the easiest way back down or continue along the ridge in either direction to get to any of the several other descents. On the skier's-right side of the ascent gully, you'll find the South Jakes Trees, which face east and hold cold snow for a surprisingly long time. The Vikingsholm Chute, named for the view from the top directly down at the mansion in Emerald Bay, is the next prominent gully to skier's right of the ascent gully. At the bottom of the Vikingsholm Chute, head skier's left to return to the bottom of the skin track or the parking area.

A more advanced descent, known as the Emerald Bay Chute, is located even farther southwest and requires a short downhill walk on the back side of the ridge to get to the entrance. The top of the Emerald Bay Chute is relatively steep and the slope is uninterrupted for its 2400-foot length down to the Eagle Falls trailhead at the west end of Emerald Bay. If the road is closed, return to the parking area by hiking north along the road about 0.8 mile back to the parking area; if the road is open, you can leave a shuttle vehicle here at the Eagle Falls trailhead.

From the top of the ascent gully, you can also head northeast for 0.25 mile, staying just on the ridge's north side, to get to the Y Chute; named for its resemblance to the letter. The Y has a couple of relatively steep entrances that funnel together after a couple hundred feet, then it heads down to join the gully you ascended. For another option along the ridgetop, 0.25 mile farther east of the Y Chute entrance brings you to the southeast face, a very long and consistent pitch that deposits you at the top of Upper Emerald Bay Road by the summer cabins.

Continuing farther along the ridge eventually brings you to the east bowl and the northeast-facing trees, routes that are typically accessed from the other side (Route 22).

SOUTH LAKE TAHOE AND DESOLATION WILDERNESS

As this region's name suggests, South Lake Tahoe sits at the southern end of the lake, surrounded by a wealth of outstanding backcountry possibilities. For the purposes of this guidebook, the South Lake Tahoe region includes the southern Desolation Wilderness and Echo Summit to the west, extends east nearly to the Nevada state line, and stretches south to the Carson Pass area. An incredible variety of terrain exists in this area, with something for everyone on the slopes that rise dramatically above town to the stark and windswept landscape of the high peaks of Desolation Wilderness. Excellent and relatively easy winter access makes this an amazing backcountry destination in both winter and spring.

US Highway 50, CA 89, and CA 88 are the three main roads that come together in or near South Lake Tahoe and provide access to the majority of the routes in this area. CA 89 stretches north up the west lakeshore to Tahoe City and is subject to winter closure through Emerald Bay during and after storms for avalanche safety and snow removal. US 50 passes west over Echo Summit on its path down to Sacramento, and it heads east through Carson City, Nevada. CA 89 continues southeast to climb over Luther Pass and meet up with CA 88, which heads south to Carson Pass and west to Kirkwood Mountain Resort.

Known for having a somewhat grittier exterior, the cities of South Lake Tahoe, California, and Stateline, Nevada, are home not only to large casinos and strip malls but a large population of hardcore backcountry enthusiasts who revel in the breadth of options so close to home. The area is significantly more developed than North Lake Tahoe, and there is no lack of dining or lodging options or places to get anything you might need while visiting the area. Once you head south on CA 88, however, there are no gas stations or stores between Meyers and Kirkwood.

The Sierra Avalanche Center provides a regular avalanche advisory for the South Lake Tahoe area (see Resources).

24 Maggies Peaks

Starting Point : Bayview trailhead, 6825 feet
High Points : Maggies South, 8699 feet; Maggies North, 8499 feet
Distances : Maggies South, 3.5 miles; Maggies North, 2.5 miles
Elevation Gains : Maggies South, 1875 feet; Maggies North, 1675 feet
Times : Maggies South, 2.5 hours; Maggies North, 2 hours
Difficulty Level : Easy
Terrain Rating : 3
Aspects : North, northeast, east
Seasons : Winter, spring
Map : USGS Emerald Bay

The twin summits of Maggies Peaks rise straight from the southwestern shore of Emerald Bay and lie just within the boundary of Desolation Wilderness. Separated by a saddle on the ridge, Maggies North and South offer a plethora of terrain on various aspects in a relatively small area. The north- and east-facing tree runs are great spots to find powder during and after storms, and a partial shuttle can be done if you are skiing the north side of the north peak when the road is open through Emerald

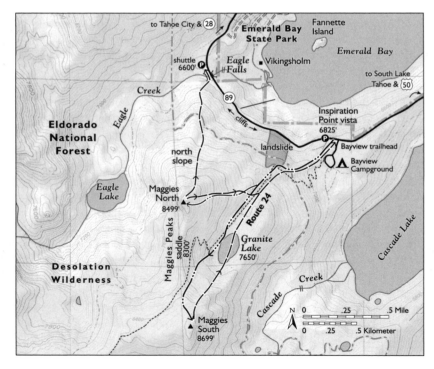

Skiing toward Emerald Bay on the north side of Maggies Peaks

Bay. The relatively short climb makes it a great spot for a quick lap, or several, with unbeatable views of Emerald Bay, Lake Tahoe, and Desolation Wilderness. CA 89 is subject to closure at Upper Emerald Bay Road during and after heavy snowfalls due to avalanche danger and potentially treacherous road conditions. When the road is closed, you can park near the closure gates (but don't block them) and approach Maggies along the snow-covered road. This adds a bit of distance, 0.8 mile from the south and 1.75 miles from the north, of easy walking to the Bayview trailhead but often makes for a very pleasant, uncrowded backcountry experience.

GETTING THERE

From the Y in South Lake Tahoe, drive north on CA 89 for 7.7 miles, or from Tahoe City, drive 20 miles south on CA 89 to a pullout for Bayview trailhead and campground on the south side of the road opposite the Inspiration Point vista. If you plan to ski the north slope, you may want to park a shuttle car at the Eagle Falls trailhead, just shy of a mile north on CA 89 from the Bayview trailhead pullout.

THE ROUTE

From the pullout, head past the gate and southwest through the closed campground. At the western end of the campground, you'll see signs for the Bayview trailhead; continue past them, heading west and up into the forest, roughly following the snow-covered path of the summer trail. Switchback up through the trees for

400 vertical feet or so, then contour northwest to the top of the landslide. Here you'll have an unobstructed view straight down into Emerald Bay. The route then turns to the southwest and into the creek drainage that comes down from Granite Lake. This is the point where the ascent routes split depending on which of the Maggies Peaks you are headed to.

Maggies South: For the south peak, continue southwest up the drainage along the climber's-right side of the creek to Granite Lake (7650 feet). Walk along the western edge of the lake, then climb west up the treed slope for 600 vertical feet to the saddle on the ridge between the peaks. Once you hit the ridge, head south, gaining 450 vertical feet to the Maggies South summit.

The view from Maggies South peak is pretty incredible: you can see all of Lake Tahoe, Emerald Bay, Granite Lake, Cascade Lake, and Fallen Leaf Lake at the same time. This is also a great vantage point for looking at the north side of Mount Tallac and the entire cirque that stretches from there to Janines Peak at the head of the Cascade Creek drainage. Be sure to look down the steep southeast slope of Maggies South, down to Cascade Creek. Some lines fill in on this slope during a big snow year, but they are extremely exposed and complex. Those with advanced routefinding and skiing skills should be able to figure this zone out on their own when everything falls into place.

For this route's descent from Maggies South peak, drop into 1000 vertical feet of fun, northeast-facing trees littered with small cliffs and rocks back down to Granite Lake. Lap it back up, or head out the way you came to return to the parking area. Some people opt to ski the landslide down to the road; while this is great ski terrain, it is frowned upon to knock slough or an avalanche onto the road when it is open.

Maggies North: From the top of the landslide, instead of heading up the creek drainage to Granite Lake, head west up the east-facing tree pitch. This slope climbs gradually at first but steadily steepens as you make your way to the top. From the top of the landslide to the top of the north peak is about 1000 vertical feet of nicely spaced east-facing trees, great for climbing and even better for skiing.

From the top of Maggies North peak, you've got options. You can head back down the east-facing trees on either side of the skin track to return the way you came. Or to drop into the north slope, from the summit head down the ridge northwest for about 50 feet before veering north and dropping into one of the steep gullies of the north face. Two short gullies are steep but relatively straightforward, separated at the top by a small rock buttress on this cliffy, tree-covered slope. Continuing farther down the ridge past these two gullies leads to some pretty complex terrain; there are a handful of ways through, but you can definitely end up in a spot you don't want to be in.

Take the north slope route down for about 1000 vertical feet, then begin to angle slightly to the northeast, down the shelfy terrain to the bridge on CA 89 that crosses Eagle Creek by the Eagle Falls trailhead. Be aware that there are many closeout lines above Emerald Bay Road (CA 89) that end in cliffs to the east of this route; it is important to ski down to the Eagle Creek drainage on your way out of here. From the Eagle Falls trailhead, shuttle back to the Bayview trailhead.

25   Janines Peak

Starting Point	Bayview trailhead, 6825 feet
High Point	9579 feet
Distance	7 miles
Elevation Gain	4000 feet
Time	4 hours
Difficulty Level	Strenuous
Terrain Rating	3
Aspect	East-northeast
Seasons	Winter, spring
Maps	USGS Emerald Bay; Rockbound Valley

Located behind the popular roadside zones of Mount Tallac and Maggies Peaks, Janines Peak sees much less traffic than its neighbors to the east and north. Janines' summit is little more than a high spot on the ridge that extends northwest from the back side of Tallac, but the broad east face is covered with rolling terrain that drops down to Azure Lake, the reward for those willing to hike just a little bit farther from the road. From the summit of Janines, a ridge extends for 0.75 mile to the north with excellent, moderately pitched terrain and exciting short rollovers dropping off its eastern flank the entire way. The best way to access Janines Peak is to hike up Maggies South (Route 24) then over it to descend to the north end of the Janines ridge. This route involves a bit more vertical than the more direct route up Cascade Creek, but it usually affords much easier passage. While the Cascade Creek route may look easier and more direct on a map, the south-facing slopes are prone to melting off quickly, resulting in some challenging hiking through complex bushy and rocky terrain. Consistent snow coverage and the chance to ski Maggies after skiing Janines with only a little more climbing make this route up and over Maggies a better option. A tour to Janines is a great introduction to skiing in Desolation Wilderness, and the mountain is ideally situated to combine with descents on Dicks, Tallac, and Maggies for a longer tour with numerous fun descents.

GETTING THERE

From the Y in South Lake Tahoe, drive north on CA 89 for 7.7 miles, or from Tahoe City, drive 20 miles south on CA 89 to a pullout for Bayview trailhead and campground on the south side of the road opposite the Inspiration Point vista.

THE ROUTE

From the Bayview trailhead, climb to the saddle (around 8300 feet) in the ridge between Maggies' twin summits, closer to the south peak (Route 24). Once you've gained the saddle, contour southwest and slightly uphill behind Maggies' south summit to the crest of the ridge that extends to the west. From here, you should have

Exploring one of the steep, narrow chutes that drop off the Janines Peak ridge

a pretty spectacular view of the broad east face of Janines Peak and ridge. This is a good time to take a photo of the zone and pick your line and entrance from the ridge.

You can generally transition into ski mode for the short descent along the west ridge that leads you down to the north end of the Janines ridge. Head west down the ridge, staying as close to the top of it as you can. Cruise as far as you can to the west before eventually transitioning back to skins for the duration of the ascent. Skin up the north end of the Janines ridge, climbing the moderately pitched slope for 1000 vertical feet to the high point on the north end of the ridge (9190 feet). From here to the summit of Janines is about 0.75 mile and 400 vertical feet of mellow ridgetop walking. The top of this slope is subject to some serious wind loading during storms and is prone to growing cornices along the ridgetop, so use caution when finding the top of your chosen descent route.

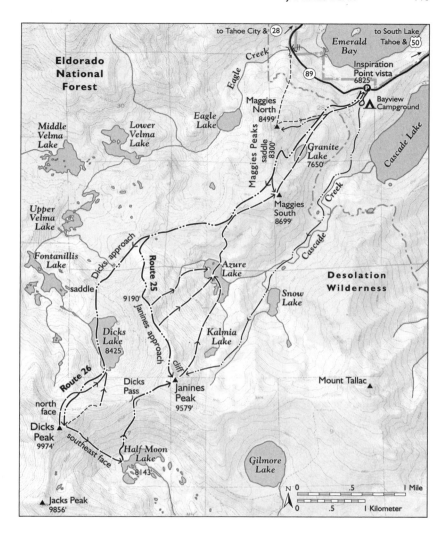

That 0.75-mile section of ridgetop has room for about 1000 sets of tracks on the massive east face down to Azure Lake. These descents vary in length from 1500 vertical feet on the north end of the ridge to around 1900 vertical feet from the summit. There are plenty of options to enter this slope, and generally speaking you can see down all of them from the top of the ridge, but just north of the summit there's a very large cliff that should generally be avoided. Enjoy the fun, moderately pitched, rolling terrain all the way down to the frozen surface of Azure Lake far below. Short rollovers on the slope will keep you guessing the whole way.

Once at Azure Lake, transition back over to skins for the short hike back to the top of Maggies South. Head to the north end of Azure Lake, then climb 500 vertical feet to the north, eventually regaining the ridge you skied down from the top of Maggies South. Head east along the ridge, following your tracks back up toward the top of Maggies South. Head back to the saddle or continue up the ridge to the summit to drop into the nicely spaced northeast-facing trees for a run down to Granite Lake. From Granite Lake, retrace your ascent route to return to the parking area.

26 Dicks Peak

Starting Point	Bayview trailhead, 6825 feet
High Point	9974 feet
Distance	10 miles
Elevation Gain	3500 feet
Time	6 hours to 2 days
Difficulty Level	Strenuous
Terrain Rating	3
Aspects	North, southeast
Seasons	Winter, spring
Maps	USGS Emerald Bay; Rockbound Valley

The summit of Dicks Peak is the third highest in Desolation Wilderness, where it sits as the centerpiece of this unique and beautiful landscape. In the summertime, Desolation is one of the most visited wilderness areas in the country. Come winter, few people venture into this amazing area—except for backcountry skiers, of course. Located far from virtually every starting location, the way to and from Dicks Peak comprises several miles of rolling terrain. The easiest way to approach Dicks is to head up to the saddle between the Maggies Peaks (Route 24), then follow the west ridge back and around Janines Peak (Route 25). Spending the day in this area is worth the trip alone, and the great skiing on the north and south sides of Dicks Peak is an added bonus. Generally not sought after for powder conditions due to its exposure to wind, Dicks is prime corn and wind buff terrain that lends itself well to linking up with nearby peaks or overnight adventures in Desolation.

GETTING THERE
From the Y in South Lake Tahoe, drive on CA 89 north for 7.7 miles, or from Tahoe City, drive 20 miles south on CA 89 to a pullout for the Bayview trailhead and campground on the south side of the road opposite the Inspiration Point vista.

THE ROUTE
From the Bayview trailhead, follow the Maggies South peak route to the saddle between the summits of Maggies Peaks (Route 24). Continue southwest behind the south summit of Maggies and gain the west ridge, following it to the north end of the Janines Peak ridge (Route 25), which towers above you to the southwest.

Kicking up chalky snow near the top of Dicks Peak's southeast face in front of the barren expanse of Desolation Wilderness

Head west from here, staying high as you wrap around the north end of the Janines ridge. Skirt the north end of the Janines ridge until you are headed south, then climb 300 vertical feet up to the saddle just north of Dicks Lake. Dicks' broad north face, as well as the north-facing terrain that drops off of Dicks' east ridge, will be clearly visible from here. Drop around 100 vertical feet down to Dicks Lake, then continue south along the flat surface of the frozen lake to its southern end.

At the south end of the lake, head southwest and climb 700 vertical feet up to the base of the peak's north face. Skin south, eventually gaining the ridge and following it west to the summit.

When coverage and conditions allow, the southeast face of Dicks drops 1800 vertical feet down to Half Moon Lake, perhaps the best run on the mountain and a great option when corn is the condition of the day. From Half Moon Lake, climb 1000 vertical feet to the north and east up to Dicks Pass, then it's a short climb up to Janines Peak and those descent options (Route 25).

The north face of Dicks is often wind scoured down the middle of the slope, with smooth wind buff on either side. From the top of Dicks, drop in for 800 vertical feet or so, then traverse skier's right under the east ridge before dropping another 800 vertical feet of turns down to Dicks Lake. You can head back the way you came to return to the trailhead—or put your skins back on to continue the tour. Once you're already this far into Desolation, I recommend hiking up to Janines Peak's west ridge and linking up with that descent (Route 25), which takes you on to the descent of Maggies South (Route 24) for three quality descents and only a little more hiking than you're already committed to.

27 Mount Tallac

Starting Point	Pullout east of Spring Creek Road on CA 89, 6315 feet
High Point	9735 feet
Distance	5 miles
Elevation Gain	3420 feet
Time	3.5 hours
Difficulty Level	Moderate
Terrain Ratings	3–4 depending on descent
Aspects	North, northeast, east, southeast
Seasons	Winter, spring
Map	USGS Emerald Bay

Mount Tallac stands proudly on the southwest shore of Lake Tahoe, dominating the view of the western skyline from South Lake Tahoe on the edge of the Desolation Wilderness. Sandwiched between Fallen Leaf Lake to the south and Cascade Lake to the north, this iconic peak has some of the longest pitches of skiing in the Tahoe area. The broad east side of Mount Tallac is more than a mile wide, offering an incredible variety of terrain that can suit just about everyone. From mellow bowls and trees to some of the steepest and most technical terrain in the region on aspects ranging from southeast to north, Mount Tallac truly has it all. Tallac is just a short drive from both North and South Lake Tahoe, with an approach on Spring Creek Road. This road used to be open in winter, cutting about 0.75 mile of flat walking off the approach. Unfortunately, the gate has been locked for the past decade or so, adding about 10 to 15 minutes of walking to your day. Even so, Tallac is great for a morning lap or an all-day adventure.

GETTING THERE

From the Y in South Lake Tahoe, drive north on CA 89 for 4.6 miles to a plowed pullout on the north side of the road, 0.25 mile east of the junction with Spring Creek Road. Spring Creek Road is closed with a locked gate in winter; please do not park anywhere near the gate. From Tahoe City, drive CA 89 south 23 miles to this pullout, but note that CA 89 is subject to closure around Emerald Bay during and after storms; to check the status of the road, visit the California Department of Transportation website (see Resources). When the road is closed, this route can be accessed from North Lake Tahoe by driving around the lake's east shore, through South Lake Tahoe, and picking up the directions from there.

Airing off a small cornice before dropping into some of Tallac's north-facing trees

THE ROUTE

From the pullout, make your way west 0.25 mile to Spring Creek Road. Walk around the locked gate and follow the road south, staying on the road as it eventually sweeps around to the west and up a slight hill. After 0.75 mile or so, at the last fork in the road, bear right and head into the forest, due west, between the summer cabins at the end of the road. Follow the path of least resistance, continuing west through this forest for about 0.25 mile, until you pop out into the relatively open manzanita slopes where you begin your ascent.

Head southwest up the gentle slopes, making your way toward the prominent ridge that splits the east side of Mount Tallac down the middle. The first steeper pitch of the climb is affectionately known as Sweat Hill because on sunny days it generally causes everyone to sweat profusely. The lowest slopes of Tallac are covered in twiggy bushes called manzanita, which are easy to travel on when there is good snow coverage; walking through here when there is no snow, on the other hand, is a lesson in frustration. Be sure to stay just on the north side of the small drainage that parallels the ridge. Follow its path, making switchbacks if necessary, up into the bottom of the large bowl (7400 feet) on the north side of the prominent east ridge.

From here the route turns northwest briefly to the base of the ridge to your north. Once on the ridge, hike just on the climber's-right (north) side of the crest, switchbacking as necessary up to the summit ridge at about 9000 feet. This ridge is called the Corkscrew by many due to the numerous switchbacks the route makes as you ascend.

Once on the ridge, the route heads south, dropping slightly through a saddle to the bottom of the north bowl. Continue south, contouring up and across the north bowl for about 500 vertical feet to the saddle just below and west of the summit. Wrap around

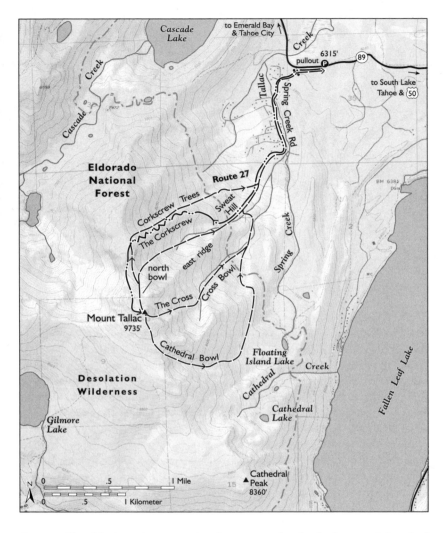

the west side of the summit, connecting the snow patches for the last couple hundred feet to the top. The summit of Tallac is the highest point along the west shore of Lake Tahoe, providing an outstanding 360-degree view. This is a great vantage point for scoping lines, including the Halls of the Gods on Angora Peak to the south and the various peaks and routes in Desolation Wilderness to the west.

A mountain as broad as Tallac has a hundred ways down it, and the various ridges and gullies that drop down its eastern face offer a wide range of aspects that allow for chasing whatever the conditions of the day might be. Most people descend the north bowl, dropping north off the summit, then bearing to skier's left near the bottom of the bowl before dropping into the open tree pitch that brings you into the large basin just south of the ascent ridge. Enjoy the rolling terrain until it flattens out at 7400 feet, then follow your skin track to return to Spring Creek Road.

If tree skiing is what you're after, the north side of the Corkscrew ridge you skinned up has 2000-plus vertical feet of nicely spaced and pitched trees. Be sure to steer back to skier's right at the bottom to return to your skin track and Spring Creek Road.

On the opposite end of the spectrum, the best corn skiing terrain on Tallac is in the Cathedral Bowl, a little over 0.25 mile south down the ridge from Tallac's summit. You lose a little elevation while making your way to the top of this broad bowl, but the smooth corn you'll find is well worth it. Once the bowl flattens out around 8000 feet, begin the traverse back around to the north to return to the Cross Bowl, then on down to Spring Creek Road.

The Cross, a classic line that drops in to the east right off the summit of Tallac, is a steep chute named for its cross shape formed by the chute and a large shelf in the cliffs that is clearly visible from South Lake Tahoe. The various entrances to the Cross are all very steep for the first couple hundred feet. The most straightforward entrance drops in directly off the summit toward the southeast, then traverses skier's right into the main gut of the chute a couple hundred feet down. Another entrance a few hundred feet south down the ridge drops slightly more into the top of the chute. Again, the top turns entering the chute are very steep and exposed; this line should be attempted only by competent, expert skiers and snowboarders. Scope this area from the top before dropping. After exiting the walls of the upper part of the chute, enjoy the rolling terrain of the lower Cross Bowl until it flattens out around 7000 feet. Traverse hard skier's left (north) through the trees around the east ridge and back to your skin track below Sweat Hill.

Experts' eyes will be drawn to exposed and committing lines like the Corkscrew, Hanging Snowfield, and Babycham, some of the most extreme terrain in the Tahoe Basin. People seeking out lines with that level of risk and exposure should have the ability to figure them out for themselves, and these descent routes are therefore not described in detail here.

28   Pyramid Peak

Starting Point : Twin Bridges on US 50, 6100 feet
High Point : 9983 feet
Distance : 6 miles
Elevation Gain : 3885 feet
Time : 4 hours
Difficulty Level : Strenuous
Terrain Rating : 2
Aspects : Northeast, southeast
Seasons : Winter, spring
Maps : USGS Pyramid Peak; Echo Lake

Named for its distinctive shape, Pyramid Peak is located on the western edge of Desolation Wilderness at the southern end of the Crystal Range, a small subrange of the Sierra Nevada. Pyramid is the highest peak in Desolation Wilderness, in the Crystal Range, and on the west side of Lake Tahoe. A run on Pyramid, at 3 miles and nearly 4000 vertical feet from the parking area, isn't a gimme but can easily be done in half a day or as part of a larger tour in Desolation. This route has a relatively low starting point, and the south-facing slope at the start of the route is often bereft of snow, even in midwinter, so be prepared for the possibility of some bushwhacking to begin and end this tour. In big winters, this route may have snow from the parking area, but it is not uncommon to start and finish this adventure on dirt. Even if this slope is bare, the rest of the route above is typically well covered, so go for it anyway. If there is snow coverage to the parking area, consider yourself lucky; the beginning of this route will be much easier and straightforward.

GETTING THERE

From the Y in South Lake Tahoe, head south (west) on US Highway 50 for 15.5 miles, passing through Meyers before going up and over Echo Summit and down to Twin Bridges. The Horsetail Falls–Pyramid Creek Loop trailhead parking area is 7 miles west of Echo Summit, just west of Pyramid Creek on the north side of the road. From Placerville, head east on US 50 roughly 41 miles to this parking area.

Pyramid Peak and the long ridgeline ascent route from US 50

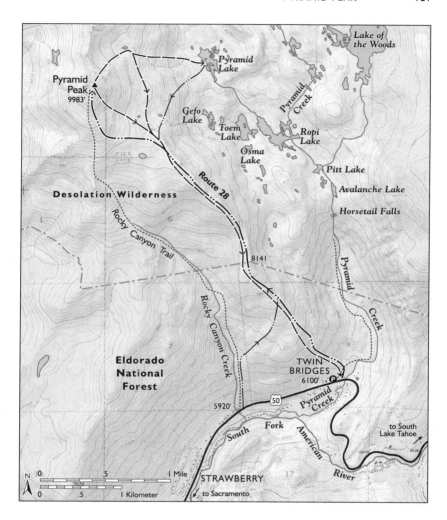

THE ROUTE

From the trailhead parking area, hike northwest up the south-facing slope above the parking area for 1000 vertical feet to gain the top of the ridge. The lowest part of this route directly above the parking area is often burned off of snow, even midwinter, so starting this route with a bit of bushwhacking is a distinct possibility. There is also the option of beginning this route 0.7 mile farther west on US 50 at 5920 feet and climbing the steep trail that parallels Rocky Canyon Creek. Again, this steep trail is south-facing but gains elevation quickly to expedite your way to the snow line. If climbing the Rocky Canyon Trail, head northeast once you reach the snow line to gain the ridge. Either way, get to the top of the ridge that serves as your ascent route all the way to the base of the east slope of Pyramid.

Once on top of the ridge, stay just on the west side of it and you'll easily make your way to the base of Pyramid Peak. In fact, this route is so mellow that you may not have to make any switchbacks until you reach the steeper south ridge of Pyramid. After about 2 miles and 3000 vertical feet from the parking area, the south ridge and east face of Pyramid Peak loom above you.

Contour west over to Pyramid's south ridge; this is the easiest way up to the summit, still nearly 1000 vertical feet above. The lofty summit of Pyramid provides a great view of Desolation Wilderness to the east, the spine of the Crystal Range to the north, and the expanse of the western slope of the Sierra down to the Central Valley.

The east face and south ridge of Pyramid are the primary ski objectives, especially if you're after smooth corn snow conditions. Enjoy a long, mellow cruise out the way you came for the easiest return to the parking area. It may also be possible to ski out the drainage just east of the ridge you hiked in on, eventually joining up with Pyramid Creek lower down, but there are more objective hazards on this route, such as small lakes, creeks, waterfalls, cliffs, and the like, so use caution if heading out this way.

The north face of Pyramid Peak can be a great ski when it fills in, but more often than not a wide band of peppery rocks pokes through the snow across the upper part of the entire face. If it does fill in, there are 1000 vertical feet of turns down to the first bench, where you have a couple options: Traverse the east slope back to the ridge you hiked in on for the easiest return to the parking area. Or for a side trip, head east down to Pyramid Lake for another 1000 vertical feet of mellower turns. Make your way back up from Pyramid Lake to the ridge you hiked in on to retrace your approach route back to the parking area.

29 Ralston Peak

Starting Points : Echo Lakes approach, 7300 feet;
south face approach, 6850 feet
High Points : Echo Lakes approach, 9235 feet;
south face approach, 9155 feet
Distances : Echo Lakes approach, 10 miles;
south face approach, 2.5 miles
Elevation Gains : Echo Lakes approach, 2100 feet;
south face approach, 2300 feet
Times : Echo Lakes approach, 6 hours;
south face approach, 2.5 hours
Difficulty Level : Moderate
Terrain Rating : 2
Aspects : North-northeast, southeast, southwest
Seasons : Winter, spring
Map : USGS Echo Lake

Ralston Peak and its north- and east-facing bowls as seen from nearby Echo Peak

At the southern edge of Desolation Wilderness, rising high above US Highway 50, Ralston Peak is a broad mountain with great skiing on several aspects. Sitting directly north and across US 50 from the Sierra-at-Tahoe ski resort, Ralston's massive south face is prime spring-conditions terrain clearly visible from the neighboring ski slopes and the road. Over the ridge, two large, prominent north-northeast-facing bowls visible from nearby peaks to the north drain down toward the Echo Lakes. Ralston's multiple skiable aspects mean that you can find great skiing here in a variety of snow conditions, sometimes with zero approach. There are a couple of ways to access Ralston Peak, depending on your objectives and the snow conditions. If spring conditions are the order of the day, I recommend approaching via and skiing the south-facing slopes above US 50. If cold snow and a longer, mellow tour are on the menu, I suggest approaching via Echo Lakes; this approach is advised when the Echo Lakes are solidly frozen and passable. This route also provides the opportunity to do additional laps on Talking Mountain (Route 30) and/or Becker Peak on the way in or out.

GETTING THERE

Echo Lakes approach: From the Y in South Lake Tahoe, take US 50 west for 9.8 miles, up and over Echo Summit. One mile past Echo Summit, turn right on Johnson Pass Road and follow it east for 0.6 mile. Park in the Sno-Park on the right side of the road (permit required). From Placerville, drive US 50 east 47 miles to Johnson Pass Road.

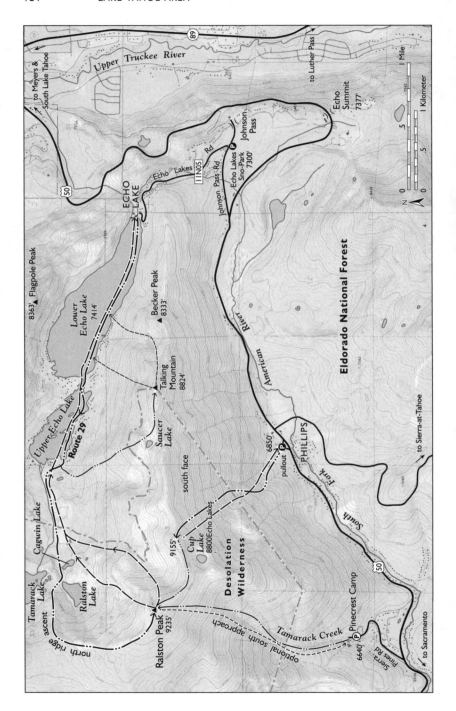

South face approach: From Echo Summit on US 50, continue west 2.8 miles, to just west of the intersection with the Sierra-at-Tahoe access road, and park in a pullout on the north side of the highway. From Placerville, drive US 50 east 45.2 miles to this pullout.

Optional south approach: From Echo Summit on US 50, continue west 5 miles to Sierra Pines Road, drive this road north 0.4 mile, and turn left and park out of the way in the Pinecrest Camp parking area. From Placerville, drive US 50 east 43 miles to Sierra Pines Road.

THE ROUTE

Echo Lakes approach: From the Echo Lakes Sno-Park, head northeast on snow-covered Echo Lakes Road (Forest Road 11N05) for 1.2 miles to the east end of Lower Echo Lake. Head west along the frozen surface of Lower Echo Lake and then Upper Echo Lake for approximately 2 miles to the west end of the lakes. Eye up the north-facing terrain of Becker Peak, Talking Mountain, and the bowls and trees that stretch to your south over to Ralston Peak as you cruise across the lakes; this terrain is easy to hit on your way back to the trailhead.

At the west end of Upper Echo Lake, begin to climb gradually, continuing west for approximately 1 mile up to Cagwin Lake and then Ralston Lake, around 7800 feet, below Ralston's north bowl. Check out your descent, then continue west up the broad ridge that leads to Ralston's north ridge. Once atop the ridge, follow it south up to Ralston's summit.

From here you have a commanding view of Desolation Wilderness and most of the peaks of the South Lake Tahoe area. Take it all in before dropping into either the bowl you climbed up or the more northeast-facing bowl to skier's right of the summit. Both options are relatively equal in vertical drop and pitch, but be advised that this ridgeline is prone to serious wind loading and is prime avalanche terrain.

At the bottom of your chosen descent, traverse east to get back to the Echo Lakes. Head back the way you came, or if you are itching for more skiing, head up from the shore of Upper Echo Lake to the top of Talking Mountain (Route 30) and/or Becker Peak for an additional run or two on the way back to the Sno-Park.

South face approach: From the plowed pullout on the north side of US 50, just west of the Sierra-at-Tahoe access road, head northwest past the summer cabins and up the forested slope. After just a few hundred vertical feet, you exit the forest onto the broad and relatively treeless expanse of the south-southeast face of Ralston Peak. Continue climbing northwest up this slope past Cup Lake (8800 feet) to the high point at 9155 feet. From here, descend the way you came.

Options: Those looking to summit Ralston Peak from this side of the mountain can traverse the ridgeline west, then return via the same route to descend the south-facing terrain. This slope is quite broad, with more than a mile of excellent open terrain stretching to the east between Cup Lake and Talking Mountain (Route 30).

Another option starts from the Pinecrest Camp off of Sierra Pines Road. This route climbs and descends the southwest slope of the mountain through sparsely tree-covered forest.

30 Talking Mountain

Starting Point : Echo Lakes Sno-Park, 7300 feet
High Point : 8824 feet
Distance : 4.5 miles
Elevation Gain : 1700 feet
Time : 2.5 hours
Difficulty Level : Easy
Terrain Rating : 3
Aspect : North-northeast
Seasons : Winter, spring
Map : USGS Echo Lake

Talking Mountain, Becker Peak, and Ralston Peak form the ridgeline that rises abruptly from the southern shores of the Echo Lakes near Echo Summit. This north-facing ridge is more than 2 miles long, with an abundance of glades and fun, playful, open terrain. The farther west along the ridge you climb toward Ralston Peak, the longer the runs become—and the longer the return trip to the parking area. Descents

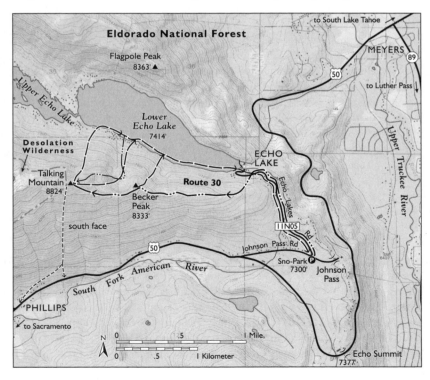

The playful terrain of Talking Mountain's northeast bowl as seen from Becker Peak

in this zone filter back down to the Echo Lakes for a casual, flat skin back to the east end of Lower Echo Lake, or you can do a steeper return back up the slope you descended for more laps. Located relatively close to South Lake Tahoe and situated just outside the southwest corner of Desolation Wilderness above the Echo Lakes, this is a convenient and truly beautiful area with excellent terrain suitable for any length of tour. With relatively short vertical runs, this zone is great for quick laps or an entire day of skiing multiple runs along this broad ridge. In spring conditions, you may also want to consider descending the long south face runs back down to US Highway 50 (see south face approach for Route 29).

GETTING THERE

From the Y in South Lake Tahoe, take US 50 west for 9.8 miles, up and over Echo Summit. One mile past Echo Summit, turn right on Johnson Pass Road and follow it east for 0.6 mile. Park in the Sno-Park on the right side of the road (permit required). From Placerville, drive US 50 east 47 miles to Johnson Pass Road.

THE ROUTE

From the Echo Lakes Sno-Park, head northwest on the snow-covered Echo Lakes Road (Forest Road 11N05) for nearly 1 mile. When the road begins to drop down toward the east end of Lower Echo Lake, bear left and start to climb the forested ridgeline to the west. Hike along the crest of this ridge for 1.25 miles to the rocky summit of Becker Peak (8333 feet). There are fun short descents from here down to Lower Echo Lake; to continue on to Talking Mountain, skirt around the south side of Becker Peak and head west along the ridgeline. Climb another 500 vertical feet over the course of 0.6 mile to the top of Talking Mountain.

From the summit, drop into excellent 1400-foot north-facing tree runs down to Lower Echo Lake or the playful bouldery terrain of the northeast bowl. Whether you are skiing down from Becker Peak or Talking Mountain, once you finish your run down onto the shore of Lower Echo Lake, you can head back up for more laps. When you're ready to return to the Sno-Park, head east on the frozen surface of the lake, or the edge of the lake when it's not frozen, to its east end and then climb up briefly out of the lake basin and follow Echo Lakes Road (FR 11N05) back to the parking area.

31 Echo Peak

Starting Point	End of Wintoon Drive, 6600 feet
High Point	8895 feet
Distance	4.5 miles
Elevation Gain	2295 feet
Time	2.5 hours
Difficulty Level	Moderate
Terrain Rating	3
Aspects	Northeast-east, east-southeast
Seasons	Winter, spring
Map	USGS Echo Lake

Situated just a few miles from the Y in South Lake Tahoe, above the town of Meyers, Echo Peak is as conveniently located as the skiing is good. Its slopes range in aspect from southeast to northeast, so you can find both corn and powder here, sometimes both in the same day, and excellent terrain to boot. A lap on Echo Peak can be done in as few as a couple hours, and since it shares a ridgeline with both Flagpole and Angora peaks (both of which are just outside Desolation Wilderness), it can serve as the start of a larger tour to some of the more exciting slopes in the area. With a 360-degree panorama from the summit that includes all of Desolation Wilderness, Lake Tahoe, and the Freel Peak region, the view alone is worth the hike.

GETTING THERE

From the Y in South Lake Tahoe, head southwest on Lake Tahoe Boulevard for 3.8 miles. As the road turns into North Upper Truckee Road, turn right to follow it for 1 mile. Turn right on Wintoon Drive and follow it 0.25 mile to the small plowed parking area at its dead end. From the south, take US Highway 50 to the junction with North Upper Truckee Road and turn northwest. Follow North Upper Truckee Road for 1.3 miles and turn left onto Wintoon Drive. Park at the end of Wintoon Drive. This parking area is popular with snowshoers, cross-country skiers, and dog walkers, so leave as much room as possible to fit vehicles in this limited space. Do not park in or block any driveway of the private homes in the immediate area.

THE ROUTE

From the parking area at the end of Wintoon Drive, head due west across the large, flat area below Echo Peak and the Angora ridge. There are some sparse trees initially, but as you exit them, you will have a great view of your route. Continue west across the open, flat terrain and into the charred forest remaining from the Angora Fire that burned 250 homes in June 2007. About 0.75 mile from the parking area, begin to climb up into the forested drainage that leads slightly southwest toward the ridge you will ascend to the summit. Switchback up through the forest, as the route turns slightly northwest, for approximately 1100 vertical feet, where you gain the ridge that extends east from Echo Peak.

Once on the ridge, look to the north and you'll see the Angora Lakes below you, the south-facing gullies—Seneca Chutes—of Angora Peak, and the ridgeline that wraps around southwest to Echo Peak. From here, the route switchbacks up the crest of the tree-covered ridge to your west for another 1000 vertical feet. As you continue to climb, you'll get views of the ridgeline that extends from Echo Peak southeast to Flagpole Peak and the multitude of other ski lines nearby. The top 200 feet or so of this ridge are significantly steeper and less tree covered, so be prepared for some more-challenging skinning right before you top out.

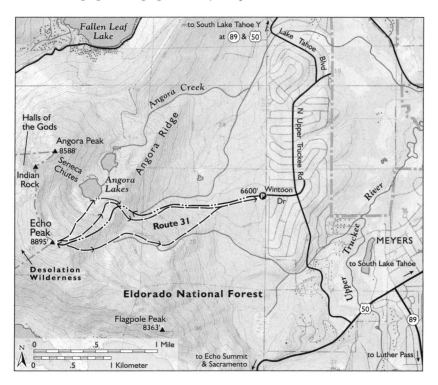

Looking south to Echo Peak and the north-facing terrain that drops below the summit

The summit of Echo Peak offers one of the best 360-degree views in all of Lake Tahoe. Take it all in and be sure to add some peaks and ski routes to your list while you're here. Some of the numerous descent options from Echo Peak require advanced routefinding and skiing skills. Very large and dangerous cornices form on the ridgeline that extends north from Echo's summit, and the upper portion of this bowl is subject to some major wind loading, so use caution.

If powder is what you came for, the sparsely treed northeast-facing terrain just to skier's left of the skin track holds cold snow longest. The slope has numerous benches with steep rollovers that will keep you guessing the whole way down. The farther to skier's left you go, the fewer trees there are, but the terrain becomes more cliffy and complex. If you descend all the way to the Angora Lakes at the bottom of the slope—and you should—you will have to climb 200 vertical feet back up to regain the ridge and the route, with more good tree skiing, back to the trailhead.

When corn skiing is the order of the day, from the summit just to skier's right, drop into the south side of the ridge you climbed to the summit. Once the pitch starts to flatten out, around 7400 feet, wrap back around the ridge to skier's left (north) to get back to your ascent route.

These runs are relatively short and sweet, but doing numerous laps is pretty easy once you're back here. However you descend the upper part of the mountain, return roughly the same way you came up. Ski near the skin track down the main drainage back to the flats you crossed on the ascent. It's usually possible to skate back across the flats, but it may be necessary for splitboarders to put skins back on here.

Options: Nearby descents include the south gullies (Seneca Chutes) of Angora Peak, the north-northeast-facing trees on Angora, and the challenging descents of the Halls of the Gods chute system that drop off the north end of the ridge by Angora Peak and Indian Rock. To the south there's the northeast-facing terrain of Flagpole Peak.

32 Trimmer Peak

Starting Point	High Meadow Trail parking area, 6535 feet
High Point	9500 feet
Distance	5 miles
Elevation Gain	2965 feet
Time	2.5 hours
Difficulty Level	Strenuous
Terrain Rating	3
Aspect	North-northwest
Seasons	Winter, spring
Maps	USGS Freel Peak; South Lake Tahoe

When viewed from North Lake Tahoe, Trimmer Peak's twin avalanche paths, the Elevens, are often mistaken for being part of Heavenly Mountain Resort. Trimmer Peak, however, is a good distance and an entire drainage southwest of the ski area. Sitting just north of Freel Peak, Trimmer Peak is some of the closest backcountry skiing to South Lake Tahoe, literally out the back door for many lucky local residents. Sitting at the north end of the ridge a few hundred feet shy of the summit, the twin north-facing slide paths are definitely the prime attraction in this area, but a wealth of amazing gladed terrain on primarily north-facing aspects awaits skiers who make the trek out here. The beginning of this route is a popular area for dog walkers,

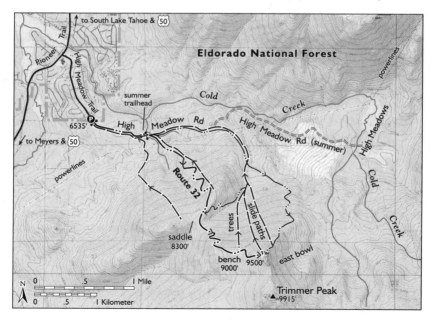

cross-country skiers, snowshoers, and outdoor recreationalists of all kinds. The parking area can fill up, but typically only a handful of cars belong to backcountry skiers. This zone can be approached a couple of different ways, but the route described here initially climbs the broad, tree-covered slope just north and in front of Trimmer Peak before ascending the west ridge to the top of the slide paths. The main approach route described here climbs up through and above lots of outstanding gladed terrain, giving you a great lay of the land and the option for two great descents with just a short second ascent between them.

GETTING THERE

From the Y in South Lake Tahoe, drive east on US Highway 50 for 2 miles, turn right on Al Tahoe Boulevard, and follow it for 1.6 miles to Pioneer Trail. Turn right on Pioneer Trail, and after 1 mile take a left onto High Meadow Trail, then continue approximately 1 mile until it dead-ends at a Forest Service gate. From the Heavenly ski area village, turn west on US 50, then take a left on Pioneer Trail. Head southwest on Pioneer Trail for 3.4 miles, take a left on High Meadow Trail, and follow it uphill for 0.8 mile to the dead end and locked gate.

THE ROUTE

Head past the locked gate and follow the path of snow-covered High Meadow Road east-southeast. After about 0.6 mile of relatively flat walking along the road, you come to another locked gate and a kiosk for the High Meadow summer trailhead parking area.

From this trailhead, bear right off the road and begin heading southeast through the forest toward the base of the steeper forested slope you will climb. After only a few hundred yards, you cross directly beneath some powerlines and through the broad swath of forest that is cut for them. Continue heading southeast as the ascent begins; this lower area is a little convoluted, with bushes and downed trees making travel somewhat awkward when the snowpack is thin.

As you tick off the vertical, the forest begins to open up into nice, widely spaced trees; continue southeast up this slope, aiming for the low saddle in the ridge at roughly 8300 feet. This pitch you are climbing offers amazing tree skiing, a great way to head back down to the parking area after your descent of Trimmer Peak. Once you reach the top of this ridge, you'll have a great view of Trimmer Peak's north-facing terrain and the rest of your ascent route. (After descending the north face of Trimmer Peak either down one of the slide paths or in the trees, you will ascend back to this point via the gully below you to return to the parking area.)

From the saddle in the ridge, head southeast and then begin climbing the forested west ridge of Trimmer Peak. This climb begins gradually but becomes progressively steeper until you hit a bench at around 9000 feet. As you head east along this bench, be aware that the slopes that drop in to your left (north) are moderately steep glades, an excellent alternative to the slide paths. Eventually the ridge ramps back up for the final ascent to the top of the slide paths, another 500 feet or so above.

Trimmer Peak's twin slide paths and the widely spaced trees that surround them

Once atop this ridge, you are standing at the top of the skier's-left slide path. This path is full of short pine trees but has nice, open lanes on either edge. The skier's-right slide path is a short traverse east through the open forest that separates the two. The skier's-right path is more wide open, with a little more-consistent fall line. On either side of and in between the slide paths are excellent tree runs through old-growth forest. Descend on either slide path to the gully at about 7600 feet far below.

At the bottom, you can descend the gully north and wrap left (west) around the ridge to your west to return to the parking area. (This descent follows the east ridge approach option described below.)

However, if you want some more turns, from the bottom of the gully switch back to skins for a 700-foot ascent up the gully southwest back to the saddle on the ridge where you ascended earlier. Head north through the saddle and find yourself a nice, wide-open run down through the trees you skinned up through on the approach; there are excellent lanes to either side or right below you. Toward the bottom of the slope, make your way back to the skin track and follow it down to the powerlines and then back to the High Meadow summer trailhead.

From here, push and skate along the road back to the parking area. Snowboarders may have a bit of difficulty traversing out through the flats at the bottom of this route, but it's well worth it.

Option: The other way to approach this area is to continue farther southeast past the summer trailhead along the road another mile, wrapping around the east end of the ridge in front of Trimmer Peak. You can then head south and climb the forested eastern ridge of Trimmer. This route also lines you up to access the east bowl of Trimmer Peak above High Meadows, which also has a great amount of terrain worth exploring.

33 Jobs Peak

Starting Point	Fay-Luther trailhead, 4800 feet
High Point	10,633 feet
Distance	8 miles
Elevation Gain	5833 feet
Time	6 hours
Difficulty Level	Very strenuous
Terrain Rating	3
Aspect	North-northeast-east
Season	Winter
Maps	USGS Woodfords; Minden

Jobs Peak is the most distracting piece of eye candy you'll see while driving south on US Highway 395 in the Washoe Valley between Carson City and Gardnerville, Nevada. A run from the summit of Jobs Peak to the Washoe Valley is one of the biggest descents possible in the greater Lake Tahoe area. This route starts in Nevada, but as soon as you begin the ascent of Jobs Canyon, you cross the state line back into California. Boasting a vertical drop of nearly 6000 feet from the summit to the parking area at Foothill Road, a descent of Jobs Peak is twice the vert of most other big descents around Lake Tahoe. This route starts in the sagebrush desert, pastures, and farmland of the Washoe Valley at 4800 feet and climbs steadily up Jobs Canyon into the alpine terrain above tree line on Jobs Peak, topping out at 10,633 feet. The scenery and staggering vertical relief to the valley far below are reason enough to undertake this long walk, as is the novelty of skiing one of the longest and most eye-catching peaks in the area. It takes an average or better winter with several cold storms in order to have adequate coverage below 6000 feet; it doesn't always fill in, and some years it may be completely unreasonable to attempt this route at all. When the stars align and conditions allow, a descent of Jobs is well worth the time and effort and should absolutely not be missed.

GETTING THERE

From the Y in South Lake Tahoe, take US 50 east 5.7 miles to just over the Nevada state line and turn right on Kingsbury Grade Road (NV 207). Take this road east and south 11.1 miles to Foothill Road (NV 206). Turn right onto Foothill Road and continue south approximately 2.5 miles to Five Creek Road, on the west side of Foothill

Road. The small parking lot is at the north end of the Fay-Luther Trail just before the locked gate of the Jobs Peak Ranch gated community. (If you know someone who lives within the gated community, ask if you can park closer to the bottom of Jobs Canyon; however, this gated community is private property, so do not enter without permission.

THE ROUTE

From the Fay-Luther trailhead parking area, hike south along the trail and follow as it circumnavigates the private homes of the gated community. Stay on the trail for about 1.5 miles as it initially heads south behind the homes on Foothill Road then cuts west and climbs toward the base of the mountains before heading south again along the edge of the gated community's massive homes. Once you cross the dead end of Nature's Edge Road, leave the Fay-Luther Trail and begin to contour west and eventually southwest, climbing gradually along the base of the slope for about 0.75 mile to enter the bottom of Jobs Canyon and your ascent route for the next

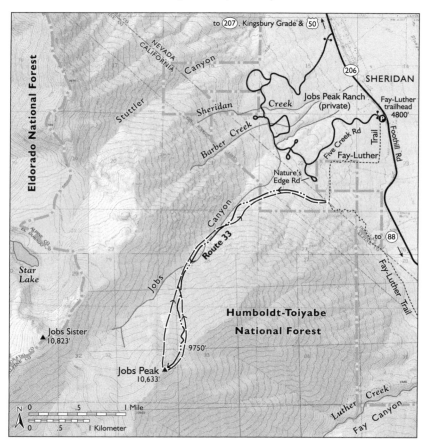

On the approach to Jobs Peak, several thousand vertical feet above the valley floor and still thousands of vertical feet below the summit

couple thousand vertical feet. As you enter Jobs Canyon, you've covered about 2.25 miles and 1000 vertical feet—the climb is just beginning.

Once in the canyon, the route becomes a bit more straightforward. Simply follow it southwest and uphill to the base of the northeast face of Jobs Peak. With low snow coverage, the bottom of the canyon is a convoluted mess of boulders and bushes, and there will typically be more snow on the north-facing (climber's-left) side of the canyon, for a smoother and easier path uphill. After about 1500 vertical feet, the canyon opens up and flattens out a bit, affording a great view of Jobs Peak and the rest of your route.

Continue heading southwest up the drainage, steadily climbing the moderate pitch toward the base of Jobs Peak's northeast face. As you get closer to the face, begin to head south toward the climber's-left gully, an easier ascent route. At about 8800 feet you enter the bottom of this massive gully, which gets progressively steeper as you ascend. Depending on conditions and snow coverage, you may be able to skin all the way to the summit, but don't be surprised if you have to switch to boot-packing at some point. As the gully gets steeper near the top, head toward the low saddle (9750 feet) to gain the ridge for the remainder of the climb. The route now follows the ridge up and west until you reach the summit.

Once atop the summit, you have an amazing 360-degree view that includes the Washoe Valley, Lake Tahoe, Desolation Wilderness, Freel Peak, Carson Pass, and Ebbetts Pass. The view is truly amazing and you've got a 5000-plus-foot descent below your feet. From the summit you have a couple of options: you can basically drop on either side of the large rock buttress that separates the gully you ascended from the gully on skier's left. The skier's-left gully is steeper off the top and generally the line that people are drawn to ski. Weigh your options based on the conditions, your skills, and the skills of your group. Either way you've got an incredible descent.

At the bottom of the steeper north face runs, continue dropping back down Jobs Canyon, roughly reversing your ascent route. While the steep upper slopes of the peak are what draw people to Jobs, the moderate cruising from there down is super fun, and there's a lot of it. Continue all the way down Jobs Canyon, then retrace your route around the private property and residences back to the parking area.

34   Powderhouse and Waterhouse Peaks

Starting Points	Powderhouse—west end of Grass Lake; Waterhouse—Luther Pass; both 7735 feet
High Points	Powderhouse Peak, 9380 feet; Waterhouse Peak, 9497 feet
Distances	Powderhouse, 2.25 miles; Waterhouse, 3 miles
Elevation Gains	Powderhouse, 1640 feet; Waterhouse, 1760 feet
Times	Powderhouse, 1.5 hours; Waterhouse, 2 hours
Difficulty Level	Easy
Terrain Rating	2
Aspects	North-northeast, southeast
Seasons	Winter, spring
Map	USGS Freel Peak

Separated by a saddle on the ridgeline, Waterhouse and Powderhouse peaks are basically the same mountain, but they have distinct, separate summits, with Waterhouse the taller of the two by just over 100 vertical feet. Both peaks offer fantastic ski descents down their tree-covered flanks. Situated atop Luther Pass on CA 89, Waterhouse and Powderhouse are popular with South Lake Tahoe's backcountry skiers for many reasons: their high starting elevation, short approach, consistent fall lines, and nicely spaced, sheltered trees are just a few. One of the best locations for tree skiing in the area, these moderately pitched north-facing slopes covered in old-growth conifers are sheltered from both the wind and sun and are generally less prone to avalanches, making this a popular spot during and right after storms. Located right next to the road, Waterhouse and Powderhouse are great for a quick lap or a full day of powder skiing along the broad slope above Grass Lake.

GETTING THERE

From the Y in South Lake Tahoe, head south on US Highway 50–CA 89 for 4.8 miles. Just after the agricultural inspection station in Meyers, turn left (south) on Luther Pass Road (CA 89 south). **Powderhouse:** Continue 6.7 miles to the pullout on the south side of CA 89 at the west end of Grass Lake. **Waterhouse:** Continue another 1.8 miles to the plowed pullout on the south side of CA 89 at the east end of Grass Lake and Luther Pass proper, closest to the Luther Pass sign. **Option:** To get to the shuttle parking for Waterhouse's southeast flank, continue south on CA 89 to CA 88 and turn right (south). In 1.5 miles, reach a pullout on the west side of the highway.

THE ROUTE

Powderhouse Peak: The true north-facing slope rises right above the parking area. From the pullout, head south past the green Forest Service gate and go downhill just briefly. The route follows the path of an old Forest Service road south through the trees across the west end of Grass Lake (a massive snow-covered meadow). Initially, the route heads very gently uphill through a sparse old-growth forest before pitching up at the base of the north-facing trees. This route simply heads south, switchbacking up the slope until you reach the summit.

Powderhouse's north slope is steeper and the trees more widely spaced than those on Waterhouse. This terrain is somewhat rockier as well, resulting in some fun pillow-esque, moundy features in the trees, especially with a thinner snowpack. Drop back down this slope on either side of the skin track and enjoy the consistent pitch and wide spacing of the trees for 1400 vertical feet before it begins to flatten out. Head back to the parking area or back up for more laps. Also, a steep, rocky, northeast-facing cirque that drops off near the summit offers some more-challenging terrain for those who are looking for that.

Waterhouse Peak: From the Luther Pass pullout, the route heads southwest, skirting across the east end of Grass Lake and through the trees toward the northeast flank of the peak. The route continues heading southwest, meandering up the moderate tree-covered slope for 1700 vertical feet to the summit.

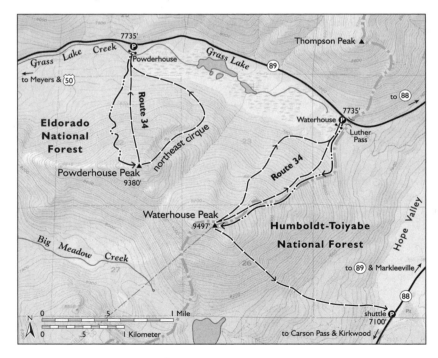

Starting the ascent of Powderhouse Peak near Grass Lake and Luther Pass

The top of Waterhouse affords a great view of the north side of Stevens Peak to the south and of the high peaks of Desolation Wilderness to the north. For the mellowest route down and the easiest return to the parking area, ski down the northeast ridge near the skin track. For a slightly steeper run, drop north from the summit; contour back to skier's right near the bottom to return to the skin track or starting point. This slope is quite broad with plenty of room to spread out and find fresh turns.

Option: There is also an option for a run down the southeast side of Waterhouse that finishes at CA 88 in the Hope Valley. This descent gets you an extra 400 vertical feet that typically involves a short car shuttle.

35 Red Lake Peak

Starting Points : East face pullouts, 7470 feet; Carson Pass, 8600 feet
High Points : East subpeak, 9845 feet; summit, 10,068 feet
Distances : Northeast ridge, 4.5 miles; east face, 3 miles;
: Carson Pass, 4 miles
Elevation Gains : East face and northeast ridge, 2600 feet;
: Carson Pass approach, 1468 feet
Times : East face and northeast ridge, 3 hours;
: Carson Pass approach, 2.5 hours
Difficulty Level : East face and northeast ridge, moderate; Carson Pass, easy
Terrain Rating : 3
Aspects : North-northeast, east-southeast
Seasons : Winter, spring
Map : USGS Carson Pass

Situated north of Carson Pass and just northwest of the small lake that is its name-sake, Red Lake Peak is a relatively popular backcountry skiing destination. Boasting a variety of terrain on virtually all aspects, the peak can accommodate nearly every snow and weather situation. Depending on the snow conditions and time of year, you've got numerous options for quality descents off of Red Lake Peak. From the mellow north-northeast-facing bowl to the impressive cliffy terrain above Crater Lake, to the massive east face, to the southeast gully, there is literally something for everyone. The potential is also endless for combinations of linkups of the various pitches and runs, so bring a camera and your imagination—there's no limit to the fun that can be had on this peak. Red Lake Peak is great for a quick roadside lap or a full day exploring the wealth of terrain that drops from the flanks off the 10,068-foot summit. Only a short drive from South Lake Tahoe, Red Lake Peak is conveniently located immediately next to CA 88, and there are a variety of ways to approach Red Lake Peak, depending primarily on whether you are doing a car shuttle and what your descent route is. A car shuttle from the top of Carson Pass can be done to shave off 1200 vertical feet of ascent. If you aren't doing a car shuttle, you'll start from below the peak's broad east face.

GETTING THERE
From the Y in South Lake Tahoe, follow US Highway 50–CA 89 south for 4.8 miles to Meyers, then turn south on CA 89. Follow CA 89 south for 11 miles to the junction with CA 88. Turn right and head west on CA 88. **East face pullouts:** Continue on CA 88 for 5.3 miles to the plowed pullouts below the peak's massive east face, just north of where the road crosses Red Lake Creek. **Carson Pass:** To do a car shuttle, continue 3.5 miles farther west to the Sno-Park (permit required) on the north side of CA 88, just past the top of Carson Pass.

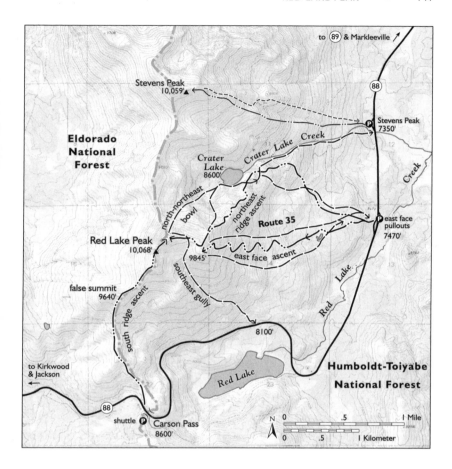

THE ROUTE

Northeast ridge: From the plowed pullouts below the peak's broad east face, start by heading northwest through the rolling terrain while contouring uphill, eventually hitting the northeast ridge just south of the Crater Lake outlet creek. Hike west along the ridge and creek up to Crater Lake (8600 feet) and take a good look around at the expansive terrain that wraps around the entire zone from Red Lake Peak north to Stevens Peak. From Crater Lake the route then heads southwest and climbs the crest of the northeast ridge up to the top of the east face. Once you hit the east face's top, you're on the east subpeak of Red Lake Peak; the true summit lies just a short distance and a few hundred vertical feet above to the west. When cold snow is the order of the day, the expansive north- and east-facing terrain above Crater Lake offers a myriad of options including bowls, chutes, cliffs—whatever you're looking for. This is a great area to scout before you drop into it and then spend the day doing numerous laps.

Breaking trail along the ridge of Red Lake Peak

East face: It is quite probable that a skin track already switchbacks directly up the east face from the pullouts near Red Lake Creek, particularly during stable spring conditions; this is a quick and straightforward alternative approach to the east face. This face is prime corn-growing terrain that holds a consistent pitch for 1600 vertical feet off the east subpeak before flattening out in the rolling terrain far below. Numerous gullies drop down this face, which is home to some of the longest and most eye-catching pitches in the area.

Carson Pass approach (south ridge): If starting from the Sno-Park atop the pass, head north, staying near the crest of the south ridge, into the south bowl. Head up the bowl and gain the ridge at the saddle between the summit and the southwest false summit (9640 feet). From here it is a short distance north up the west side of the ridge to the true summit. A large southeast gully drops in from near the true summit, perfect spring slash-turn terrain all the way down to the road at 8100 feet.

Option: Red Lake Peak's neighbor to the north, Stevens Peak (10,059 feet), is also home to fine ski terrain. An ascent of Stevens Peak starts from a plowed pullout on CA 88 just north of Crater Lake Creek. (This pullout can also be used as a shuttle for Red Lake Peak's descent along Crater Lake Creek.)

36 Elephants Back

Starting Point	Carson Pass, 8600 feet
High Point	9585 feet
Distance	4 miles
Elevation Gain	1000 feet
Time	2 hours
Difficulty Level	Easy
Terrain Rating	2
Aspects	North, northeast-east, southeast
Seasons	Winter, spring
Map	USGS Carson Pass

Elephants Back is the shortest route and most easily accessed peak in the Carson Pass area. For that reason, it is a great introductory tour or is often linked up with other objectives for a longer tour in the Mokelumne Wilderness. Elephants Back, conveniently located on the way back from descents on Round Top Mountain (Route 37) and the east bowl above Winnemucca Lake, is easily added to a longer tour for little extra vertical. Elephants Back's northeast-facing bowl is prime powder skiing terrain, and the east-facing chute off the summit is a good option for those looking to add a little spice to their run. Elephants Back's longer southeast face also serves up 1300-foot corn runs down to Forestdale Creek. The short approach and moderate terrain are perfect for those just starting out in the backcountry, and the stunning scenery and ease of access will have you coming back for years. While it is just a short hike from the bottom of Elephants Back to return to Carson Pass, many people do a car shuttle and finish their descent at Red Lake, scoring an extra 700 vertical feet or so of rolling descent.

GETTING THERE

From the Y in South Lake Tahoe, follow US Highway 50–CA 89 south for 4.8 miles. Just past the agricultural inspection station in Meyers, turn south on CA 89 and follow it for 11 miles up and over Luther Pass to the junction with CA 88. Turn right on CA 88 and follow it west through the Hope Valley for 8.75 miles to the top of Carson Pass and park in the Sno-Park (permit required) on the left (south) side of the road. From the west, Carson Pass is on CA 88, 5 miles east of Kirkwood Mountain Resort. **Red Lake pullout:** For a shuttle at Red Lake, 2.3 miles before Carson Pass, park in the parking area at the gated Forest Service road on the south side of the highway by Red Lake, then continue up to the pass.

THE ROUTE

From the Sno-Park at Carson Pass, head south, following the heavily traveled path of the summer trail toward Winnemucca Lake. Carson Pass is a popular spot for

The scoured hump of Elephants Back and its northeast bowl as seen from Red Lake Peak

snowshoeing and cross-country skiing, so there is often a well-beaten path from the parking area in this direction. The majority of this route is relatively flat as you hike along the west side of this broad ridge. Follow the contours of the terrain as you climb gently for 1.5 miles. Here, the route splits depending on your objective.

Northeast bowl: To reach the large bowl below the cliffy ridgeline, head east to the saddle on the ridge just north of Elephants Back. From this saddle you can traverse into the bowl. If the snow is good, the northeast bowl is a great place to do a few 500-vertical-foot laps, and a variety of short terrain in the immediate area is worth exploring as well. To return to the top of the pass, hike back to the ridge just north of Elephants Back's north ridge, then retrace the route back down to the parking area. If you dropped a car at Red Lake for a shuttle, from the bottom of the bowl head northeast and push across the flats for a few hundred feet, then sample some of the fun, rolling, north-facing terrain down to Red Lake. Traverse to the east end of Red Lake to get to the parking area.

East chute: If you're planning to drop into the east chute from the summit, from where the route splits at 1.5 miles continue hiking south while contouring up the west slope of Elephants Back. If snow coverage is good, you may be able to skin to the top of the peak, but this west-southwest-facing slope gets both wind scoured and warmed by the sun, so you may need to hike on dirt a short way to the top. The summit of Elephants Back provides an incredible view of the surrounding mountains, so take it all in before descending.

The east chute off Elephants Back takes off from the south side of the summit. This steep east-facing chute drops for a few hundred feet before wrapping around to the northeast and joining with the northeast bowl descent line below the peak's cliffy face. Enjoy the moderate pitch of the bowl until it flattens out below, and either ascend back to the ridge for a ski down to Carson Pass or descend north, then east, to the Red Lake parking area if you have a shuttle car there.

Southeast face: From the ridge just south of the summit, the southeast face is the perfect aspect for growing and farming corn snow, and it holds its pitch for 1300 vertical feet down to Forestdale Creek. From the creek you can hike back up to either descend to Carson Pass or follow the northeast bowl descent to the Red Lake pullout—or you can take a longer descent to Red Lake: follow Forestdale Creek down a short distance and then turn north and climb through a low saddle, then continue north to the Red Lake parking area.

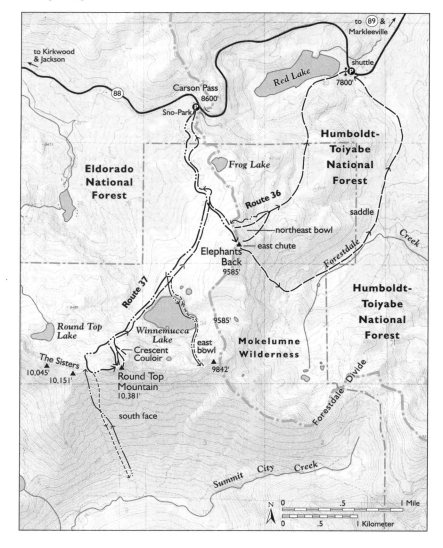

37 Round Top Mountain

Starting Point	Carson Pass, 8600 feet
High Point	10,381 feet
Distance	6 miles
Elevation Gain	2080 feet
Times	Couloirs and east bowl, 4 hours; south face, 6 hours
Difficulty Level	Moderate
Terrain Ratings	Couloirs 4; south face and east bowl 3
Aspects	North-northeast, south
Seasons	Winter, spring
Map	USGS Caples Lake, Carson Pass

Round Top Mountain dominates the skyline south of CA 88 above Carson Pass, its impressive north face split by a trio of short, steep chutes. The most notable of these is the Crescent Couloir, named for its striking resemblance to a crescent moon. One of the steepest lines in the Lake Tahoe area, the Crescent has an intimidating, blind, exposed, narrow entrance and stays walled in for 500 vertical feet. The top of the Crescent and the alternate chute immediately to skier's right that joins the Crescent at the bottom are very steep; if you plan to climb either of these lines, you may want an ice axe and crampons for safety. Another variation farther east along the face of Round Top is a slightly less steep diagonal chute. Those looking for some legitimate steep skiing close to Tahoe in Mokelumne Wilderness can definitely find it here. The varied terrain adjacent to Round Top has plenty to offer as well, with skiable slopes on all aspects and something for all ability levels. The east bowl above Winnemucca Lake offers some shorter playful terrain, and the south side of Round Top also hides one of the longest pitches in the Tahoe area, with 2500 vertical feet of south-facing fall line down to Summit City Creek. This area is home to phenomenal ski terrain where you can check off one of the steepest lines in Tahoe or spend the day on a longer, more casual tour.

GETTING THERE

From the Y in South Lake Tahoe, follow US Highway 50–CA 89 south for 4.8 miles. Just past the agricultural inspection station in Meyers, turn south on CA 89 and follow it for 11 miles up and over Luther Pass to the junction with CA 88. Turn right on CA 88 and follow it west through the Hope Valley for 8.75 miles to the top of Carson Pass; park in the Sno-Park (permit required) on the left (south) side of the road. From the west, Carson Pass is on CA 88, 5 miles east of Kirkwood Mountain Resort.

THE ROUTE

From the Sno-Park, follow the summer trail along the west side of the ridge toward Elephants Back (Route 36), then split off from that route to stay on the west side of

Taking it all in on the approach to Round Top

the ridge and climb very gradually west of Elephants Back before descending slightly to Winnemucca Lake, roughly 2 miles and a gradual 550 vertical feet to the south from Carson Pass.

From Winnemucca Lake, the imposing north face and couloirs of Round Top should be clearly visible. Hike southwest, contouring along the north side of the peak and up to the apron below the chutes. At this point you can either climb up the line of your choice or continue to contour uphill southwest to the saddle at 10,000 feet on the west side of the peak, then climb the west ridge to the summit. Getting to the summit via the west ridge is somewhat easier than climbing directly up the chutes, although it involves a bit of rocky scrambling and doesn't afford you the chance to directly assess the snow conditions in the chutes.

The entrance to the Crescent is a blind, steep rollover that begins on a hanging snowfield with lots of exposure beneath. Coverage varies from year to year, but the top of the Crescent is generally so narrow that you must make a couple turns down the hanging snowfield before traversing skier's right into the chute where it is a little wider. The top of the Crescent is very steep and exposed and is a no-fall zone, so this line should be attempted only by competent expert skiers and snowboarders. If the Crescent Couloir is above your ability level, there is plenty of moderately pitched terrain in the bowls throughout this area.

If the Cresent is skied out, the chute immediately to skier's right, known as the Hidden Chute, is another option that is similarly steep and funnels into the bottom of the Crescent. Another diagonal chute lies even farther to skier's right on the north face of Round Top.

From the bottom of these chutes, return to Carson Pass by going back the way you came. The return along the ridge is mostly gently downhill, and with the right conditions it is possible for skiers to skate and coast all the way back, while snowboarders may have to transition back to skins.

Options: If you're looking for corn snow, the south slopes of Round Top drop 2500 vertical feet down to Summit City Creek and the bottom of the north face of Deadwood Peak. This is an excellent place to harvest corn when high pressure dominates for extended periods. From the saddle west of Round Top, pick a line on this broad face and ski it all the way to the creek, then reverse your ski route for a steep skin back to the saddle. This adds a couple of miles in distance, as well as 2500 vertical feet of gain per lap.

Those looking to extend their tour may do so in the east bowl: the north-northwest-facing rolling, rocky terrain directly above Winnemucca Lake. Several fun, short chutes here usually get passed up by people heading to Round Top. Those with energy to burn may also opt to hit Elephants Back (Route 36) on the way out of this area.

EBBETTS AND SONORA PASSES

These two major mountain passes cross the Sierra between Tahoe and Yosemite, and both roads close seasonally for the winter, reopening as weather and snowpack allow. Motorized travel is allowed to access these remote areas in winter, so they are popular with snowmobilers, although most backcountry skiers wait, rightly so, for the roads to open to get there. Once the gates open in the late spring or early summer, it becomes easy to reach the backcountry skiing buffet available beyond. The Ebbetts and Sonora passes area south of Lake Tahoe has an incredible amount of terrain worthy of exploration.

Ebbetts Pass is the high point on CA 4 between the small town of Angels Camp to the west and Markleeville to the east. The western road closure of CA 4 is near Lake Alpine and the Bear Valley Mountain ski area, which offers some of the easiest western-slope winter backcountry access in the entire range. Mount Reba sits just above the road and has a variety of great moderate terrain. Once the road opens, access to routes like Silver Peak becomes reasonable, although snow coverage, or lack thereof, can often be an issue.

Sonora Pass is the high point on CA 108 between the small foothill town of Sonora to the west and Sonora Junction on US Highway 395 to the east. Sonora Pass is closed in winter and may reopen anytime from mid-April to late May, depending on the snowpack, and may close at anytime after it has reopened for the summer due to inclement weather. The distance associated with accessing this area when the road is closed makes it prohibitively far for most backcountry skiers unless they have a snowmobile. Once the road opens, however, skiers flock to this area for late-season turns. There is a ton of excellent moderate terrain in the bowls near the top of the pass, as well as the superclassic Y couloir on Leavitt Peak. Plenty of skiing up here is not described in detail in this guidebook, so have a good look around (much of it is pretty self-explanatory).

Both passes are situated relatively in the middle of nowhere, and the nearest amenities of any kind are located in the small towns far to the east or west, so come prepared. You can check the status of these roads on the California Department of Transportation website (see Resources) by typing in the highway number. Ebbetts Pass is considered the far southern end of the Sierra Avalanche Center's advisory area (see Resources). The Bridgeport Avalanche Center (see Resources) provides an avalanche advisory and observations for the Bridgeport Winter Recreation Area terrain in the Sonora Pass region that is generally accessed by snowmobile in winter.

38   Mount Reba

Starting Point	Lake Alpine Sno-Park, 7580 feet
High Points	8842 feet; summit, 8755 feet
Distances	Point 8605, 3 miles; summit, 6 miles
Elevation Gains	Point 8605, 1025 feet; summit, 1200 feet
Times	Point 8605, 2 hours; summit, 4 hours
Difficulty Level	Point 8605, easy; summit, moderate
Terrain Rating	2
Aspects	South, southwest, west, east
Seasons	Winter, spring
Maps	USGS Mokelumne Peak; Big Meadow; Spicer Meadow Reservoir; Pacific Valley

Located on the western slope of the Sierra adjacent to the Bear Valley Mountain ski area, just south of Mokelumne Wilderness and west of the winter closure of CA 4 at Ebbetts Pass, Mount Reba offers a wealth of moderate ski terrain on a variety of aspects. The relatively short pitches and mellow slopes are perfect for people just getting into backcountry skiing, while those with more experience can have plenty of fun doing multiple laps or getting into some of the more complex areas. The various ridges of Mount Reba offer skiing on virtually all aspects, so no matter the snow conditions you're likely to find good snow somewhere on the mountain. The best way to familiarize yourself with the area is to ascend the ridge that separates Poison Canyon and Bee Gulch and eventually joins the main ridge of Mount Reba. This ridgeline approach affords you a great view of the terrain that drops off to either side, excellent for scoping the short gullies and tree pitches that go down into Poison Canyon and Bee Gulch. Farther up the ridge you eventually intersect the east-west ridge of Mount Reba, with the summit just a short distance along the ridge to the west. The

The ascent ridge of Mount Reba

longest pitches drop southwest from near the summit down into Horse Canyon next to the Bear Valley Mountain ski area. Whether you are doing a quick lap or an all-day adventure, Mount Reba is one of the best and easiest-to-access backcountry ski spots on the western slope of the Sierra.

GETTING THERE

From Angels Camp, at the intersection of CA 49 and CA 4, drive 47 miles east on CA 4 to its winter closure at Lake Alpine just before Ebbetts Pass. The Sno-Park is on the right, just past the turnoff on the left for Mount Reba Road (CA 207), the Bear Valley access road. There is also another Sno-Park 0.25 mile up CA 207, on the right at the mouth of Poison Canyon. Either Sno-Park (permit required) is a fine place to start this tour.

THE ROUTE

From either Sno-Park, head northeast and begin the gradual ascent of the long, mellow ridgeline that separates Poison Canyon and Bee Gulch. After only a few hundred vertical feet of ascent, you gain the crest of the ridge and continue heading northeast along it. As you walk, check out the moderate terrain that drops off the ridge on both sides, into either Poison Canyon or Bee Gulch; your route on Mount Reba depends on the conditions and your objectives.

Point 8190: You reach the first prominence (8190 feet) at about 0.6 mile. All the terrain you are hiking above is good moderate skiing; the 600-vertical-foot shots are perfect for doing a lot of quick, short laps down to the Sno-Park or off either side of the ridge, and they continue as you proceed north. You can drop in here and do some short laps and/or continue up.

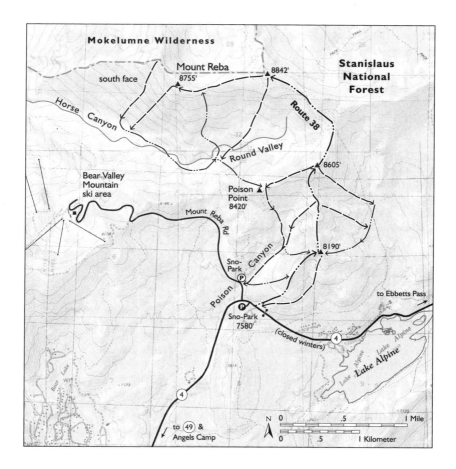

Point 8605: After about 1.5 miles and around 1000 vertical feet of ascent from the parking area, you hit another prominent point in the ridgeline, at 8605 feet. From here you can descend via either the large south- to west-facing bowl of Poison Canyon or the more east-facing terrain down into Bee Gulch. If you drop into either of these side canyons, be aware of the multitude of terrain traps in the gullies below you. Also remember which side of the ridge you're on and how to get back up to it for more laps or the return to the parking area. Or you can carry onward and upward to gain the east-west summit ridge.

Point 8842: Continuing on up toward the summit from the second prominence (8605 feet), you lose a small amount of elevation as you head north along the ridge for 0.25 mile, then head northwest for 0.75 mile and gain around 400 vertical feet to the highest point along the summit ridge, although it's not the named summit. Once atop this ridge (8842 feet), you have a variety of options, including skiing a south-facing run down to Round Valley or continuing along the ridge to Mount Reba's summit.

Summit (8755 feet): Off the summit, these south-facing slopes are great for harvesting spring corn and will provide you with about 1000-vertical-foot runs down into Horse Canyon. Once at the bottom of Horse Canyon, head east up it and into Round Valley; you can head north from here back up to the ridge for more laps, or return to the parking area by heading southeast up to Poison Point (8420 feet) for a cruise down into Poison Canyon to return back to the parking area.

39 Silver Peak at Ebbetts Pass

Starting Point	Noble Canyon trailhead, 6904 feet
High Point	10,772 feet
Distance	6 miles
Elevation Gain	3900 feet
Time	4 hours
Difficulty Level	Strenuous
Terrain Rating	4
Aspect	North-northwest-west
Seasons	Late spring, early summer
Map	USGS Ebbetts Pass

The Ebbetts Pass area is one of the Sierra passes least visited and utilized by skiers since it is one of the last Sierra passes to be cleared of snow. Sadly, by the time the road opens, many of the great ski routes in the area are no longer in condition for skiing; however, skiers with snowmobiles can access this area midwinter. Despite being one of the longest walled-in chutes in the Sierra north of Sonora Pass, Silver Peak's northwest chute, a.k.a. the Glider Chute, is one such route that sees little traffic due to its out-of-the-way location. Visible from the higher peaks in the Tahoe region, this chute is 1000 feet long, with 2500 feet of incredible terrain below it. Getting lucky with snow coverage and the opening of the road for the season is crucial for a successful attempt on Silver Peak. For a long and unique multisport day, those with a sense of adventure often use bikes to approach this area when the road is melted out but not yet opened for the season. Hopefully if you can drive to the trailhead, there will still be decent snow coverage on Silver Peak. While the northwest chute may be the crown jewel of the Ebbetts Pass region, a multitude of other peaks and lines wait to be explored off the top of CA 4.

GETTING THERE

From Markleeville, on CA 89 south of Lake Tahoe, continue south on CA 89 for 4.8 miles; when CA 89 turns left up toward Monitor Pass, continue straight, west, on CA 4 for 8.25 miles to the Noble Canyon trailhead, about 0.25 mile past the Silver Creek campground at a right switchback in the road. From Angels Camp, drive east on CA 4 for 67 miles to 5.4 miles east of the top of Ebbetts Pass to reach this trailhead.

THE ROUTE

From the trailhead, go south along the trail toward Noble Canyon and begin a gradual ascent just on the west side of Noble Canyon Creek. Follow this trail uphill for just over 0.5 mile and 400 vertical feet, and as the terrain begins to flatten out, find a place to safely head southeast across the creek, at around 7228 feet. Once you cross the creek, climb east up the slope to a prominent high point at 7844 feet. From here you should have a good vantage point of the rest of your ascent, which follows the ridge southeast with a bit of up and down, then up a big ramp to the south summit of Silver Peak.

Head southeast, staying on the top of the prominent ridgeline that climbs gradually at first but steadily gets steeper as you ascend. Over the course of 1.25 miles you gain around 1500 vertical feet, and the ridge opens up to more of a steep ramp. From here the route becomes much steeper and you gain 1500 more vertical feet in 0.5 mile until you reach Silver Peak's south summit. Once atop the summit, take in the incredible views in all directions. From here you have a choice: descend the line you just ascended assuming snow coverage allows, or head north along the summit ridge to the top of the northwest chute, a.k.a. Glider Chute, that drops in from the saddle between the north and south summits.

The steep chute starts as a wider face that funnels into much narrower and walled-in confines a few hundred feet down the line. After about 1000 vertical feet, the chute opens up into a much wider gully. Be aware while in the chute, as frequent rockfall occurs here. Once you exit the chute, continue down as far as the snow coverage allows

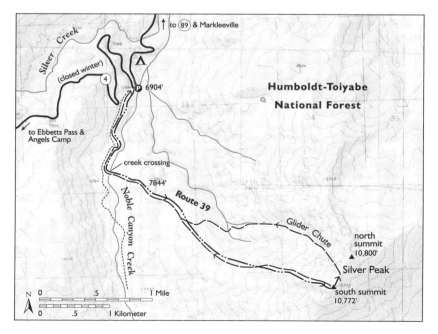

Silver Peak and the Glider Chute from Hawkins Peak

before traversing hard to the left (west) to regain the ridge you ascended. Once you have regained the ridge, return the way you came back to the trailhead. The convoluted terrain on the lower part of this mountain can be confusing, and the drainages can suck you in and lead you away from where you want to go. It is important that you make your way back to the prominent 7844-foot point and cross Noble Canyon Creek at approximately the same place you did on the way up, then return the way you came to the trailhead.

40 Leavitt Peak

Starting Point	Mouth of Blue Canyon, 8800 feet
High Point	11,569 feet
Distance	5 miles
Elevation Gain	2770 feet
Time	3.5 hours
Difficulty Level	Moderate
Terrain Rating	3
Aspect	North
Seasons	Late spring, early summer
Map	USGS Sonora Pass

Prior to the opening of Sonora Pass on CA 108 in the late spring, the area is primarily accessed by snowmobile and used by the US Marines from the Mountain Warfare Training Center. Once the pass opens, however, snowmobiles are no longer necessary to reach the backcountry skiing bounty that the road accesses. Sonora Pass is often overlooked for the bigger skiing farther south in the Sierra, but there is a lot of interesting, albeit somewhat smaller, terrain within striking distance of this road, the most impressive of which is Leavitt Peak in Emigrant Wilderness. Leavitt's classic Y couloir is probably the most notable and sought-after descent in the area. With two steep entrances that come together in the shape of a backward Y, this 1000-foot chute is definitely worth checking out. There are various ways to access the north side of Leavitt Peak: some people hike in from the top of the pass, but in my opinion it is easier to hike up the Blue Canyon drainage. This route avoids unnecessary sidehilling

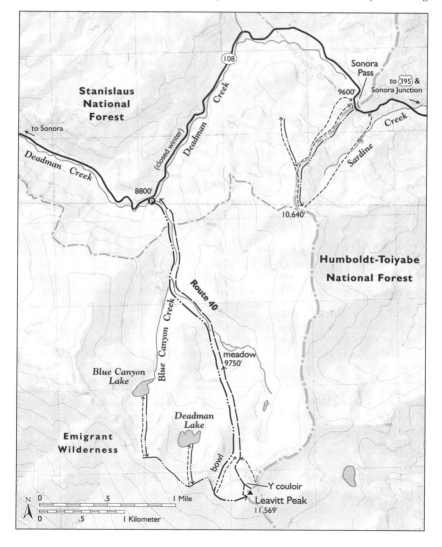

Approaching Leavitt Peak in late spring after the peak and the top of the Y couloir have just come into view

on the way both in and out as well as the need for a car shuttle back to the top of the pass after your tour. Much of this route follows creek drainages, so be careful when crossing them, especially later in the day when the snow is softer. Numerous other descent options, including neighboring couloirs and a mellower bowl, offer something for everyone in this little slice of backcountry skiing heaven. The Bridgeport Avalanche Center (see resources) provides an avalanche advisory for the Bridgeport Winter Recreation Area which includes the Sonora Pass region.

GETTING THERE

From Sonora, drive east on CA 108 for roughly 63 miles to the switchback at the mouth of Blue Canyon Creek; this sharp corner is the first true switchback west of the pass. Park in a small pullout on the north side of the road just uphill of the switchback; there's room for about four or five vehicles. From Sonora Junction at US Highway 395 and CA 108, head west on CA 108 for 17.6 miles to this pullout, roughly 2 miles west of Sonora Pass.

THE ROUTE

Within the first 50 feet from where you parked on the road, your crossing of Deadman Creek is often the crux of this route. Depending on the season's snowpack, this crossing can be anything from very easy to extremely treacherous. The creek will generally be swollen with spring snowmelt, and a misstep could certainly ruin your day before it even starts. Take your time and look around; you can generally step from rock to rock. Be especially wary of weak snow bridges that could possibly break beneath you; please use caution.

Once across the creek, turn south into the drainage that comes down from Blue Canyon Lake. Head south, staying on the west side of and following Blue Canyon Creek for roughly 0.75 mile. At 9500 feet, a ridge splits the drainage; continuing south would bring you to Blue Canyon Lake, but you want to head left (southeast) and more directly to the bottom of the north face of Leavitt Peak. Shortly after heading southeast at the split, you enter a broad meadow at 9750 feet, and the top of Leavitt Peak will come into view, about a mile away directly south. Head southeast to the far end of the meadow, then begin the gradual climb south for 750 vertical feet up into the basin below the face of Leavitt.

Contour south around the base of the ridge that forms the west wall of this basin and into the large bowl just west of Leavitt Peak. At this point you can decide whether to skin up the bowl or boot-pack up the chute. I think it is much easier to climb southwest up the bowl and do a short ridge walk east to the summit, but do whatever suits you and your group. Then take in the incredible 360-degree view from the top.

The Y couloir has two entrances: skier's left is significantly steeper and often guarded by a cornice; skier's right is less steep and much more straightforward. After about 150 vertical feet, both entrances funnel together into a 50-foot-wide chute with a fall line that heads skier's left for another 600 vertical feet to the apron below.

Once you're finished skiing on Leavitt Peak, the fun is far from over. There's still 2000 vertical feet of mellow terrain back down the drainage to the road. Watch for open water near the creeks and be careful crossing the creek once you get back to the road.

Options: If the conditions in the Y look bad or the line is above your ability level, the large bowl to the west of the peak offers around 1000 vertical feet of fun, moderate turns, essentially along your ascent route. The east-facing (skier's-left) side of the bowl also has a better aspect for growing corn if north faces are still frozen. Another chute, to skier's right of the Y, tops out in the ridge just northeast of the summit, good for an extra lap or as an alternative descent route.

For those who enjoy exploring, the ridge that extends west from Leavitt Peak has a variety of fun, short lines above Deadman and Blue Canyon lakes.

For those looking for a shorter option, from the top of the pass, head southwest along the ridgeline to ski a number of moderate short bowls in close proximity.

41 Mount Emma

Starting Point	Little Walker River bridge, 7700 feet
High Point	10,525 feet
Distance	4 miles
Elevation Gain	2800 feet
Time	3 hours
Difficulty Level	Moderate
Terrain Ratings	East gully 2; north gullies 3
Aspects	East, northeast, northwest
Seasons	Winter, spring
Map	USGS Fales Hot Springs

When driving south on US Highway 395 near Sonora Junction, as you exit the Walker River Canyon the mountains of the Little Walker River Canyon sit in plain view straight ahead of you. Most people just drive on by in search of more prominent objectives farther south, but when conditions allow, the Little Walker River drainage offers some excellent terrain off the beaten path that is worth exploring. Mount Emma, the closest peak in this zone, has fine moderate skiing on a variety of aspects

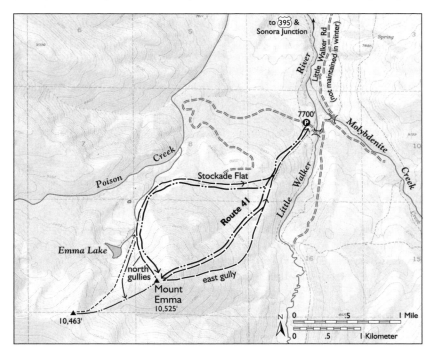

The view of Mount Emma (center) from Little Walker Road

off the summit. Getting back into this area can often be the crux of this route, as Little Walker Road is not plowed or maintained and may be snowbound, making for a very long approach. This route is best attempted when the snow level is higher, or later in the season as the snow recedes, when you can drive a few miles in toward Mount Emma on this relatively smooth dirt road. When this road is snowbound, you can certainly hike in on the road's path, although I suggest attempting other routes that have a shorter approach.

GETTING THERE

From Sonora Junction at US 395 and Sonora Pass Road (CA 108), head south on US 395 for 0.7 mile and turn south onto Little Walker Road. From Bridgeport on US 395, drive north 16.5 miles to this turnoff. Drive 3.4 miles on this road if possible, staying right and crossing Molybdenite Creek and then the Little Walker River on bridges. Park just beyond the bridge that crosses the Little Walker River. If you cannot make it this far by vehicle, drive as far as is reasonable and park where you can, then hike the road to just beyond the bridge over the Little Walker River.

THE ROUTE

From across the bridge, head southwest up the open slope for approximately 0.75 mile and 600 vertical feet to the east end of a broad bench known as Stockade Flat. At this point, you have two choices, depending on your objective: the east gully or the north gullies.

East gully: To head to the enticing east gully, continue climbing gradually to the southwest and up the open, sparsely treed slope leading directly to the summit. You gain another 2300 vertical feet or so over 1.5 miles. From the summit, you can descend the slope you just hiked up or the prominent east gully just to skier's right. Either way, drop in and descend for more than 2000 vertical feet of excellent, moderately pitched fall-line skiing. As the pitch begins to flatten out at the bottom of the east gully, begin traversing left (north) to return to Stockade Flat, then continue back down to where you started.

North gullies: Hidden behind Mount Emma's north ridge are a couple of long northwest-facing chutes. This terrain is somewhat steeper, albeit somewhat shorter, than the east gully. Anyone wishing to ski this side of the mountain should approach these routes from below to assess coverage and conditions. To do so, from Stockade Flat head west across the flats for about 1 mile and begin to contour around the base of the north ridge and into the Emma Lake drainage. As you contour around to the south, the northwest-facing terrain of Mount Emma will come into view. Climb the gully of your choice or head south from Emma Lake to gain the ridge for a less exposed but potentially wind-scoured rocky ascent to the summit. After descending your chosen gully, retrace your ascent route to return to the bridge over the Little Walker River.

Option: There is also some moderate skiing in the bowl just west of Mount Emma above Emma Lake.

Opposite: *Booting up Hurd Peak's north face high above South Lake*

PART IV
EASTERN SIERRA

THE EASTERN ESCARPMENT OF THE SIERRA NEVADA is one of the most beautiful and impressive geologic features in the United States, if not the entire world. Stretching from Bridgeport in the north to Lone Pine in the south, the east side of the High Sierra is an impressive sight, with mountainsides that drop precipitously from the rugged Sierra crest to the high desert far below. The mountains and vertical relief from summit to valley get progressively bigger the farther south you go, with numerous peaks over 14,000 feet—including the highest peak in the Lower 48 states, Mount Whitney—before dropping off quickly to the southern end of the range. Perhaps even more impressive is the abundance of amazing skiable terrain as well as relative ease of access to these gorgeous mountains. The eastern Sierra offer what is arguably the best backcountry skiing in the entire country, with an incredible variety of topography to suit everyone's tastes.

US Highway 395 parallels the Sierra to the east, the main artery for access to this backcountry wonderland. Numerous towns dotting the highway, home to local backcountry skiers and snowboarders, are places to refuel and rest on the way to and from or between forays into the mountains. Various other roads head west from US 395 into the mountains, providing access to the routes described in this guidebook. Some of these roads are cleared of snow all winter long, while others are snowbound until they melt or are cleared of snow for the fishing season in the late spring.

BRIDGEPORT TO LUNDY CANYON

The small town of Bridgeport on US Highway 395 is the unofficial northern end of the eastern Sierra. Although it has a population of fewer than 600 year-round residents (as of the 2010 census), several of whom are hardcore backcountry skiers, this tiny burg is a popular destination for fishermen in the summer and backcountry enthusiasts in the winter.

Bridgeport has a gas station, a general store, and several small motels and restaurants. Some restaurants are closed for the winter and reopen for the fishing and summer season in the late spring. Known for expensive gas and a couple of popular hot springs—Travertine and Buckeye—Bridgeport is also renowned for its amazing mountains and backcountry access. Twin Lakes and Virginia Lakes are the primary entry points for skiers and snowboarders, with a wealth of terrain located relatively close to both.

Twin Lakes Road is cleared of snow all winter to the Mono Village resort and campground at the west end of the west Twin Lake; this is a great starting point for many routes, including the can't-miss classic the Matterhorn.

Virginia Lakes Road offers incredible access to this area but is often closed in winter more than 6 miles from the trailhead at the Virginia Lakes. This road closure varies from year to year based on the snow line, snowpack, and weather, but when it is open, the abundance of moderate to advanced terrain is very easy to reach.

Lundy Canyon, just one drainage south of the Virginia Lakes area, also has a wealth of ski terrain. Access to this area is off of Lundy Lake Road, which has a winter closure gate about a mile east of Lundy Lake; the road reopens each spring when snow coverage allows.

42   Monument Peak

Starting Point : Mouth of Tamarack Creek, 7100 feet
High Point : 11,785 feet
Distance : 10.5 miles
Elevation Gain : 4685 feet
Time : 6 hours
Difficulty Level : Strenuous
Terrain Rating : 3
Aspect : North-northeast
Seasons : Winter, spring
Maps : USGS Twin Lakes; Dunderberg Peak

Monument Peak is visible just briefly from US Highway 395 as you drive through Bridgeport. Tucked behind the Crater Crest at the head of Tamarack Creek, just outside Hoover Wilderness, Monument Peak's triangular summit and aesthetic northeast-facing couloir beckon would-be skiers from afar. The crux of this route is the distance to get there: quite a bit of relatively flat walking awaits. A run down Monument's northeast couloir is certainly worth the walk, as are a number of other fun gullies in the cirque to the east of the summit, on Monument Ridge. Those looking for a more moderate descent may find it in the broad gullies just west of the northeast couloir. For really fit hikers, this route can be linked up with a run on Crater Crest (Route 43) for a longer tour.

GETTING THERE

From Bridgeport on US 395, turn west onto Twin Lakes Road and follow it for 10 miles to the east end of East Twin Lake. Turn onto South Twin Road and continue for 0.6 mile to Tamarack Creek. After recent snowfall, this road may be snowbound; if so, park as close to the Twin Lakes campground as you can get and ski the remaining 0.5 mile or so past the campground to the creek.

THE ROUTE

From South Twin Road at Tamarack Creek, cross the creek and turn south into the creek drainage to climb the steep lower slope on the west side of the creek. After about 800 vertical feet, you hit a bench, and the pitch moderates. Continue south, climbing gently up the Tamarack Creek drainage for 2.7 miles to Tamarack Lake (9630 feet). From here it is another mile farther south to Hunewill Lake at the base

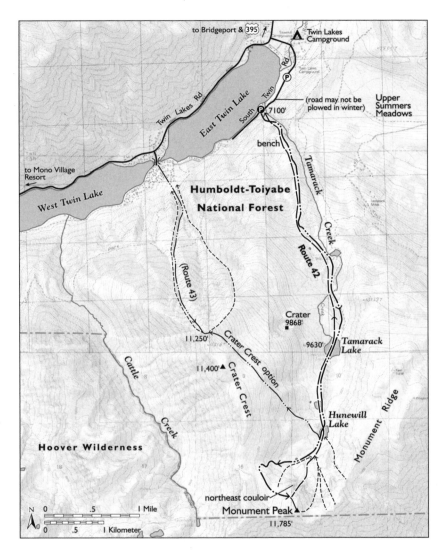

of the north face of Monument Peak. From Hunewill Lake the route begins to climb to the west up the mellow east-northeast-facing bowl. At the top of the bowl, around 11,100 feet, head southeast up the slope toward the summit.

The top of the northeast couloir should be quite obvious at around 11,500 feet. This relatively wide and moderately pitched couloir drops in here, almost 300 vertical feet shy of the summit. Ski the couloir, enjoying the 900 or so feet of walled-in skiing before entering the apron above Hunewill Lake, then return the way you came via the Tamarack Creek drainage.

Hiking across the flats of Hunewill Lake on the way to Monument Peak (Oscar Havens)

Options: From the top of the northeast couloir, it's a relatively short walk to the summit, but it is often wind scoured and rocky. However, those looking for a more moderate run, or extra vertical and more skiing, may find it off the summit, dropping east and then turning north into the Monument Ridge cirque. The short shots in the Monument Ridge cirque drop to the east of the summit.

Or from Hunewill Lake, you can make a long sidehill slog northwest to the top of Crater Crest (Route 43) for those descents.

43 Crater Crest

Starting Points	Gully and ridge ascents, 7100 feet
High Point	11,250 feet
Distances	Gully ascent, 4 miles; ridge ascent, 5 miles
Elevation Gain	4200 feet for both ascent routes
Time	3.5 hours for either route
Difficulty Level	Strenuous
Terrain Rating	3
Aspect	North
Seasons	Winter, spring
Map	USGS Twin Lakes

The gullied north face of Crater Crest rises 4200 vertical feet above Twin Lakes, just outside of Bridgeport. Named for the odd volcanic crater hole on its eastern flank, this crest, along with the many hot springs nearby, tell the story of the area's fiery past. This route's close proximity to the road, relatively short approach, and long north-facing gullies make it a fantastic half-day adventure. Crater Crest's north-facing

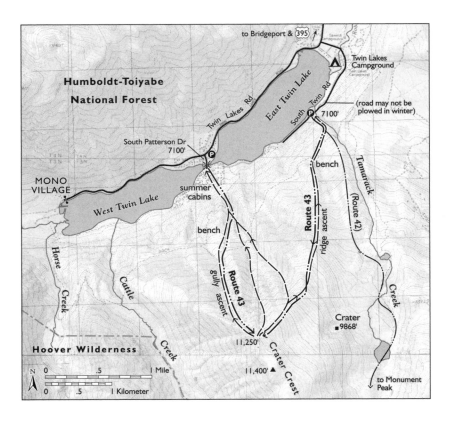

aspect keeps snow cold during the winter and holds snow well into the spring, when you can find smooth, consistent corn snow on this broad face overlooking the Twin Lakes. The most direct approach to Crater Crest is to start at South Patterson Drive between the Twin Lakes. This starting point, the main access to cabins on the south side of the lakes, is not cleared of snow beyond the bridge, so in winter, people generally walk, ski, or snowmobile to their cabins. For a significantly mellower tour or to avoid avalanche hazard on the ascent, skiers may wish to approach via the northeast ridge, from the east end of the East Twin Lake near Tamarack Creek. Though the northeast ridge is significantly longer, it is a good alternative that is far less steep and exposed.

GETTING THERE

Gully ascent: From Bridgeport on US Highway 395, turn south on Twin Lakes Road and follow it for 11.8 miles to the junction with South Patterson Drive. Turn left on South Patterson Drive and park in the small dirt parking area on the left just a few hundred feet down this road.

Crater Crest (center), Monument Peak (left), and the Matterhorn (right)

Ridge ascent: From Bridgeport on US 395, turn south on Twin Lakes Road and follow it 10 miles to South Twin Road, then turn left and follow this road as it wraps around the east end of East Twin Lake toward the northeast ridge of Crater Crest. Follow South Twin Road approximately 1 mile and find a good spot to park below the northeast ridge just west of Tamarack Creek. After recent snowfall, this road may be covered with snow, making for a longer approach; follow it as far as possible, then ski the rest of the way toward Tamarack Creek.

THE ROUTE

Gully ascent: From the South Patterson Drive parking area, cross the bridge between the Twin Lakes and walk south along the road, past the summer cabins and directly toward the bottom of the prominent drainage that comes down the center of the peak. A large ridge that starts at the highest point on the face splits Crater Crest almost perfectly down the middle, with large gullies on either side. Bear in mind that all of the gullies on this face are avalanche paths, so plan your route accordingly based on the current snow and avalanche conditions.

If the snow stability is good, you can hike directly up any of the main gullies that connect to the ridges near the summit. I prefer the gully to climber's right, which eventually reaches the northwest ridge and follows that to the top. When the drainages split near the bottom, at around 7700 feet, head climber's right and up onto the large bench at the base of the gully. Skin up this main gully as high as you can; in the right conditions you may be able to skin the whole way, but you'll typically end up switching to boot-packing several hundred feet from the ridge. However you have to, gain the ridge and follow it to the top. The true summit of Crater Crest lies just south of the top of the face, but gaining this summit does not provide any additional skiing. Be sure to take in the outrageous views of the Matterhorn (Route 44), Sawtooth Ridge, Twin Peaks, and the Robinson Creek drainage.

Any of the main gullies down the north face offer equally good skiing—in fact, the entire face is good ski terrain, but the top hundred feet or so are often windswept and may have some peppery rocks poking just out of the snow. It may be necessary to cautiously pick your way down through this pepper to get to your chosen descent route. The gullies offer subtle changes in aspect from one side to the other, so scout around to find the best snow for your descent. The pitch mellows out the farther down you go, but some fun rollovers off the front of the bench near the bottom are easy to find if you look around.

Ridge ascent: From a parking spot on South Twin Road just past Tamarack Creek, head south on the west side of the creek, up the slope and onto the prominent bench at around 7900 feet. From here, follow the northeast ridge all the way to the top of the north face.

You can descend either the way you came up or via the north face gullies described above. If you descend the north face, head east along the snow-covered road along the south side of the lake to return to your starting point.

44 Matterhorn Peak

Starting Point	Mono Village campground, 7100 feet
High Point	12,279 feet
Distance	10 miles
Elevation Gain	5179 feet
Time	6 hours
Difficulty Level	Strenuous
Terrain Rating	Ski Dreams 3; couloirs 4
Aspect	North-northeast
Seasons	Winter, spring
Maps	USGS Matterhorn Peak; Buckeye Ridge; Dunderberg Peak

The couloirs on Matterhorn Peak in Hoover Wilderness have seen traffic since the late 1960s, when Sierra backcountry skiing pioneers like H. J. Burhenne were laying tracks down them on bear-trap bindings, leather boots, and Firn Gliders. Backcountry skiing gear has certainly changed a lot since then, but the adventurous spirit of skiers has not. The impressive jagged summit of the Matterhorn, clearly visible from US Highway 395 in Bridgeport, continues to draw skiers to its classic couloirs and rolling lower slopes. Named for its resemblance to its iconic namesake in the Swiss Alps, the Matterhorn is the northernmost 12,000-plus-foot peak in the Sierra. Choose from three great descents on the Matterhorn: from the steeper west couloir and east couloir to the more moderate Ski Dreams and the bowls below, there is plenty of great terrain to make everyone happy. This true Sierra classic should absolutely be on everyone's list.

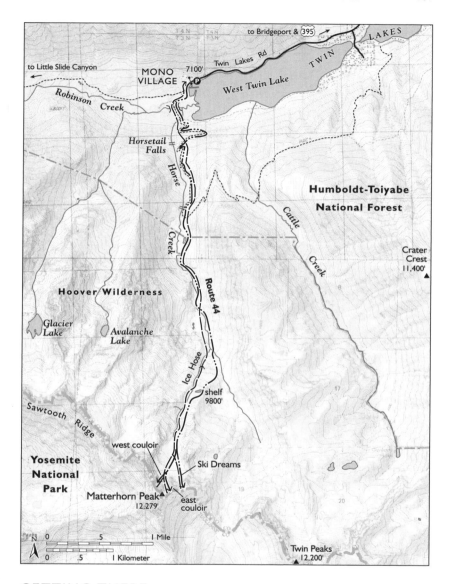

GETTING THERE

From Bridgeport on US 395, turn south onto Twin Lakes Road. Follow it for 13.4 miles to the gate at the Mono Village resort and campground. In winter, the gate is closed and you have to park here. In late spring, if this gate is open, drive into Mono Village and park at the south end of the parking area just past the marina, 0.25 mile closer.

A late-spring approach to the Matterhorn

THE ROUTE

From the car, walk south along the west end of West Twin Lake. The beginning of this route can offer some routefinding difficulties, but the main goal is to head up the Horse Creek drainage, which lies almost directly south from the parking area. At the south end of the parking area, follow signs for the Horse Creek Trail, crossing Robinson Creek on the bridge and following the trail if it is visible. Whether there is snow or not on this lower slope, follow the hiking trail as it switchbacks up along the east side of Horse Creek. I've always had the best luck hiking the Horse Creek drainage by staying on the east (climber's left) side of the creek. This is where the summer trail is, and if the snow is nonexistent or intermittent, you can hike along the trail until you reach the snow line.

Once you crest the first pitch, hiking becomes a little flatter as you continue south up Horse Creek. You soon come to a short, steep headwall and a beautiful waterfall, about 1 mile in, at roughly 8200 feet. Once you pass this spot, the drainage flattens out significantly, and as you enter the Hoover Wilderness, the creek widens into a marshy area of shallow ponds. Continue south along the bottom of the drainage, with the Matterhorn and its couloirs slowly becoming closer.

After roughly 2 miles, at about 8600 feet, the drainage steepens again. Continue south up the slope as it pitches up to around 9200 feet. At the top of this rise, turn southwest and climb the ridge toward the Matterhorn (continuing due south from here leads to Twin Peaks). Switchback your way up this ridge to a shelf at 9800 feet. At this shelf, continue southwest, dropping downhill for just a bit into the wide drainage that you climb for 1000 vertical feet to the moraine at the base of the couloirs on the

Matterhorn. From here you'll have a great view of all the routes: from east to west, they are Ski Dreams, the east couloir, and the west couloir. From this vantage point you can evaluate the snow conditions and coverage and choose the line that looks best for you and your group. You can typically skin to the base of the rocks that form the couloirs, at which point the pitch usually requires you to switch to boot-packing, possibly with crampons and an ice axe, depending on conditions.

These chutes are relatively short, only about 600–800 feet within the walls, but they're quite steep and good for multiple laps if you've got energy. Ski Dreams has the most moderate pitch and is the widest of the three runs. The east couloir is the most likely to be wind scoured but is a fantastic and surprisingly steep run when in good condition. You can climb to the summit of the Matterhorn via a short scramble from the top of the east couloir. The west couloir, my favorite, is I believe the steepest of the three options.

Once out of the run of your choice, follow the main drainage back down. At 9800 feet, continue following the drainage down and over the bench, into the narrow, walled-in confines of the Ice Hose, a moderately pitched chute that leads you back down to Horse Creek. From here return the way you came, cruising out several miles of mellow slopes back down to West Twin Lake.

45 Incredible Hulk and Kettle Peak: Little Slide Canyon

Starting Point	Mono Village campground, 7100 feet
High Points	Incredible Hulk, 11,335 feet; Kettle Peak, 10,994 feet
Distance	10 miles for either route
Elevation Gains	Incredible Hulk, 4300 feet; Kettle Peak, 3900 feet
Time	6 hours for either route
Difficulty Level	Strenuous
Terrain Ratings	Kettle Peak 3; Incredible Hulk 4
Aspects	Northwest, east-northeast, north
Seasons	Winter, spring
Maps	USGS Matterhorn Peak; Buckeye Ridge

Little Slide Canyon in Hoover Wilderness holds an abundance of great skiable terrain, most notably on Kettle Peak and the Incredible Hulk. This amazing zone remains almost completely hidden from view until you hike a couple miles west up the Robinson Creek drainage from West Twin Lake and turn south into Little Slide Canyon. Situated on opposite sides of the canyon, Kettle Peak and the Hulk both feature a couple of long, steep couloirs. On the east side of the valley, Hulk Right and Hulk Left both face northwest and frame the classic rock-climbing routes on this huge tooth of granite. The climber's-left couloir, Hulk Left, tops out on the ridge

Skiing down the Hulk Right Couloir within the massive granite walls of the Incredible Hulk

and is very steep and narrow and sometimes blocked by a rock crux a couple hundred feet from the top. The climber's-right couloir, Hulk Right, tops out in the cliffs just shy of the ridge and is wider and slightly less steep. On the west side of the canyon, facing the Hulk couloirs, sits Kettle Peak with the aesthetic Irie Chute and Jah Bless Couloir. The interesting reggae names refer to the classic Reggae Pole rock-climbing route that ascends one of the walls of the Irie Chute. The northeast-facing Irie Chute and Jah Bless Couloir are both slightly shorter than those across the way on the Hulk but well worth the hike any day. The Jah Bless Couloir, the skier's-right chute, is skinnier and steeper and tops out in a col close to the summit. The Irie Chute is skier's left and after a few hundred feet in rock walls, it opens up to a big face that leads up to the summit.

GETTING THERE

From Bridgeport on US Highway 395, turn south onto Twin Lakes Road. Follow it for 13.4 miles to the gate at the Mono Village resort and campground. In winter, the gate is closed and you park here. In late spring, if this gate is open, drive into the Mono Village resort and park at the south end of the parking area just past the marina, 0.25 mile closer.

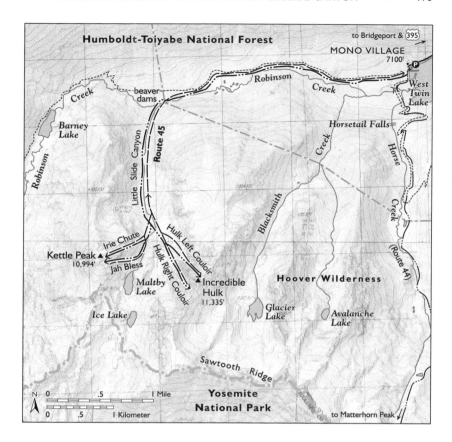

THE ROUTE

From the campground, head west into the Robinson Creek drainage. Follow the path of the summer trail that heads this way as it stays north of the creek, which prevents you from heinous bushwhacking near the creek. Head west up the drainage for roughly 2.5 miles, gaining approximately 600 vertical feet, to the mouth of Little Slide Canyon. At this point you head south into Little Slide Canyon. Crossing the creek here is often the crux of the route; fortunately, busy beavers in this area provide a beaver dam or downed tree, which is usually your best option for the crossing. Once you enter Little Slide Canyon, the route steepens and your objectives begin to come into view as you head south up the drainage. After a mile or so, the route splits, depending on your objectives.

Incredible Hulk: To get to the Hulk couloirs, begin to head southeast and up onto the large apron below the two chutes. Choose the line that is right for you: both are more than 1000 vertical feet—the Hulk Left Couloir is somewhat steeper than Hulk Right—and both may require the use of crampons and/or an ice axe depending on conditions. Climb your chosen chute as high as you can before dropping in for steep and beautifully walled-in turns back down to the bottom.

Kettle Peak: At the point where the ascent route splits, the Irie Chute basically rises above you to the west, across the drainage from the Hulk. Head southwest and climb up to the bottom of the chute walls. This chute isn't all that steep, but the narrow confines generally require you to switch over to boot-packing until you reach the ramp up above it. This line is within walls for around 500 vertical feet before it opens up onto the broad ramp that leads up to the summit. Continue southwest up this ramp to gain the summit.

The Jah Bless Couloir approach is located slightly farther south into Little Slide Canyon. From where the Irie Chute ascent begins, continue south up the drainage toward Maltby Lake for about 0.25 mile before turning right and climbing up to the base of skinny and steep Jah Bless Couloir. This couloir is skinnier and steeper than the Irie Chute and tops out at a col in the ridge just south of Kettle Peak's summit.

No matter which of the routes you descend in Little Slide Canyon, head north back down to the Robinson Creek drainage, retracing your approach route to return to the parking area.

46 Dunderberg Peak

Starting Points	Virginia Lakes Road pullout, 9500 feet; Trumbull Lake campground, 9675 feet
High Points	West summit, 12,374 feet; east summit, 12,300 feet; south chute saddle, 12,175 feet
Distances	Southeast face or south chute, 3 miles; north couloir, 4.25 miles
Elevation Gains	South chute, 2700 feet; southeast face, 2800 feet; north couloir, 3900 feet
Times	Southeast face or south chute, 2.5 hours; north couloir, 4.5 hours
Difficulty Level	Moderate
Terrain Rating	3
Aspects	South-southeast, north
Seasons	Winter, spring
Map	USGS Dunderberg Peak

The Virginia Lakes area on the edge of Hoover Wilderness offers a multitude of great skiing options that are very easily accessible once the road is clear of snow. However, Virginia Lakes Road is generally not cleared in winter, so it is often closed about 0.5 mile west of US Highway 395, which makes it prohibitively far to walk to attempt these routes. Instead, snowmobiles and snowcats are often used to access the terrain in the Virginia Lakes area in midwinter. Nestled at the end of Virginia Lakes Road,

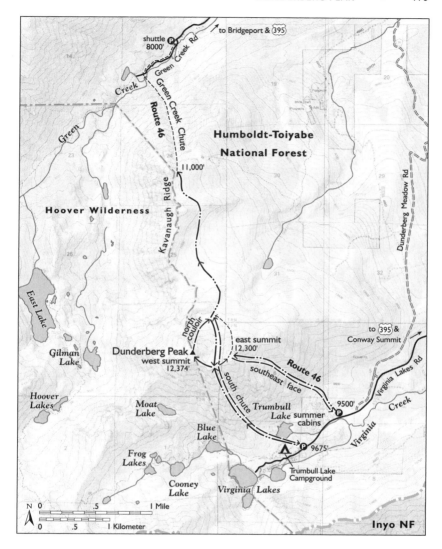

the Virginia Lakes are surrounded by several peaks that offer moderately pitched bowl skiing. The tallest of these peaks is Dunderberg, which has several lines on both sides of its twin summits. The southeast face is a classic corn descent and a superb route for a first trip to the eastern Sierra, sure to be repeated over the years. The other runs on Dunderberg include a steeper south chute that drops off the saddle between the twin summits and an even steeper chute that drops north off the west summit. The north side of Dunderberg can also be linked up with the Green Creek Chute for an outstanding point-to-point tour, adding a couple of miles of hiking and requiring a car shuttle up to the end of Green Creek Road.

Looking back at Dunderberg Peak en route to the Green Creek Chute

GETTING THERE

From US 395 at the top of Conway Summit, midway between Bridgeport and Lee Vining, turn west onto Virginia Lakes Road and follow it uphill for 5 miles. **Virginia Lakes Road pullout:** For the southeast face, find a spot to park near the summer cabin tract on the north side of the road, around 9500 feet. **Trumbull Lake campground:** For the south chute, continue up the road until you reach the campground, around 9675 feet.

THE ROUTE

Southeast face: From the Virginia Lakes Road pullout, head north past the cabins through the trees and directly toward the bottom of the southeast gully, below the southeast bowl. Once you emerge from the trees, it's a short walk on some mellow uphill terrain to where the route begins to steepen. If the snow is burned off of these lowest slopes, follow a faint old dirt road to keep out of the sagebrush as you climb to the snow.

The first 600 feet or so of the southeast face are somewhat constricted into a gully compared to the wide-open bowl higher up. Make your way up this first pitch; the slope then slackens up to the bottom of the upper face. Choose your line to the top; I usually skin as high as I can up the gut of the upper slope before boot-packing a few hundred feet to the top of the east summit. Skinning up toward climber's right to gain the ridge then following the ridge to the top may be more effective for people who prefer to skin the whole way. The southeast face offers some really nice, moderately pitched skiing back down the way you came.

South chute: From the Trumbull Lake campground, head directly northwest, just past the south side of Trumbull Lake, a short distance to the bottom of the chute. Continue up the significantly steeper and narrower south chute to where it meets the summit ridge at the saddle between the two summits. Descend the way you came—or continue to the west summit for the north couloir and other options (see below).

North couloir: From the east summit or the saddle between the two summits, it's a short talus walk west along the ridge to the higher west summit of Dunderberg. The steep north-facing chute off the west summit opens up into a nice bowl that also leads you down to the plateau at about 11,000 feet on the north side of the peak. From here, head south back up to the saddle between Dunderberg's summits to return down the south side of the mountain to either parking area.

From the summit of Dunderberg, check out all the other possibilities on the south side of the Virginia Lakes: Black Mountain (Route 47), South Peak, and Mount Olsen to the east all have great moderate ski terrain. Look southwest for a unique perspective of the mountains in the Tioga Pass region. Around to the north you can see toward Twin Lakes (Routes 42–45), Bridgeport, and even the historic mining town of Bodie in the hills east of US 395.

Options: From the east summit, you can ski north for a relatively mellow 1200-foot run down to the plateau on the north side of the peak. From the saddle, you can ski down the north bowl to this plateau.

Green Creek Chute: Linking the runs on the north side of Dunderberg with a run down the Green Creek Chute is a great way to spend a spring day in the Sierra. This option requires a vehicle shuttle, so both Virginia Lakes Road and Green Creek Road must be clear of snow to access the starting point and endpoint. This tour and shuttle adds significantly more skiing with only a little more hiking. To park a shuttle vehicle, from Bridgeport on US 395, drive south 4.5 miles to Green Creek Road and turn west; follow it for 8.5 miles to parking at the end of the road by the locked gate (8000 feet). Those looking for free camping will find several beautiful spots about two-thirds of the way down this road. Then return to the Virginia Lakes parking spots and get to the top of Dunderberg and ski its north face to the plateau at about 11,000 feet. Hike north along this plateau, staying east of Kavanaugh Ridge, for about 1.5 miles, climbing 200 vertical feet over a short ridge and out to the prow at the top of the Green Creek Chute (11,100 feet). This 3000-foot north-facing gully holds a perfect pitch all the way down to Green Creek. Fight your way through the aspens at the bottom of the chute, carefully cross the creek, then walk east down the dirt road to your shuttled car.

47 Black Mountain

Starting Point : Virginia Lakes trailhead, 9820 feet
High Point : 11,797 feet
Distances : Northeast bowl, 2.5 miles; north gullies, 3 miles;
: north chute, 2.5 miles
Elevation Gain : 2000 feet
Times : Northeast bowl, 2 hours; north gullies, 2.5 hours;
: north chute, 2 hours
Difficulty Level : Easy
Terrain Ratings : Northeast bowl and north chute 2; north gullies 3
Aspects : North, northeast
Seasons : Winter, spring
Maps : USGS Dunderberg Peak; Lundy

Black Mountain sits at the head of the Virginia Creek drainage, looming directly above the Virginia Lakes. With excellent ski terrain on both the east and north sides of the peak, and the relatively short vertical and approach, this is ideal introductory backcountry ski terrain, perfect for doing laps. Early and late in the season, or anytime the road is open, Virginia Lakes Road provides incredibly easy access to

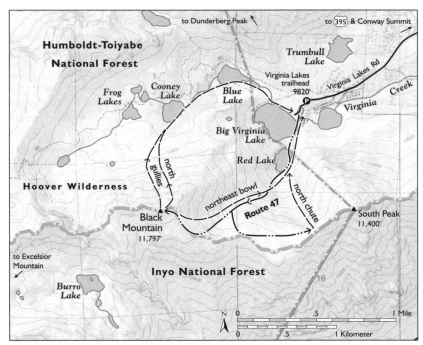

The view of Black Mountain from the top of nearby Dunderberg Peak

Hoover Wilderness for fishermen and backcountry enthusiasts. If the road is not plowed, you may want to wait until later in the season as it may be prohibitively far to walk; otherwise, drive as far up the road as you can and walk up the road to the trailhead. The entire area has a great variety of skiing on all aspects, with something to suit every snow condition and ability level. Along with neighboring Mount Olsen (11,100 feet) and South Peak to the east, Black Mountain creates a massive ridgeline that separates the Virginia Lakes from Lundy Canyon to the south. There is also a variety of terrain on nearby Dunderberg Peak (Route 46) and Excelsior Mountain (Route 48). When Virginia Lakes Road is open, it provides some excellent high-elevation access, and this area is worth spending several days exploring.

GETTING THERE

From Bridgeport on US Highway 395, drive south 13 miles to the top of Conway Summit, then turn west on Virginia Lakes Road and follow it uphill 6 miles to its end at the gravel parking area at the trailhead. From Lee Vining on US 395, Conway Summit is 12 miles north on US 395.

THE ROUTE

From the trailhead, head southwest along Big Virginia Lake and up to Red Lake at the bottom of the large northeast-facing bowl of Black Mountain. Climb southwest up this large bowl, eventually gaining the ridge at around 11,200 feet. Ascend the ridge northwest and west up to the summit of Black Mountain. The view from the top of Black Mountain, despite its relatively low elevation, is quite incredible: Lundy Canyon and the Tioga Pass region are immediately south, and Dunderberg and the mountains of the Green Creek and Twin Lakes areas are to the north.

Northeast bowl: The moderately pitched northeast bowl offers great turns all the way back down to Red Lake.

North gullies: From the summit of Black Mountain, you can also drop down any of the numerous gullies on the north side of the peak. These gullies drop down 1200 vertical feet to Cooney and Frog lakes below. To return to the trailhead, follow the drainage east around the northeast ridge of Black Mountain past Blue Lake back to the trailhead. (If you are skiing on this side of the peak, you could also approach this same way, hiking up the drainage west from the trailhead and climbing the north-facing gullies.)

North chute: For anyone looking to add a little spice to their run, from the northeast bowl you can also head east along the ridge between Black Mountain and South Peak to find a variety of fun, short north-facing chutes dropping off the ridge down to Red Lake.

48 Excelsior Mountain

Starting Point	Virginia Lakes trailhead, 9820 feet
High Point	12,454 feet
Distance	9 miles
Elevation Gain	3100 feet
Time	5 hours
Difficulty Level	Moderate
Terrain Rating	3
Aspect	East-northeast
Seasons	Winter, spring
Map	USGS Dunderberg Peak

Excelsior Mountain lies just a few miles west of Virginia Lakes at the head of Lundy Canyon, at the boundary between Hoover and Yosemite wilderness areas. This peak offers an abundance of skiable terrain on a variety of aspects, so you can generally find good snow out here regardless of the snow cycle. With Excelsior Mountain's summit elevation of nearly 12,500 feet, the route out has relatively little vertical gain when approached from the Virginia Lakes trailhead. What this route lacks in vertical it makes up for in distance, but all things considered, this summit is easier to reach than most that are over 12,000 feet. This is a classic peak descent and beautiful tour with great skiing in the peak's upper cirque. If the road is not plowed, you may want to wait until later in the season as it may be prohibitively far to walk; otherwise, drive as far up the road as you can and walk up the road to the trailhead. When conditions are

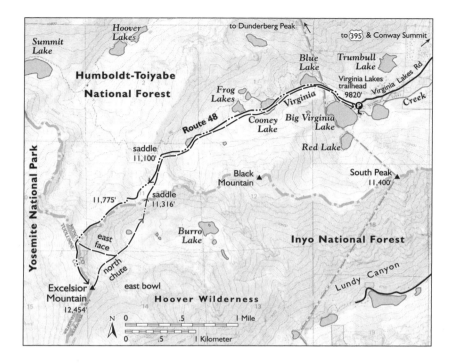

right it may also be possible to do a car shuttle for a tour starting from Virginia Lakes and finishing in Lundy Canyon (Route 49), making for a truly incredible point-to-point experience.

GETTING THERE

From Bridgeport on US Highway 395, drive south 13 miles to the top of Conway Summit, then turn west on Virginia Lakes Road and follow it 6 miles uphill to its end at the trailhead. From Lee Vining on US 395, drive 12 miles north to Conway Summit. For a car shuttle to Lundy Canyon, from US 395 at Conway Summit, drive south 5 miles to Lundy Lake Road and turn west onto it. Follow Lundy Lake Road west for 3.4 miles to the Lundy Dam Road parking area (the road is often closed in winter about 1 mile shy of this spot).

THE ROUTE

From the Virginia Lakes trailhead, head northwest for about 0.5 mile and follow the drainage to Blue Lake. At Blue Lake the route turns west and continues up the drainage for another 0.5 mile to Cooney Lake. At Cooney Lake continue west and begin to bear slightly southwest as you head for the saddle in the ridge about 1 mile away, at 11,100 feet. Once you reach this saddle, the rest of the route to the summit of Excelsior should be in view.

Sliding into one of the north-facing gullies from the top of Excelsior Mountain

Continue southwest from the saddle and dip down just slightly before climbing gently toward the ridge you will follow for the duration of the route. On your way out of this zone, you climb back over this ridge as you exit Excelsior's cirque. Climb this ridge to a high point at 11,775 feet, where you will have a commanding view of the skiable terrain you are approaching. The route continues southwest, following the ridgeline for another 0.5 mile to 12,220 feet; the snow is often burned off this ridge, making for some talus walking. At this point, you are standing above a large east face that can be prime corn skiing terrain; the summit lies another 0.5 mile and 275 vertical feet south along the ridge.

From the summit, a couple of short, steeper north-facing lines are visible and a large east-facing bowl drops down toward Lundy Canyon. Do a lap, or a couple, and to return back the way you came, head northeast to the base of the short slope you have to climb to an 11,316-foot saddle in the ridge you ascended. You gain around 400 vertical feet as you go up this slope.

Continue 0.4 mile north-northeast from this saddle to the 11,100-foot saddle you crossed on your approach. From here, head generally east, retracing your approach route just north of Black Mountain and down to Cooney Lake and then Blue Lake. From Blue Lake, turn southeast and follow the drainage down to Big Virginia Lake to return to the trailhead.

49 Gilcrest Peak

Starting Point	Lundy Dam Road, 7770 feet
High Point	11,565 feet
Distance	5 miles
Elevation Gain	3800 feet
Time	4 hours
Difficulty Level	Moderate
Terrain Rating	3
Aspects	North, east
Seasons	Winter, spring
Map	USGS Lundy

Named after the mining-era surveyor who first mapped the mountain, Gilcrest Peak towers high above Lundy Lake at the eastern end of Lundy Canyon. Featuring a collection of east- and north-facing gullies and chutes and a beautiful lofty summit, Gilcrest Peak is an often-overlooked gem. The relatively short approach and vertical gain also make for a reasonably quick hike to fabulous terrain in this incredible area. Several north-facing lines—as well as a long, moderate east-facing gully—drop straight down to the shore of Lundy Lake from the saddle just east of the summit. Access to this area is quite easy when the road is open and cleared of snow, although in midwinter the road is often closed about a mile east of the parking area near Lundy Dam, making for a slightly longer approach.

GETTING THERE

From Bridgeport on US Highway 395, drive south 18 miles and turn west onto Lundy Lake Road. Follow the road west for 3.4 miles (if possible) to the Lundy Dam Road parking area. If the road is not cleared of snow and the gate is locked, follow the snow-covered road to the parking area. From Lee Vining on US 395, Lundy Lake Road is 6.7 miles north.

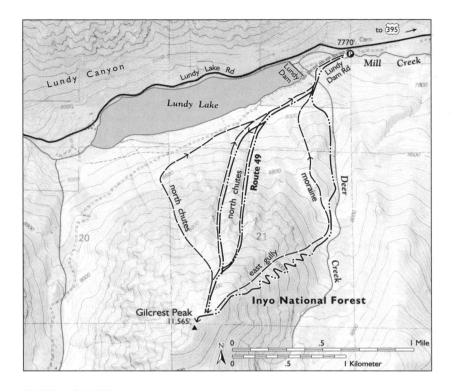

THE ROUTE

From the Lundy Dam Road parking area, your route may vary, depending on your objective.

North chutes: To head for one of the north-facing gullies or chutes, bear southwest and begin the gradual ascent toward the line of your choice. There are three major lines down this face; once you are beneath the line you want, simply climb up it. Skin for as long as possible before switching to boot-packing as you get higher. After about 3500 vertical feet, you top out on the ridge just below and east of the summit. It is a short scramble from here to the lofty summit of Gilcrest Peak. The view from here is expansive: Mono Lake, Mount Warren, Mount Scowden, the entire Lundy Canyon drainage, Mount Conness (Route 51), and North Peak (Route 50). Drop back down the line of your choice.

East gully: To reach the east gully, head south from the dam and up the Deer Creek drainage. Continue south to 9200 feet or so, when you should be able to see up the large east-facing gully that drops down from the summit ridge. Hike up through the trees to climber's left of this gully; it may be possible to skin all the way to the top, but switch to boot-packing if necessary. Once on the ridge, head west to get to the summit. Descend the way you came, but once you have exited the gully, head north (skier's left) to the top of the moraine for more great turns down to Lundy Lake.

Slashing powder turns down the east gully of Gilcrest Peak above Mono Lake

TIOGA PASS

Tioga Pass Road (CA 120) stretches west from US Highway 395 at Lee Vining through Yosemite National Park, renowned for some of the Sierra's most beautiful mountains. This road is closed in the winter, but when it reopens from the east side to the park gate in the spring, it offers access to one the highest concentrations of incredible ski terrain anywhere. Numerous classic descents sit within close proximity to this high-elevation pass near the Tioga Pass entrance to Yosemite National Park. No park entry fee is required unless you enter the park, and all the routes described here don't require entry. Until Tioga Pass Road opens for the season, however, access to this area is somewhat limited, though not impossible, and starts much lower: from near the winter closure gate off of Poole Power Plant Road, which is open all winter.

The small town of Lee Vining sits just north of the junction of CA 120 and US 395 near Mono Lake. The town has a small market, a couple of gas stations, some restaurants and motels, and the Mono Lake Visitors Center, an interesting place to spend a few hours. Come fishing season, the Mobil Mart reopens and features a gas station, general store, and the best food in town at the Whoa Nellie Deli.

The Tioga Pass area is the northern end of the regular avalanche advisory by the Eastern Sierra Avalanche Center (see Resources). The Tioga Pass Road reopens each spring as snowpack and weather allow. Road information can be found on the websites of the National Park Service and the California Department of Transportation (see Resources).

50 North Peak

Starting Point	Saddlebag Lake Road, 9520 feet
High Point	12,251 feet
Distance	11.5 miles
Elevation Gain	2900 feet
Time	5 hours
Difficulty Level	Strenuous
Terrain Ratings	Southeast face 3; north couloirs 4
Aspects	North, southeast-east
Season	Late spring
Map	USGS Tioga Pass

North Peak is a Sierra spring classic. The steep north couloir has long served as a rite of passage for many backcountry skiers and often remains skiable well into the summer in a good snow year. This couloir tops out at nearly 50 degrees in pitch, and while it isn't all that long, it definitely is quite steep. There are actually three couloirs on the north face, all of which are similarly steep, but the one to skier's left is the most popular. The mountain's southeast face can often be found in perfect corn and is ideally situated to link up with the terrain in the Conness Glacier area (Route 51). Access to this peak may vary slightly depending on snow coverage and road openings. Since North Peak is accessed from Tioga Pass Road (CA 120), which is closed in winter, these descents are best saved for late spring once the road has opened from the east side up to the Yosemite National Park entrance at the top of the pass, when the approach is still long but much more reasonable. Typically, when Tioga Pass Road opens, Saddlebag Lake Road will still be covered in snow from Tioga Pass Road to Saddlebag Lake. Sometimes the gate will still be closed even when much of the snow has melted off the road. When this is case, you can ride a bicycle to the lake. Occasionally, the road will open to Saddlebag Lake, shaving 2.5 miles off the beginning of this route. However, this route is described for when Saddlebag Lake Road is closed. When there is still skiable snow in the north couloirs but Saddlebag Lake is no longer frozen, there may be the unique opportunity to access this area midsummer using the Saddlebag Lake water taxi (see Resources). Due to the distance associated with this route and the wealth of great ski terrain, many people often opt to spend a night or two out in this area.

GETTING THERE

From the junction of US Highway 395 and Tioga Pass Road (CA 120) just south of Lee Vining, drive west up CA 120 for 9.9 miles to the junction with Saddlebag Lake Road. The plowed pullout is on the north side of CA 120 at a sweeping left-hand curve, 1 mile past the Ellery Lake dam and just before the Tioga Pass Resort.

The view of North Peak and Mount Conness from Dunderberg Peak

When Saddlebag Lake Road is snowbound (usually until early summer), park here and be sure not to block the road entrance in case spring snowclearing operations are in progress. Later in spring or early summer, if Saddlebag Lake Road is plowed or open, either walk or pedal on the road or drive 2.5 miles to the south end of Saddlebag Lake.

THE ROUTE

From the pullout at Saddlebag Lake Road, head northwest along the road as it contours along the hillside just above Lee Vining Creek for 2.5 miles to the dam at the south end of Saddlebag Lake (10,070 feet). When the lake is frozen solid, the easiest way to the other side is along the frozen surface, 1.2 miles northwest from the dam. If the lake is no longer frozen or the ice's integrity is questionable, follow summer trails on either shore of the lake to this same point. From the northwest end of Saddlebag Lake, head west up the short slope to Greenstone Lake (10,144 feet), where the route splits depending on which side of North Peak you intend to ski.

Southeast face: From Greenstone Lake, continue west toward the Conness Lakes and the base of the southeast face, approximately 1.3 miles and 800 vertical feet away. At the base of the southeast face, pick a route up this broad slope, ascending another 0.5 mile and 1300 or so vertical feet to the ridge above. Descend this moderately pitched slope and retrace your approach route to the parking area.

North couloirs: From Greenstone Lake, head northwest for 0.5 mile to Wasco Lake (10,308 feet). From this lake head west for nearly 1 mile, gaining 1100 or so vertical feet, until you are beneath the steep north couloir. Climb straight up it—be prepared with an ice axe and crampons for the ascent. The north couloir is very steep and should be attempted only by expert skiers and snowboarders. Retrace your approach route to return to the parking area.

Options: If conditions warrant it, from the bottom of the south face, ascend back up to the top and return via the north couloir for a loop—or vice versa. After skiing the south face of North Peak, it is also easy to link up with nearby routes on Mount Conness (Route 51) or the Greenstone Ridge to make for a big day. There is a lot of great terrain out here, so those with extra energy and time may want to link up more short runs on the way out from this zone.

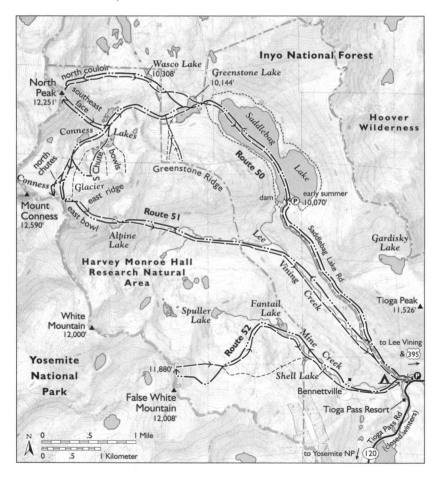

51 Mount Conness

Starting Point	Saddlebag Lake Road, 9520 feet
High Point	Top of east ridge, 12,370 feet; summit, 12,590 feet
Distances	East bowl, 9 miles; north chutes, 12 miles
Elevation Gain	3000 feet
Times	East bowl, 5 hours; north chutes, 6 hours
Difficulty Level	Strenuous
Terrain Rating	3
Aspects	East, north
Seasons	Late spring, early summer
Map	USGS Tioga Pass

Mount Conness dominates the skyline north of Tioga Pass, its massive fortress like rock ridges hiding the Conness Glacier on the peak's north side. Mount Conness is named for a former California senator who is credited with carrying the bill that organized the Geological Survey of California. Once Tioga Pass Road (CA 120) opens from the east side up to the Yosemite National Park entrance at the top of the pass in the late spring, access to this area becomes relatively easy, although still quite far, and the incredible ski terrain on both the east and north sides of the mountain is tough to ignore. Mount Conness can be approached a couple of ways, depending on your objective. You can follow Saddlebag Lake Road to Saddlebag Lake and then wrap west around to the Conness Glacier and the north side of the peak, or you can follow Lee Vining Creek through the Harvey Monroe Hall Research Natural Area up the east bowl and onto the east ridge. These two approaches can also be combined to make this tour into a loop. The massive east bowl is visible for miles around, and a number of fun, short chutes lie hidden on the north side of the east ridge above what remains of the Conness Glacier. As the spring progresses, it may be possible to drive as far as Saddlebag Lake, but most trips to Mount Conness begin from 2.5 miles farther away, at the junction of Tioga Pass Road and Saddlebag Lake Road, making for a longer, albeit relatively flat, approach. If the road to the lake has been plowed or is closed but clear of snow, you can ride a bike to the lake; if the road is open, drive all the way up it. Later in summer, a boat (see Resources) ferries hikers to the northwest end of the lake, a truly novel way to approach a ski route. As a day tour, Mount Conness involves a significant amount of distance with relatively short vertical gain; for that reason, this area is a great spot to spend a night or two and combine with nearby descents like North Peak (Route 50), White Mountain, or Greenstone Ridge.

GETTING THERE

From the junction of US Highway 395 and CA 120 just south of Lee Vining, drive west up CA 120 for 9.9 miles to the junction with Saddlebag Lake Road. This plowed

Booting up one of the north-facing chutes on Mount Conness with the southeast face of North Peak in the background

pullout is on the north side of CA 120 at a sweeping left-hand curve, 1 mile past the Ellery Lake dam and just before the Tioga Pass Resort. If Saddlebag Lake Road is still snowbound (usually until early summer), park here and be sure not to block the entrance to the road in case spring snow clearing operations are in progress. Later in spring or early summer, Saddlebag Lake Road may be plowed or open and you can walk or pedal on the road or drive 2.5 miles to the south end of Saddlebag Lake.

THE ROUTE

East bowl: From the pullout on CA 120, follow Saddlebag Lake Road to the northwest as it parallels Lee Vining Creek for approximately 0.75 mile. In a large clearing, where the road begins to climb onto the forested hillside and away from the creek, head west and drop a few feet down to Lee Vining Creek, then begin to follow it northwest. Eventually find a safe spot to cross the meandering creek and get on its west side as you continue to parallel it northwest for another 1.25 miles.

At this point the drainage forks, with one branch coming from the north (climber's right) and the dam at Saddlebag Lake and the other from the west (climber's left) and Mount Conness. Follow the left-hand drainage west for another mile, ascending ever so gradually to the base of the lower pitch of the east slope of Mount Conness. Here the route actually begins to climb, and you continue west up the slope for 1000 vertical feet to Alpine Lake (11,050 feet).

From Alpine Lake, continue up the huge and somewhat benchy east bowl of Mount Conness for another 1200 vertical feet. The very top of the bowl is somewhat steep for a couple hundred feet and generally requires boot-packing to the crest of the east ridge. Once atop the ridge, it is a rocky 0.5-mile ridgeline walk to Mount Conness's summit. Unless you plan on dropping into one of the several chutes on the north side of this ridge, you may want to leave your skis or board near the top of the east bowl for a side trip to the summit.

Descend the east bowl to Alpine Lake, then down to the Lee Vining Creek drainage. The next 3 miles of very gradual downhill along the creek typically involve a lot of pushing and skating. Snowboarders will generally want to convert their splitboards back into skis for the slow push and slide back out.

North chutes: From the pullout on CA 120, follow Saddlebag Lake Road to the northwest as it parallels Lee Vining Creek. Over 2.5 miles you gain roughly 500 vertical feet of elevation up to the dam at the south end of Saddlebag Lake. From the dam, hike along the frozen surface of the lake (or either shore trail if the lake isn't frozen) northwest for another 1.25 miles. At the northwest end of the lake, the route turns west to head into the drainage flanked by North Peak's southeast face and Mount Conness's east ridge. Moments after leaving Saddlebag Lake, you come to Greenstone Lake (a variety of fun, short north-facing terrain rises directly above it to the south, known as Greenstone Ridge). Continue past Greenstone Lake, following the creek for another mile as it snakes up to the Conness Lakes (10,700 feet).

The long east ridge of Mount Conness offers a wealth of north-facing terrain from near the mountain's summit to the Conness Lakes. On the east end, moderate, large, open bowls frame the ever-popular S chute, offering 1000 vertical feet of fun turns. Head farther west and up onto the moraine of the Conness Glacier to access the north chutes, which drop north off the ridge (12,350 feet) down to the large bowl of the Conness Glacier below.

You can also cross over to the east ridge of Mount Conness to combine these two approach routes and make this tour into a loop. Otherwise, head back down the drainage you ascended to cross back over Saddlebag Lake and make your way back down Saddlebag Lake Road.

52 False White Mountain

Starting Point	Saddlebag Lake Road, 9520 feet
High Point	12,008 feet
Distance	6.5 miles
Elevation Gain	2500 feet
Time	3 hours
Difficulty Level	Moderate
Terrain Rating	2
Aspect	East
Seasons	Late spring, early summer
Map	USGS Tioga Pass

False White Mountain's eye-catching east face is one of the easiest ski objectives to reach in the Tioga Pass region. False White sits in plain view from Tioga Pass Road (CA 120); it is just east of White Mountain, and as its name suggests, it almost completely blocks White Mountain from view. Since Tioga Pass Road is closed in winter, most routes in this area are usually not in play until the road opens in the late spring. Once the road opens from the east side up to the Yosemite National Park entrance at the top of the pass, however, False White's east face is prime for corn harvesting by skiers of all abilities. The relatively short approach and moderate ski terrain make this route a great introductory tour for less experienced backcountry skiers and snowboarders. False White is also conveniently situated to link it up with descents on nearby peaks like Mount Conness (Route 51) or White Mountain to make a longer day in the mountains.

GETTING THERE

From the junction of US Highway 395 and CA 120 just south of Lee Vining, drive west on CA 120 for 9.9 miles to the junction with Saddlebag Lake Road. This plowed pullout is on the north side of the road at a sweeping left-hand curve, a mile past the Ellery Lake dam and just before the Tioga Pass Resort.

False White Mountain's broad east face is prime corn skiing terrain

THE ROUTE

From the parking area, follow Saddlebag Lake Road for a couple hundred feet, then head west and cross Lee Vining Creek on the bridge that leads into the summer campground. Head southwest and follow Mine Creek as it contours around to the northwest and slightly uphill for 0.6 mile to the small mining settlement of Bennettville (9764 feet). From here the route continues northwest for another mile, following the creek past Shell Lake and on to Fantail Lake. From Fantail Lake, the route heads west and then southwest to climb rolling terrain for another mile and 1300 vertical feet to the base of the east face of False White Mountain.

From the base of the east face, head directly up it to gain the summit ridge. The summit is at the south end of this ridge, while the longer fall-line skiing starts from the north end of the ridge. This wide slope has room for a hundred sets of tracks, and on a busy weekend in the late spring, it might actually see half of that.

After skiing the east face, enjoy the rolling terrain back down the way you came or traverse hard to skier's right before dropping down to Mine Creek for a longer pitch and less time pushing through the flats on the way out. Once you reach Mine Creek, follow it back out the way you came to return to the parking area.

53   Dana Plateau: Ellery Bowl

Starting Points	Tioga Lake pullout, 9740 feet; Ellery Lake dam, 9500 feet
High Point	Top of Ellery Bowl, 11,500 feet
Distance	2.75 miles one-way
Elevation Gain	1830 feet
Time	2 hours with car shuttle
Difficulty Level	Easy
Terrain Ratings	3–4
Aspects	North, northeast
Seasons	Winter, spring, early summer
Maps	USGS Tioga Pass; Mount Dana

Few places in the world have as many classic and incredible ski routes as the Dana Plateau at the edge of Yosemite National Park. The sheer cliff walls are split by numerous chutes and bowls that spill down the mountainside for thousands of feet. With Ellery Bowl, Power Plant Bowl (Route 54), the east face, the Kidney Lake Chute, and the east end of the plateau (all in Route 55), there are enough lines to keep you busy for a lifetime. The Dana Plateau sees little traffic before the spring opening of Tioga Pass Road (CA 120). Once CA 120 opens, however, skiers flock to the amazing terrain and world-famous California corn to be found just a short hike from higher up on the pass. Your route will vary depending on the line you choose, and where you park may also vary depending on whether CA 120 is open or you do a car shuttle; the route described here assumes a car shuttle. When the road is open,

Scoring some late-season powder turns in Ellery Bowl (Oscar Havens)

the typical approach starts at the south end of Tioga Lake. Ellery Bowl is the closest and easiest objective to reach.

GETTING THERE

From US Highway 395 just south of the town of Lee Vining, turn west onto Tioga Pass Road (CA 120). **Ellery Lake dam:** Drive to the east end of Ellery Lake, 9.5 miles from the junction with US 395, and park in the pullout on the south side of the road right near the small dam to leave a shuttle car or to access Ellery Bowl from the bottom. **Tioga Lake pullout:** When the road is open, drive another 1.5 miles to the plowed pullout on the left (east) side of the road at the south end of Tioga Lake (ample parking, pit toilets), about 0.5 mile shy of the Yosemite National Park entrance.

THE ROUTE

From the plowed pullout at the south end of Tioga Lake, the route drops down for 100 vertical feet and heads east across the south end of Tioga Lake. The beginning of the ascent climbs into Glacier Canyon, the valley that separates Mount Dana from the Dana Plateau. Hike east up the creek that drains down out of Glacier Canyon for approximately 1 mile and about 1000 vertical feet. As the trees start to open and the canyon begins to really flatten out, head northeast up a little draw and climb 400 vertical feet up onto the western end of the plateau. Once atop the plateau, at about 1.5 miles from the parking area, the hiking becomes dramatically easier, and

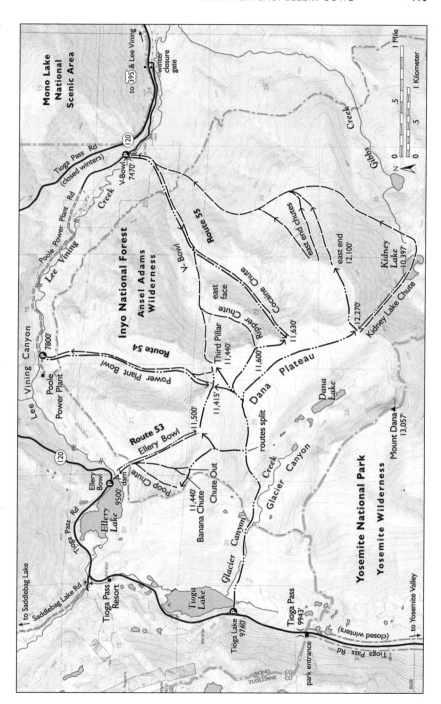

you generally head in a straight line toward your objective. To reach the top of Ellery Bowl, head north up the gentle slope for about 0.3 mile and 400 vertical feet to the top (11,500 feet) of the large, north-facing open bowl that enters the slope farthest west on the plateau.

Ellery Bowl: As the closest and easiest objective to reach, Ellery Bowl is among the most popular routes off Tioga Pass Road. The main drop-in of Ellery Bowl, the easiest way down, is actually quite steep for a few turns before mellowing out into fun, rolling terrain.

Chute Out and Banana Chute: Farther west along the ridge of Ellery Bowl is the Chute Out. The entrance to this steep chute is about 0.25 mile west of the drop-in for the Ellery Bowl run, and it can be somewhat difficult to find. It takes some guessing and checking to find the top, but once you've found it, you can see right down it; as you search, beware of the large cornices that often form on the ridge. Just west of the Chute Out is the Banana Chute, which joins into the Chute Out after a short run.

Poop Chute: Then 0.25 mile farther west beyond that is the Poop Chute, on the far western edge of the Ellery Bowl zone. The Poop Chute is named for dark rock that stains the snow that comes out of this short, steep chute.

All these chutes join the Ellery Bowl run to the bottom. Drive your shuttle car from the Ellery Lake dam back to the parking area at Tioga Lake. If you parked here at the Ellery Lake dam, you can hike straight up Ellery Bowl, about 1.75 miles round-trip and 1975 vertical feet.

54 Dana Plateau: Power Plant Bowl

Starting Points	Tioga Lake pullout, 9740 feet;
	Poole Power Plant Road, 7800 feet
High Point	Top of Power Plant Bowl, 11,415 feet
Distance	4 miles one-way
Elevation Gain	1770 feet
Time	2.5 hours with car shuttle
Difficulty Level	Easy
Terrain Rating	3
Aspects	North, northeast
Seasons	Winter, spring, early summer
Maps	USGS Tioga Pass; Mount Dana

Power Plant Bowl is sandwiched between Ellery Bowl and the east face of the Dana Plateau. The bowl's steep entrances filter down to a long run that leads all the way to Poole Power Plant Road far below. If Tioga Pass Road is open and there is good snow coverage on the lower portions, it is possible to do a shuttle run starting high up on the pass and finishing down at Power Plant Road. The typical approach for the shuttle run starts at the south end of Tioga Lake. Prior to the spring opening of

The top of Power Plant Bowl is steep!

Tioga Pass Road, Power Plant Bowl and all the routes in the Dana Plateau area can be accessed by climbing up Power Plant Bowl from Poole Power Plant Road, which is cleared of snow all winter long.

GETTING THERE

From US Highway 395 just south of the town of Lee Vining, turn west onto Tioga Pass Road (CA 120). **Poole Power Plant Road:** Drive CA 120 west for 3 miles and turn left onto Poole Power Plant Road (the winter road closure gate is on the highway just beyond here). Follow it west for a little over 4 miles to the end of the road and park a shuttle car near the end of the road after it crosses to the south side of Lee Vining Creek. You can also park here to access the Power Plant Bowl from the bottom. **Tioga Lake pullout:** When the road is open, drive another 8 miles to the plowed pullout on the left (east) side of the road at the south end of Tioga Lake (ample parking, pit toilets), about 0.5 mile shy of the Yosemite National Park entrance.

THE ROUTE

From the plowed pullout at the south end of Tioga Lake, the route drops down 100 vertical feet and heads east across the south end of Tioga Lake. The beginning of the ascent climbs into Glacier Canyon, the valley that separates Mount Dana from the Dana Plateau. Hike east up the creek that drains down out of Glacier Canyon for approximately 1 mile and about 1000 vertical feet. As the trees start to open and the canyon begins to really flatten out, head northeast up a little draw and climb 400 vertical feet up onto the western end of the plateau. Once atop the plateau, at about 1.5 miles from the parking area, the hiking becomes dramatically easier, and this is where your route splits, depending on your objective; you generally head in a straight line toward your objective as the gentle slope leads to various routes.

From where the approach splits by the west end of the plateau, continue east for about 0.4 mile, then head northeast for another 0.3 mile to reach the top of Power Plant Bowl. Two very steep lines enter the bowl from the low spot in the ridge between Ellery Bowl and the east face of the Dana Plateau. The main entry is dead center in the bowl; the other is a couple hundred feet to skier's right along the ridge. In big snow years, other entrance variations may fill in as well.

Both entrances are incredibly steep for about 400 vertical feet before flattening out about 1000 feet below the plateau. From here, descend north and follow the bottom of the canyon down to the end of the Poole Power Plant Road for your car shuttle back up to Tioga Lake. Or you can climb back up this route, which also provides access to the plateau in midwinter when CA 120 is closed. The climb up Power Plant Bowl is 1.6 miles and 3600 vertical feet to get on the plateau.

You can also reach this route from the top of the Ellery Bowl (Route 53); from Ellery Bowl, cut due east for 0.4 mile to the top of Power Plant Bowl.

55 Dana Plateau: East Face and East End

Starting Points	Tioga Lake pullout, 9740 feet; V-Bowl approach, 7470 feet
High Points	East face, 11,630 feet; Kidney Lake Chute, 12,270 feet; east end, 12,100 feet
Distances	East face, 5 miles; Kidney Lake Chute, 7 miles; east end, 6.25 miles
Elevation Gains	East face, 2000 feet; Kidney Lake Chute, 2800 feet; east end, 2700 feet
Times	East face, 3 hours; Kidney Lake Chute or east end, 4 hours
Difficulty Level	East face chutes, moderate; Kidney Lake Chute and east end chutes, strenuous
Terrain Ratings	East face 4; east end/Kidney Lake Chute 3
Aspects	Northeast, east, southeast
Seasons	Winter, spring, early summer
Maps	USGS Tioga Pass; Mount Dana

An expert skier's playground, the Dana Plateau's east face, east end chutes, and Kidney Lake Chute offer a wealth of runs just northeast of Mount Dana. Despite the impressive east face being a 1500-foot cliff in Ansel Adams Wilderness, a variety of steep skiable lines split it, clearly visible from US Highway 395. The routes described

Boot-packing the last few hundred feet of the Cocaine Chute to the Dana Plateau

here all funnel down to the top of the V-Bowl, which is the descent route to the lower parking area on Poole Power Plant Road. Where you park may vary depending on whether CA 120 is open up to the pass or you do a car shuttle from Poole Power Plant Road. When the road is open, the typical approach starts at the south end of Tioga Lake. This route description assumes a car shuttle from the V-Bowl parking and a start from Tioga Lake. The hike from the lake to reach these routes deposits you farther from the top of the pass than the Ellery Bowl (Route 53) or Power Plant Bowl (Route 54). With runs that take as few as a couple hours and options to do laps or go for a longer tour, the east end of the Dana Plateau is one of the best spots to make some late-season turns on the entire east side of the Sierra. These routes are often coupled with a descent of Mount Dana (Route 56) by climbing from Glacier Canyon up onto the plateau for a day of truly epic proportions.

GETTING THERE

From US 395 just south of the town of Lee Vining, turn west onto Tioga Pass Road (CA 120). **V-Bowl parking:** Drive CA 120 west for 3 miles and turn left onto Poole Power Plant Road (the winter road closure gate is on the highway just beyond here). Follow it west for just over 1 mile to the first dirt parking area on the left and leave a shuttle car here. In the winter a bridge across Lee Vining Creek also accesses V-Bowl from the bottom. **Tioga Lake pullout:** When the road is open, drive another 8 miles to the plowed pullout on the left (east) side of the road at the south end of Tioga Lake (ample parking, pit toilets), about 0.5 mile shy of the Yosemite National Park entrance.

THE ROUTE

From the plowed pullout at the south end of Tioga Lake, the route drops down 100 vertical feet and heads east across the south end of Tioga Lake. The beginning of the ascent climbs into Glacier Canyon, the valley that separates Mount Dana from the Dana Plateau. Hike east up the creek that drains down out of Glacier Canyon for approximately 1 mile and about 1000 vertical feet. As the trees start to open and the canyon begins to really flatten out, head northeast up a little draw and climb 400 vertical feet up onto the western end of the plateau. Once atop the plateau, at about 1.5 miles from the parking area, the hiking becomes dramatically easier, and this is where your route splits. From here, you generally head in a straight line toward your objective; the gentle slope leads to all the various routes. As you head farther east, the edge of the plateau turns south above the impressive and sheer east face.

East face: From where the approach splits by the west end of the plateau, continue east for about 0.4 mile, then head northeast for another 0.3 mile toward the top of Power Plant Bowl (Route 54). The east face's first line, just a few hundred feet to skier's right of Power Plant Bowl, drops in just skier's left of the pointy rock prow known as the Third Pillar. A classic rock-climbing route, the Third Pillar forms the skier's-right wall of this very steep and committing northeast-facing line. About 500 vertical feet from the plateau, the rock walls choke and a rock can often be found protruding from the snow here, so be sure to give this line a good look from the top before dropping in.

About 0.4 mile farther southwest along the edge of the plateau is the steep, narrow Ripper Chute, which also descends the east face. The top of this line can be found in a cleft in the top of the cliff face where the rock changes color from dark to light. The Ripper and the Third Pillar both deposit skiers into the same basin.

Just 0.3 mile south beyond the Ripper is the wider Cocaine Chute, the mellowest of the three chutes dropping off the east face (it is by far the easiest to climb up if you are accessing this area from the bottom in midwinter or doing laps). There are a couple of entrances to this massive chute; skier's right has a better fall line.

From the bottom of these three chutes, follow the contours of the mountain as it funnels down to the top of V-Bowl. V-Bowl drops another 1500 vertical feet down to Lee Vining Canyon below. At the bottom of V-Bowl, bear northeast through the forest, and for the easiest crossing of Lee Vining Creek to the road, be sure to find the bridge by the parking area.

Kidney Lake Chute: From the point where the approach splits near the west end of the plateau, continue southeast for 1.5 miles up the broad plateau to the saddle between the highest points at the far southeast end of the plateau, the top of the Kidney Lake Chute. This wide, southeast-facing chute drops off the plateau at 12,270 feet all the way down to Kidney Lake (10,397 feet). This run puts you into the basin between the plateau and Mount Gibbs. From the lake, traverse northeast all the way around the east end of the plateau to the bottom of V-Bowl at the parking area on Poole Power Plant Road. Or you can climb back up the chute to the plateau to do some more runs.

East end: The plateau's east end, sometimes referred to as East Peak, seems like its own mountain, but it is still considered part of the plateau. From the southeast end of the plateau, near the top of the Kidney Lake Chute, traverse east on the north side of the ridge across a big bowl about 0.5 mile to the high point at the far east end of the ridge. From here, a number of 2000-vertical-foot east-facing chutes drop east off the ridge. At the bottom of these runs, drop down the broad slopes to the north, eventually contouring around the ridge to the bottom of V-Bowl at the winter parking area on Poole Power Plant Road.

V-Bowl approach: You can reach these routes in winter when CA 120 is closed from the V-Bowl parking area. Be sure to find the bridge over Lee Vining Creek for the easiest crossing, then climb from the bottom of the V-Bowl up the Cocaine Chute, 2.5 miles and 4300 vertical feet of gain.

56 Mount Dana

Starting Points	Tioga Lake pullout, 9740 feet; Tioga Pass entrance, 9943 feet
High Point	13,057 feet
Distance	5.5 miles
Elevation Gain	Glacier Canyon approach, 3400 feet; west slope approach, 3100 feet
Time	4.5 hours
Difficulty Level	Moderate
Terrain Rating	4
Aspect	North-northeast
Seasons	Late spring, early summer
Maps	USGS Tioga Pass; Mount Dana

At 13,057 feet, Mount Dana's summit is the second-highest point in Yosemite National Park. Located on the northeastern edge of the park boundary and on the border between Yosemite and Ansel Adams wilderness areas, Mount Dana is among the most popular spots in the eastern Sierra for spring backcountry touring once Tioga Pass Road opens, and for good reason. The massive sheer cliff on the north face of Mount Dana is framed beautifully by two of the most classic couloirs in the range: the Dana Couloir and the Solstice Couloir. Both runs, rites of passage for Sierra backcountry skiers, usually offer great skiing into early summer. There are two main ways to approach Mount Dana: the northwest ridge–west slope or Glacier Canyon. I prefer to climb the gradual west slope that connects from Tioga Pass by Yosemite's Tioga Pass entrance, but some people choose the Glacier Canyon approach from Tioga Lake so they can assess snow conditions as they climb their chosen line prior to skiing it; this approach is also advisable when the top of the Solstice Couloir has an impassable cornice. Tioga Pass Road (CA 120) is closed in winter, making a midwinter ski of Mount Dana an arduous overnight endeavor. Come spring, the opening of Tioga Pass Road to the park entrance provides quick and easy access to this area, a reason for backcountry enthusiasts to celebrate.

GETTING THERE

From US Highway 395 just south of Lee Vining, turn west onto Tioga Pass Road (CA 120). **Glacier Canyon approach:** Follow CA 120 west for 11 miles to a plowed pullout on the left (east) side of the road at the south end of Tioga Lake (ample parking, pit toilets). **West slope approach:** Follow CA 120 west for approximately 12 miles from US 395 to the park's Tioga Pass (east) entrance station; park as close to the pass as possible, making sure to park completely off the road.

THE ROUTE

West slope approach: From the park's Tioga Pass entrance station, head directly east, aiming for the south (climber's-right) side of the prominent rock buttress at the end of Mount Dana's northwest ridge. Meander through the sparse trees and among the little ponds that sit at the top of Tioga Pass, heading toward the open slope that climbs up onto the peak's west flank. The steepest part of this ascent is the first pitch, which climbs 1200 feet up to the more gradual slopes above. Switchback up the open slopes, heading east. Once you crest the top of this first pitch, you'll have a view of the rest of the west slope as it climbs moderately toward the summit.

The west slope can also be accessed by starting on the Glacier Canyon approach (see below), then climbing the slope on the north (climber's-left) side of the rock buttress at the end of the northwest ridge. From this point, this Glacier Canyon start route joins the regular west slope approach.

From here the approach to the summit is straightforward and relatively easy; you can basically walk in a straight line all the way to the top. However, the corniced ridgeline from the top of the Solstice Couloir to the summit is exposed above 1000-plus feet of sheer cliff, so scrambling on the rocks may be a safer alternative.

Glacier Canyon approach: From the pullout at the south end of Tioga Lake, drop east down the short slope next to the road and cruise across the flats above the south side of Tioga Lake toward the drainage that exits Glacier Canyon. Put on your skins, then begin climbing east up into Glacier Canyon, generally following the creek. Once you're in the canyon, walk along its bottom as it wraps around southeast toward the base of the north face of Mount Dana. At roughly 2.5 miles, you arrive at Dana Lake, and both couloirs should be clearly visible: the Dana Couloir is to climber's left of the

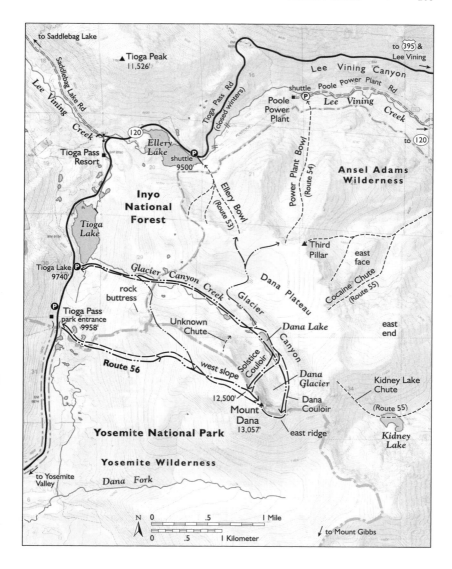

imposing north face; the Solstice Couloir is to climber's right. Climb the couloir of your choice, and be aware that it may be impossible to top out on the Solstice Couloir due to a cornice at the top (see Solstice Couloir, below); also be aware that others may be accessing the routes from the west slope approach and dropping in from above.

Solstice Couloir: On the northwest ridge, west of and 500 vertical feet below the summit, is the entrance to the Solstice Couloir (12,500 feet). It is often guarded by a very large cornice, and just having a look into this couloir from the top can be incredibly dangerous; exercise extreme caution in this area. One of the safest ways to look at the

Dropping into late-season powder after negotiating the massive cornice at the top of the Solstice Couloir (Mike Vaughan)

entrance is to climb a couple hundred feet east of and above the couloir and have a look back down. Some years, the cornice stretches the entire way across the top of the Solstice Couloir, preventing entry from the top altogether. Most years, however, you are able to sneak in from the skier's-left side, doing a very short traverse to skier's right over exposure and into the top of the couloir under the cornice. This short traverse may be especially difficult for goofy-footed snowboarders, who have to enter here on their heelside edge. The couloir drops for 1500 vertical feet, starting around 45 degrees for the first couple hundred feet or so, down to the bottom of Glacier Canyon.

Dana Couloir: This chute is located east of the summit of Mount Dana. From the Solstice Couloir, proceed east to the summit, taking care on this exposed, possibly corniced ridgeline (see Solstice Couloir, above). Take in the inspiring view of Yosemite National Park to the southwest, the Dana Plateau and Mono Lake to the northeast, and Mount Gibbs immediately south. Then descend the east ridge for 600 vertical feet to the top of the Dana Couloir. The top is significantly less steep than that of the

Solstice Couloir, but the rollover into it can be very intimidating. After 100 vertical feet or so, you should be able to see the drop to the north all the way to the bottom in Glacier Canyon.

After skiing the couloir of your choice, exit via Glacier Canyon by following the path of least resistance along the creek drainage to the south end of Tioga Lake. From the lake, climb up the short slope to the west to the pullout. Exiting via Glacier Canyon saves you from having to climb back up to the summit ridgeline and ski back out the way you came in, but it does require either a car shuttle or a road walk from Tioga Lake back up to the pass.

Options: If conditions are not favorable for a descent of the couloirs, or for a much mellower alternative, you can ski the gradual west slope back down to the park's east entrance at Tioga Pass.

A number of chutes often fill in farther to skier's left down the northwest ridge from the Solstice Couloir. These routes are prone to melting out faster and are much narrower than either the Dana or Solstice Couloir. Have a good look around if you're on the Glacier Canyon approach to see if there is enough coverage to warrant skiing any of these lines. One of them is the Unknown Chute, which drops in off the first large, rocky prow to the northwest of the entrance of the Solstice Couloir.

Those looking to extend their tour can add some Dana Plateau runs (Routes 53–55), which usually involves a car shuttle. From the bottom of the Dana and Solstice couloirs, head northwest on the Glacier Canyon exit a short way, and at the north end of Dana Lake climb north, contouring up onto the Dana Plateau.

JUNE LAKE AREA

The June Lake area, located on the June Lake Loop Road (CA 158), includes the modest June Mountain ski area as well as access to Mounts Wood, Lewis, and Gibbs. The June Mountain ski area's open-boundary policy makes for quick and easy access (with a lift ticket) to the Negatives and Carson Peak.

The town of June Lake has a small year-round population, many of whom are backcountry enthusiasts. The town has a number of restaurants and motels, and there is a gas station at the June Lake Junction.

The June Lake Loop Road stretches between its northern junction with US Highway 395 just a few miles south of Lee Vining to the June Lake Junction at US 395 in the south. This loop road is closed in winter between Silver Lake, just west of the town of June Lake, and the northern junction with US 395. Access to several routes in this region becomes much easier as the snows recede and the road opens, allowing you to get closer to the base of these peaks before starting your approach.

The Eastern Sierra Avalanche Center provides a regular avalanche advisory for the region (see Resources).

57 Mount Gibbs

Starting Points	Bohler Canyon road, 8000 feet; Poole Power Plant Road, 7400 feet; Gibbs Lake trailhead, 8000 feet
High Point	12,500 feet
Distances	East face, 4 miles; north face, 7–8 miles
Elevation Gains	East face, 4500 feet; north face, 4500–5100 feet
Times	East face, 4 hours; north face, 6 hours
Difficulty Level	Strenuous
Terrain Rating	3
Aspects	Southeast-east, northeast, north
Seasons	Winter, spring
Maps	USGS Mount Dana; Koip Peak

It's hard not to be distracted by the numerous chutes and gullies that split the east face of 12,773-foot Mount Gibbs as you drive north on US Highway 395 between June Lake and Lee Vining. This cluster of 4000-vertical-foot runs in Ansel Adams Wilderness are prime ski terrain, and their nearly roadside location makes them even more attractive to skiers and snowboarders. Depending on the season's snowpack, however, getting to the bottom of them can be as easy as driving up a rugged dirt road or as arduous as a 3-mile slog across the flats each way from the snow line near US 395. I recommend attempting this route when you can get at least halfway in by road; otherwise, you are in for a long, flat walk in and out from the road's end. Either way, the east face of Mount Gibbs has fantastic ski terrain with a great aspect for growing sweet spring corn. Additionally, a wealth of terrain lies hidden on the north side of Mount Gibbs above Gibbs and Kidney lakes. While it is generally approached differently than the east side of the mountain, the north side of Mount Gibbs is an incredible zone that is worthy of exploration as well.

GETTING THERE

Bohler Canyon road: From US 395, 3.3 miles south of Lee Vining, turn right (west) onto Oil Plant Road. Follow it for 1.3 miles and at a fork turn right onto Forest Service Road 1N106. Follow it for roughly 1 mile, take a left, and then after another 0.3 mile turn right onto the rugged dirt road that parallels the creek up into Bohler Canyon; a high-clearance vehicle is recommended for this narrow double-track road. The road travels through a dense old-growth aspen forest full of 1950s-era Basque shepherd carvings that are interesting to look at; the aspens, however, are prone to falling and blocking the road, so bring a chain saw or large handsaw if you suspect that you are the first party up the road for the season. Late in the spring, or when the snow line is high, it may be possible to drive all the way to the end of this road. Farther up, deep snowdrifts linger in the shadows of the dense pine forest, so don't be surprised if you can't make it all the way. If the road is snowbound, be ready for a

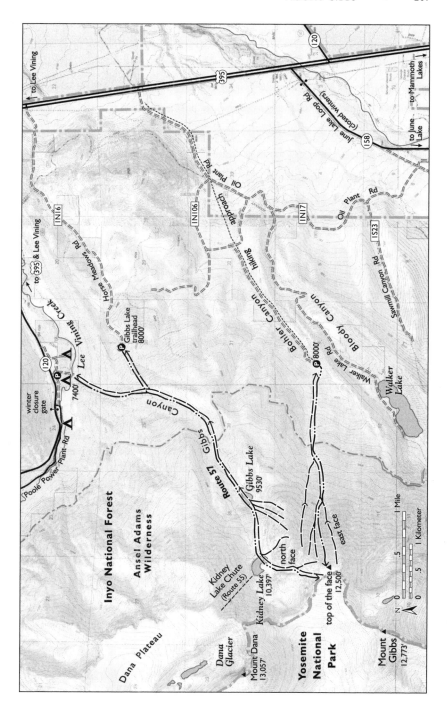

long approach to the east face (about 3 miles), following Oil Plant Road 1.3 miles and then cutting straight southwest from the first turn up to the mouth of Bohler Canyon. Drive as far as possible on the road, then ski or walk the path of the road up Bohler Canyon. After about a 4.3-mile drive from the highway, the road ends in a large sagebrush meadow at the base of the east face gullies (8000 feet).

Poole Power Plant Road: From the junction of US 395 and CA 120, drive west on CA 120 for 3 miles, then turn left onto Poole Power Plant Road (the winter road closure gate is just past here) and immediately left again. Park at one of the entrances to the campgrounds that are closed in winter (7400 feet). This starting point for the north face can be used in winter when there is snowpack below 8000 feet.

Gibbs Lake trailhead: From US 395, drive south of Lee Vining 2 miles, turn west onto Horse Meadows Road, and follow this rough dirt road uphill for 2.5 miles (if possible) to the Gibbs Lake trailhead (8000 feet). This starting point for the north face can be used later in spring.

THE ROUTE

East face: From the meadows at the end of the Bohler Canyon road, walk west in a straight line up this gradual pitch for about 0.75 mile to the bottom of the main gully (9000 feet). Skin up this to around 9500 feet, where it splits into several separate and distinct gullies. All of them are roughly the same length and pitch, so pick whichever one you like for your ascent to the top of the face. Under the right conditions, it may be possible to skin most of the way up this face, but as the pitch steepens near the top, it will generally be necessary to switch to boot-packing.

The top of the east face of Mount Gibbs is roughly 12,500 feet, though the peak's true summit lies almost a mile to the southwest. Since there is little to no ski terrain between here and the summit, most people make the top of the face the end of their ascent. From this ridge, you get an incredible view of Mount Dana and the Kidney Lake basin to the north and Mount Lewis, Mount Wood, and the eastern escarpment of the Sierra to the south. Be sure to peer over the edge straight down the north face of Mount Gibbs as well.

The numerous gullies below you vary in aspect from facing due east on skier's right to southeast on skier's left, so chose wisely based on the solar radiation and snow conditions of the day. Then drop in for 4000 vertical feet of turns back down to the meadows below. Retrace your route back to your starting location from here.

North face: From the Poole Power Plant Road parking area, immediately head south through the closed campgrounds and find a good spot to cross Lee Vining Creek—there are generally a number of large trees across it that are often used for this. Once across the creek, continue south and up into the obvious drainage that climbs into Gibbs Canyon. Climb this forested slope for about 1000 vertical feet, following the drainage south. At around 8400 feet, the pitch becomes more gradual as you follow the creek that comes out of Gibbs and Kidney lakes. As you follow the creek, you begin to head southwest where the Gibbs Lake Trail enters the drainage.

Climbing the stairway up the north side of Mount Gibbs above Kidney Lake

From the Gibbs Lake trailhead at the end of Horse Meadows Road, follow the summer trail southwest for about 0.75 mile until it enters Gibbs Canyon at around 8800 feet, where you meet the approach from Poole Power Plant Road described above.

Both approaches join to now continue southwest, climbing gradually for another mile to Gibbs Lake (9530 feet). A number of fun-looking northeast-facing chutes drop off the east ridge of Mount Gibbs down to the lake—some good options for extra credit on the way out or for future exploration.

Continue west another 0.5 mile and 850 vertical feet up to Kidney Lake (10,397 feet) and the basin formed by Mount Gibbs and the southeastern end of the Dana Plateau. From the frozen surface of this kidney bean–shaped lake, the lines of the north face of Mount Gibbs are directly above you to the south, the south-facing Kidney Lake Chute (Route 55) to your north, and the large but somewhat mellower headwall to the west. Climb the route of your choice and enjoy the view from the top of the face. Descend your chosen route, then retrace your approach to return to your starting location.

58 Mount Lewis

Starting Points : Parker Lake trailhead, 7775 feet;
                   : Sawmill Canyon Road, 8100 feet
High Points : Mount Lewis, 12,352 feet; top of north couloir, 11,500 feet
Distances : East gully, 8.5 miles; north couloir, 5.75 miles
Elevation Gains : East gully, 4600 feet; north couloir, 3450 feet
Times : East gully, 5 hours; north couloir, 4 hours
Difficulty Level : Strenuous
Terrain Rating : 3
Aspects : Southeast-east, northeast, north
Seasons : Winter, spring
Map : USGS Koip Peak

Mount Lewis is another of the beautiful roadside giants just south of Lee Vining and
Mono Lake in Ansel Adams Wilderness. Nestled between Mounts Gibbs and Wood,
Lewis is often overlooked for the more classic descents on its more popular neighbors, but Mount Lewis features a wealth of terrain on a variety of aspects. Lewis's
massive east gully rises for more than 4000 vertical feet to a steep headwall that tops
out on the summit. On the mountain's north side sits the somewhat hidden north
couloir, which drains down toward Walker Lake, and the broad northeast face offers
3000 vertical feet of open slopes and tree skiing. There is terrain suitable for everyone's tastes and snow conditions on the flanks of this lesser-traveled peak. Mount
Lewis is accessed from the June Lake Loop Road (CA 158), and when the road is
closed in winter near its northern intersection with US Highway 395, this adds an
almost prohibitively long road walk until snow recedes later in the spring. When
you can get past the winter closure gate, however, you can cut down the approach
distance dramatically, making this approach much shorter and more reasonable.

GETTING THERE

From US 395, 5 miles south of Lee Vining, turn right on June Lake Loop Road
(CA 158). In winter this road will be closed very near this intersection, which adds 3.6
miles of relatively flat road walking to Parker Lake Road. If the roads are snowy, your
approach will start from as far as you can get by car. When the snow line is higher, or
later in the spring as the snow recedes, you may be able to continue much farther by
car. Whether walking or driving, head southwest on CA 158 for 1.25 miles to Parker
Lake Road; from here, your approach depends on your objective—but Mount Lewis's
summit is most easily reached from the east gully. If June Lake Loop Road is closed
just past its northern junction with US 395 due to snow at this elevation, pull off the
road just before it intersects Parker Lake Road for a more direct approach to Sawmill
Canyon Road; otherwise, bear right onto Parker Lake Road. **Sawmill Canyon Road:**
Follow Parker Lake Road about 0.4 mile and take the first right, following it north

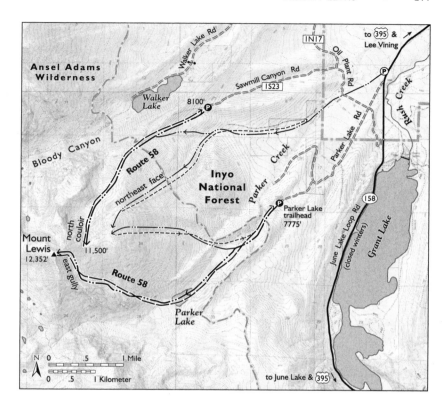

for 1 mile to Sawmill Canyon Road; turn left onto this road and follow it west and uphill to the end of the road, about 2 miles. **Parker Lake trailhead:** Follow Parker Lake Road southwest for 2.4 miles to the trailhead. If you can't drive this far, hike along the road to the trailhead.

THE ROUTE

East gully: From the Parker Lake trailhead, head southwest, following the summer trail into the Parker Creek drainage. Follow this drainage for 1.8 miles to Parker Lake. Make your way across or around the lake, then to the base of the east gully just beyond. Head up this large, moderately pitched gully and over a series of benches for 3000 vertical feet to the base of the steeper headwall that leads up to the summit. The pitch steepens from here as the route heads north up toward the col east of the summit before turning west and traversing above some moderate exposure on the final push to the top.

Mount Lewis's summit offers a unique view of Yosemite National Park's highest peaks just a short distance to the west. After savoring the top, drop back down the way you came and be sure to enjoy the long cruise in the gully back down to Parker Lake. Return the way you came to the trailhead.

A view of Mount Lewis's hidden north couloir

Option: You can also approach the northeast face from the Parker Lake trailhead. A little under a mile from the trailhead, head due west (right) to the top of the north ridge of the northeast face (11,500 feet). The run descends this ridge between the east gully and the northeast face.

North couloir: From the end of Sawmill Canyon Road, head southwest about 1.25 miles and contour around the base of the north ridge of the northeast face; the north couloir lies hidden behind this ridge.

If you parked on June Lake Loop Road just before it intersects Parker Lake Road, take a more direct line southwest toward the base of the north ridge of the northeast face. Cross the road to Sawmill Canyon and follow the drainage as it heads southwest then west through the high-desert meadows, gradually climbing up into the forest. After about 3.5 miles, you join the Sawmill Canyon Road approach at the base of the north ridge of the northeast face.

From this point, the main approach continues southwest into the large bowl and apron beneath the north couloir. Continue south up the north couloir by whatever means necessary to reach the top. The north couloir tops out at a col in the east ridge of Mount Lewis at around 11,500 feet, a short distance west of the top of the northeast face.

Head back down this aesthetic, moderately pitched chute toward Bloody Canyon and Walker Lake. Be sure to contour back northeast around the north ridge, retracing your approach route to your starting point.

59 Mount Wood

Starting Points	Silver Lake (winter), 7240 feet; Grant Lake, 7180 feet
High Point	12,657 feet
Distances	Grant Lake approach, 5.25 miles; Silver Lake approach, 9.5 miles
Elevation Gain	5500 feet
Times	Grant Lake approach, 5 hours; Silver Lake approach, 7 hours
Difficulty Level	Strenuous
Terrain Rating	3
Aspect	East
Seasons	Winter, spring
Maps	USGS Koip Peak; June Lake

The east face of Mount Wood dominates the western skyline on US Highway 395 between the towns of Lee Vining and June Lake. A truly massive mountain, this

Looking north from June Mountain at the massive east face of Mount Wood

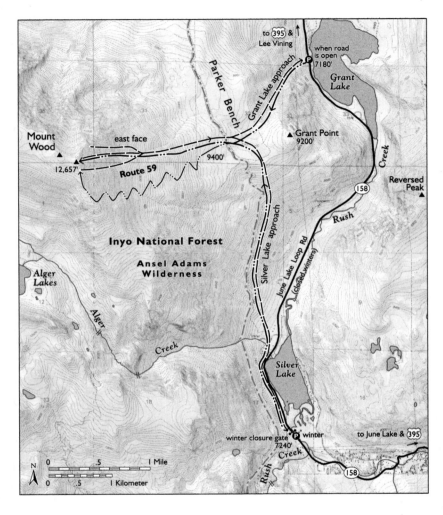

eastern Sierra giant in Ansel Adams Wilderness is as impressive in its width as its height. The potential for 5500-vertical-foot roadside descents is very real in this part of the state, and few mountains are as close to the road as this one. As with most mountains in the eastern Sierra, the route up Mount Wood is not set in stone. Conditions and snow coverage will dictate the best way up on any given day. Although it is most popular starting from Grant Lake in spring, Mount Wood is accessible all winter long from the winter closure of the June Lake Loop Road near Silver Lake. The view from the summit is reason enough to climb Mount Wood, but with good coverage and snow conditions, the east face is one of the most fun, and visible, descents in the area.

GETTING THERE

From US 395, turn west onto the June Lake Loop Road (CA 158) from either end. When the road is open later in the spring, Mount Wood can be accessed from either end of the loop road, starting from Grant Lake or Silver Lake, wherever the snow coverage is better. **Silver Lake approach:** When the loop road is closed in winter, the easiest access is from the southern winter closure gate at Silver Lake just past the town of June Lake. If the lower pitch is burned off, a hiking trail climbs from the shore of Silver Lake all the way up onto the Parker Bench below the east face. **Grant Lake approach:** When June Lake Loop Road is closed, you can often drive around the northern winter closure gate (closer to Lee Vining) to access Mount Wood from Grant Lake if snow coverage allows.

THE ROUTE

Whether you start from the winter closure gate at Silver Lake or from Grant Lake, you begin by ascending to the first major bench on the mountain, Parker Bench, at around 9000 feet, underneath the east face of the mountain.

Grant Lake approach: The easiest route from Grant Lake is up the gully just north of the prominent rock buttress of Grant Point. Snow is generally the easiest surface to climb on, and the minor aspect changes of the lower slopes may afford good snow for skinning or boot-packing. Climb this gully for about 1 mile to Parker Bench, and the summit should be clearly visible.

Silver Lake approach: From the gate, head north, following the road along the lakeshore for about 1 mile, then at a narrow creek gully head diagonally up the slope along the path of the summer trail for about 2 miles to the bench just west of Grant Point.

From Parker Bench, it might seem like the summit isn't too far off, but the top of the mountain is still nearly 4000 vertical feet away. If you prefer to try and skin as far as possible, head toward the ridge to climber's left of the three chutes, switchbacking up just to the south of the summit. When snow conditions are right, you may be able to skin all the way to the ridge then on to the summit along that ridge.

Otherwise, skin toward the base of the three prominent gullies that come directly off the summit. When the going gets too steep to skin, switch to crampons and boot-packing. Climbing straight up one of these gullies brings you directly to the summit in about 1.5 miles.

Mount Wood is extremely broad, so choose the descent route that most appeals to you based on snow conditions and your skiing ability. For a steeper run, the three gullies that drop straight off the summit start off quite steep before the pitch slackens dramatically once you exit the rocks onto the apron. The middle portion of the run below the gullies is a massive 2000-vertical-foot glory run. If you don't want to tackle the steeps of these gullies, drop in down the ridge just south of them and descend the slightly mellower slopes below. Whatever way you choose to go, enjoy the view and the ride—it's a long way down. At Parker Bench, descend the lower pitch toward whichever lake you parked near.

60 The Negatives

Starting Points	June Mountain, 10,090 feet;
	mouth of Yost Creek, 7400 feet
High Point	South end of Negatives ridge, 11,237 feet
Distances	June Mountain approach, 4.5 miles;
	Yost Creek approach, 8 miles
Elevation Gains	June Mountain approach, 1800 feet;
	Yost Creek approach, 3890 feet
Times	June Mountain approach, 3 hours;
	Yost Creek approach, 5 hours
Difficulty Level	June Mountain approach, moderate;
	Yost Creek approach, strenuous
Terrain Rating	3
Aspects	Northeast, east, southeast
Seasons	Winter, spring
Map	USGS June Lake

The Negatives zone is some of the easiest-to-access backcountry skiing in the eastern Sierra. Situated on a ridge that extends north from the summit of San Joaquin Mountain, just one small drainage west of the June Mountain ski area and just outside Ansel Adams Wilderness, the Negatives sit in plain view and entice backcountry skiers to the beautiful east-facing bowl that features a variety of chutes, gullies, and open terrain that ranges in difficulty from moderate to expert. While the Negatives are generally east facing, the bowl shape of the zone provides for skiing on a variety of aspects from northeast through southeast. Couple this terrain with that of Dream Mountain and Hemlock Ridge, both just north of the Negatives along the same ridgeline, and the wealth of gladed slopes that drop from the bottom of this area down to the June Lake Loop Road, and you've got a lot of options to choose from. There are two ways to access the Negatives, and both routes meet in the upper part of the Yost Creek drainage at the base of the Negatives. Accessing this area is simple, with the help of June Mountain ski area's open-boundary policy and a bump from the resort's chairlifts (lift ticket required) to the top, shaving a couple thousand vertical feet off the approach. Those without a ski pass or who don't want to buy a lift ticket can access this zone under their own power by climbing the forested slope of the Yost Creek drainage up to Yost Meadow from the June Lake Loop Road.

GETTING THERE

From US Highway 395 at June Lake Junction, 11 miles south of Lee Vining and 14.6 miles north of Mammoth Lakes, turn west on June Lake Loop Road (CA 158). **June Mountain approach:** Follow CA 158 west for 3.9 miles from US 395 to the June Mountain ski area parking lot (7510 feet). Purchase a ski pass or lift ticket. Ride the

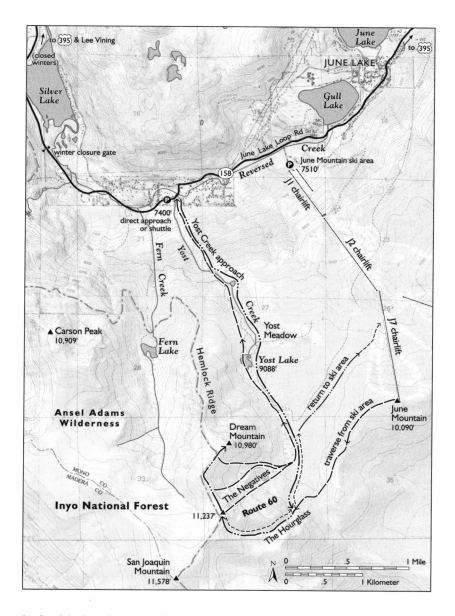

J1 chairlift, then the J2 chairlift, and then the J7 chairlift to June Mountain's summit.
Yost Creek approach: Continue west on CA 158 past the ski area parking lot for
about 1 mile to a pullout on the north side of the road near the base of the Yost Creek
drainage. You can also park a shuttle vehicle here to shorten the return back to the
June Mountain ski area parking lot.

The fun and easily accessible terrain of the Negatives as seen from the top of June Mountain

THE ROUTE

June Mountain approach: From the top of June Mountain, the Negatives should be in plain view, as is your route to the base of the Hourglass, your ascent path; scope your lines from here, as this is one of the best views you will have of the zone. From the top of the chairlift, head west and exit the ski resort boundary. Continue west and downhill for a short distance before heading southwest while contouring along the west side of the low ridge that extends south from the summit of June Mountain. Grab a few turns and let gravity help you traverse for as long as possible before you come to a stop in the upper reaches of the Yost Creek drainage at approximately 9500 feet. This is the point where the ski area approach and the Yost Creek approach meet.

Yost Creek approach: From the bottom of Yost Creek, head south through the tangle of aspens and up into the Yost Creek drainage. Climb south up this forested slope for 1400 vertical feet until the pitch slackens as you reach a bench around 8800 feet. Continue south and into Yost Meadow, up past Yost Lake, under the face of Dream Mountain, and eventually beneath the face of the Negatives. Continue south and begin to climb toward the Hourglass, where you meet the main route.

Switch over to skins and head west up what is known as the Hourglass, the large funnel-shaped bowl immediately south of the Negatives. The Hourglass's moderate pitch makes for relatively quick and easy work of the 1800-foot ascent to the top of the ridge.

Once you're at the top of the high point of the Negatives (11,237 feet), you will have a pretty good view of most of the terrain that lies beneath you. There are many lines on a variety of aspects, so choose wisely based on the conditions and your abilities. Most of the descent options are quite steep off the top of the ridge, so those looking for a more moderate descent may want to consider heading back down the Hourglass.

From the bottom of the Negatives, you can head back up via the Hourglass for more laps or check out the terrain on neighboring Dream Mountain or Hemlock Ridge to the north. When you are done skiing in this zone, head back to the ski area with a short skin northeast, paralleling your traverse approach. Or to enjoy the 1400 vertical feet of tree skiing down to the June Lake Loop Road, follow the Yost Creek drainage north and ski the steep gladed pitch on either side of Yost Creek down to the road. Then walk the short distance back to the ski area or use a shuttle vehicle to return to the ski area parking lot.

61 Carson Peak

Starting Points	June Mountain, 10,090 feet; Fern and Yost lakes trailhead, 7300 feet
High Points	North bowl, 10,750 feet; summit, 10,909 feet
Distances	June Mountain approach, 6 miles; trailhead approach, 4 miles
Elevation Gains	June Mountain approach, 2000 feet; trailhead approach, 3500 feet
Times	June Mountain approach, 3 hours; trailhead approach, 4 hours
Difficulty Level	June Mountain approach, moderate; trailhead approach, strenuous
Terrain Rating	3
Aspects	North-northeast, south-southeast
Seasons	Winter, spring
Maps	USGS Mammoth Mountain; June Lake

Carson Peak rises dramatically above Silver Lake along the June Lake Loop Road just west of the town of June Lake. This picturesque mountain just inside Ansel Adams Wilderness is eye-catching and hard for backcountry enthusiasts to ignore. Considered an eastern Sierra classic, Carson Peak offers a variety of skiable terrain, from its moderately pitched north bowl to the Devils Slide or the steep and extremely exposed Petes Dream. Carson Peak can be approached in a couple of ways: either via a chairlift ride to the top of June Mountain followed by a short climb and a long traverse or more directly via the Fern Creek drainage and ascent of the north bowl to the summit ridge. The June Mountain approach adds just over 2 miles of distance but cuts about 1500 vertical feet off the direct approach via the trailhead; the direct approach is much shorter but has around 3500 vertical feet of elevation gain. Either way, Carson Peak is an approachable mountain with a maximum ascent of roughly 3500 feet and a low summit, relative to other peaks of the eastern Sierra. Both the views and the terrain are hard to beat, and a run on the north bowl to the Devils Slide is a classic that should be on everyone's list.

GETTING THERE

From US Highway 395 at June Lake Junction, 11 miles south of Lee Vining and 14.6 miles north of Mammoth Lakes, turn west on June Lake Loop Road (CA 158). Follow it west through town. **June Mountain approach:** Follow CA 158 for 3.9 miles from US 395 to the June Mountain ski area parking lot and purchase a lift ticket for the top of June Mountain (Route 60). You can drop a shuttle car at the Yost and Fern

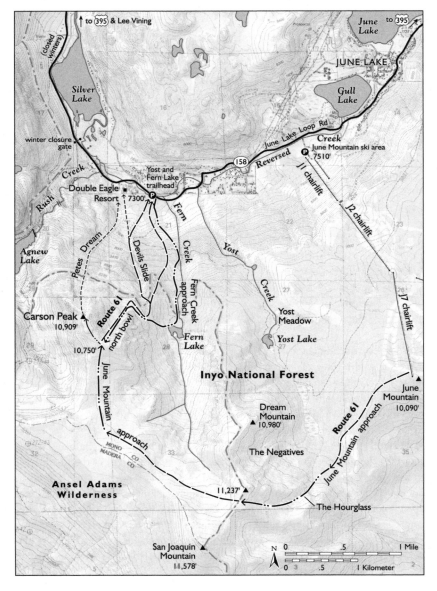

Slashing the white wave near the top of the Devils Slide in a low snow year

Lake trailhead for an easier return to the ski area parking lot. **Trailhead approach:** Continue on CA 158 past the ski area for an additional 1.4 miles to the Yost and Fern Lake trailhead parking area, or another 0.2 mile past that to the Double Eagle Resort at the bottom of the Devils Slide (approximately 7400 feet).

THE ROUTE

June Mountain approach: Ride the chairlifts to the top of June Mountain and follow the route up the Negatives (Route 60) to the top of the south end of the Negatives ridge. From here, follow a broad ridge to the northwest for 2.2 miles by traversing above the head of the Fern Creek drainage, as far as you can coast, to a broad saddle before putting skins back on for the short, mellow hike north to the top of north bowl.

Trailhead approach: From the Fern and Yost lakes trailhead (or the Double Eagle Resort at the bottom of the Devils Slide), head south and ascend the gladed slope of the Fern Creek drainage (or climb the Devils Slide to join this route above Fern Lake). At around 9000 feet you reach Fern Lake; head west and begin to look for a route through the cliff bands above you that lead to the base of the north bowl. While this slope may look quite intimidating, there is a route, albeit exposed, through here to the north bowl. After cautiously making your way northwest through the exposed uphill traverse, wrap around into the bottom of the north bowl.

Once in the north bowl, continue on skins southwest up the moderate lower pitch to the steeper part of the upper bowl. When the going gets too steep, switch to boot-packing to reach the top of the bowl and the summit ridge (10,750 feet). The actual summit (10,909 feet) is a short distance north for those who want to take in the amazing views of the range to the west and check out the relief down the way you came.

Drop back down the north bowl, keeping in mind the massive exposure that exists below you, to reach the point where the trailhead approach traverses into the bottom of the bowl. Follow this ascent route through the exposed traverse back down to the top of the Devils Slide, skier's left of the ascent through the Fern Creek drainage. Enjoy the 1500 vertical feet of the natural half-pipe that is the Devils Slide. If you prefer, you can return to Fern Lake to ski the protected north-facing trees between the Devils Slide and the Fern Creek drainage of the trailhead approach. At the bottom of the slope, return to your parking spot.

Options: Petes Dream drops in north from the summit of Carson Peak. This steep and exposed line is very committing and should only be attempted in safe conditions by competent, expert skiers with the navigational skills to scope and negotiate this complicated route.

Those with limited time or energy can consider doing a shorter ascent of the Devils Slide for a run of just under 2000 vertical feet.

MAMMOTH LAKES TO ROCK CREEK

The town of Mammoth Lakes sits at the base of the Mammoth Mountain ski area, just west of US Highway 395 in the heart of the eastern Sierra. This town is a year-round outdoor playground, and most local residents and tourists come here for the abundant and diverse recreational opportunities. In winter the focus turns to snow, and not only is there incredible terrain that rises right above town, but it is also in striking distance of access to many other routes only a short distance north and south along US 395. Besides the outstanding backcountry skiing in the area, Mammoth Mountain ski area is a world-class resort and a wonderful place to spend a storm day or to shred the mountain's signature wind buff or corn.

The town of Mammoth Lakes has all the modern conveniences, restaurants, lodging, groceries, and gear shops. A number of popular hot springs are also nearby, just south of town and west of US 395.

Several roads in and near Mammoth Lakes are cleared of snow all winter long, providing midwinter access to several zones and classic routes. Lake Mary Road is plowed to its winter closure near the Tamarack Lodge Cross-Country Ski Center, the approach for routes like the Mammoth Crest (Route 63) and Sherwin Ridge (Route 62). Just south of Mammoth Lakes, Convict Lake Road is plowed all winter between US 395 and Convict Lake, allowing for convenient winter and spring access to Mount Morrison (Route 65), Laurel Mountain (Route 66), and Red Slate Mountain (Route 67), to name just a few.

At the top of the Sherwin Grade, Rock Creek Road climbs up into the Rock Creek drainage and is cleared of snow for 6 miles to the winter closure and the only Sno-Park in the eastern Sierra. Accessing the routes described in the Rock Creek area in this guidebook gets much easier as the snow recedes and you can drive farther up the road. Access via other roads like McGee Creek Road and Laurel Lakes Road depends on snow coverage and varies from year to year, typically opening up later in the season or at times with high snow lines.

The Eastern Sierra Avalanche Center provides a regular avalanche advisory for this area (see Resources).

62 Sherwin Ridge: The Sherwins

Starting Point : Lake Mary Road gate, 8600 feet
High Points : 9700–10,200 feet (varies by route)
Distances : 2.6–5 miles (varies by route)
Elevation Gains : 1100–1600 feet (varies by route)
Times : 1–2 hours (varies by route)
Difficulty Level : Easy
Terrain Ratings : 2–3 (varies by route)
Aspect : North-northeast
Seasons : Winter, spring
Maps : USGS Crystal Crag; Bloody Mountain

The runs on Sherwin Ridge—known as the Sherwins—are the closest and easiest-access terrain in the Mammoth area. Clearly visible just to the south of town, Sherwin Ridge beckons people to its variety of excellent terrain. This broad ridge stretches for more than a mile with 2000 vertical feet of primarily north-facing trees, gullies, avalanche paths, and even a few short chutes down to Old Mammoth and the Snowcreek Golf Course on the outskirts of town. A car shuttle shaves a bit of vertical off the route, and many local residents also access this area after exiting the ski

The Sherwins, with amazing coverage, viewed from Old Mammoth Road

resort. People often get to this zone, considered by many to be a "side-country" area, without skins or splitboards due to the short and relatively easy ascent. Be aware that despite the ease of access, this area is still an uncontrolled backcountry environment. Cornices may form at the ridgetop, and this area is most definitely prone to avalanches, as evidenced by the massive slide path, Main Avy Path, in the center of the ridge. Access issues have arisen in recent years at the base of these ski runs, so it is important to respect private property when exiting this area. People have finished their runs by crossing the Snowcreek Golf Course and taking one of the neighborhood roads to their shuttle vehicle on Old Mammoth Road, but I urge you not to do this. Please avoid the private property of the golf course and any residences altogether by exiting this area at the dead end of Tamarack Street or farther northeast by the junction of Sherwin Creek Road and Old Mammoth Road.

GETTING THERE

From US Highway 395, take CA 203 west to the town of Mammoth Lakes and head west on Main Street (CA 203) to the stoplight at the junction with Minaret Road. Continue straight as the road becomes Lake Mary Road. Follow Lake Mary Road for 2.3 miles and park at the winter closure gate just above the Tamarack Lodge Cross-Country Ski Center. **Shuttle options:** The most conflict-free parking area is near the intersection of Old Mammoth Road and Sherwin Creek Road: from the intersection of Main Street (CA 203) and Old Mammoth Road, turn left onto Old Mammoth Road, follow it south 0.9 mile, and turn onto Sherwin Creek Road; park by the winter closure gate (7850 feet). Near the Snowcreek Athletic Club has long been a preferred location for many people: from the junction of Main Street (CA 203) and Old Mammoth Road, drive south on Old Mammoth Road 1.6 miles to Club Drive. A bus stop there can also be used for public transportation for your shuttle.

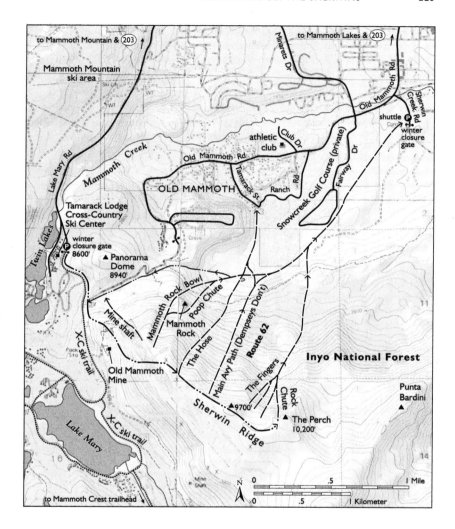

THE ROUTE

From the parking area by the winter closure of Lake Mary Road at the Tamarack Lodge Cross-Country Ski Center, head south on the groomed track. Please obey all posted signs and be sure to use the left side of the groomed ski track, designated for backcountry skiers, snowshoers, and hikers, on the way in or out of this area. Follow this groomed road for approximately 0.75 mile, and you'll see the rocky northern end of the Sherwin Ridge rising above you. Leave the groomed path and head southeast up this windswept and rocky ridge. More often than not, there will already be a boot-pack heading up this direction. Most of this route is often wind scoured down to rocks, and you will likely be hiking on them for much of this short climb.

After several hundred feet, pass above the site of an old mine, at which point you traverse to climber's right under a cliff band. The traverse puts you at the bottom of a short talus-filled chute for the duration of the climb to the plateau on top of the ridge. Once atop the ridge at 9700 feet, simply follow it southeast and climb gradually to the descent of your choice. The Perch, at the far southeast end of the Sherwin Ridge, is about 1 mile away and 500 vertical feet higher than the north end.

Starting from the north end of the ridge, the first run you encounter is the Mineshaft, which drops down just to the east of the ascent route and deposits you back near the groomed cross-country trail. Just past the Mineshaft, Mammoth Rock Bowl filters skiers down around the north side of Mammoth Rock or to the Poop Chute, a steep, narrow, short chute lower down the slope on the southeast side of Mammoth Rock.

Beyond that, the Hose is a beautiful, tree-lined gully that cuts an eye-catching swath down the mountain. Next is the Main Avy Path, sometimes called Dempseys Don't, a broad slide path left from a naturally occurring avalanche in the winter of 1986. Between the Main Avy Path and the rocky outcrop of the Perch is a trio of gullies known as the Fingers. The ridgeline above the Fingers is often wind scoured; consequently the Fingers may be wind loaded, so use caution. The Fingers share a nice open bowl below them with a run called the Rock Chute, a steep, narrow chute through the cliffs of the Perch.

All the runs on the Sherwin Ridge filter down to the flats at the base of the slope. Exit this zone to your waiting shuttle vehicle, but please avoid private property, including the Snowcreek Golf Course. It is also not out of the question to return from the bottom of these runs back to the ascent route or the starting-point parking area by hiking west and up through the saddle between the north end of the Sherwin Ridge and Panorama Dome.

Option: There is also excellent skiing nearby on Punta Bardini. These north-facing trees and gullies, however, are generally accessed by an approach from Sherwin Creek Road.

63 Mammoth Crest

Starting Point	Lake Mary Road gate, 8600 feet
High Points	Red Cone, 10,200 feet; top of TJ Bowl, 10,850 feet
Distances	Red Cone, 6 miles; top of TJ Bowl, 7 miles
Elevation Gains	Red Cone, 1700 feet; top of TJ Bowl, 2200 feet
Times	Red Cone, 2.5 hours; top of TJ Bowl, 3.5 hours
Difficulty Level	Easy
Terrain Rating	2
Aspect	North-northeast
Seasons	Winter, spring
Maps	USGS Crystal Crag; Bloody Mountain

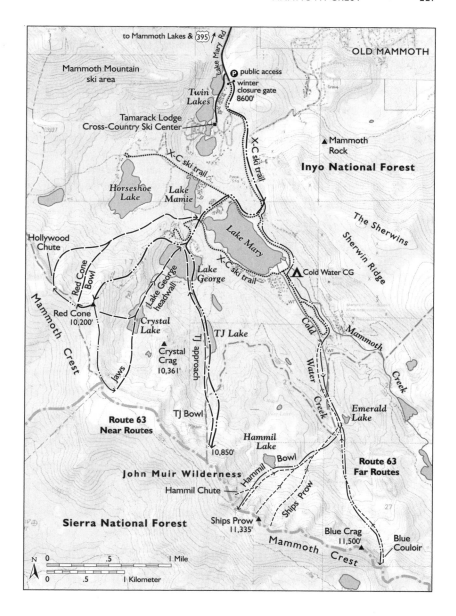

Situated just south of Mammoth Mountain ski area and just west and above the Tamarack Lodge Cross-Country Ski Center at Lake Mary, the Mammoth Crest is some of the closest and easiest-access backcountry skiing to Mammoth Lakes. This broad, northeast-facing ridgeline stretches for nearly 4 miles, offering an abundance and variety of fun, short, skiable lines the whole way. Of the many options out here, this route description touches on just a few major ones. There's lots of terrain perfect for a quick lap or up to a full day of exploring and taking runs off the ridge. Access to this entire zone starts from the winter closure of Lake Mary Road, and all the approaches start on the groomed cross-country trails of the Tamarack Lodge Cross-Country Ski Center. Routes in this area fall into two categories, near and far, with the far routes inside John Muir Wilderness and the near routes just outside the boundary—and even the closer routes have a 2.5- to 3-mile flattish approach. That said, the groomed ski track makes quick work of it. Near routes include the terrain above Lake George, Crystal Crag, and TJ Lake, including Red Cone, Jaws, and TJ Bowl. Far routes, roughly another mile on the way in and out, depending on your route, include Hammil Bowl, Ships Prow, and the Blue Couloir. The lakes provide a direct route for travel in this area when they are well frozen, but be wary of thin ice, especially later in the day.

GETTING THERE

From US Highway 395, take CA 203 west to the town of Mammoth Lakes and head west on Main Street (CA 203) to the stoplight at the junction with Minaret Road. Continue straight as the road becomes Lake Mary Road. Follow Lake Mary Road for 2.3 miles and park at the winter closure gate just above the Tamarack Lodge Cross-Country Ski Center.

THE ROUTE

From the cross-country area, head south on the groomed surface of Lake Mary Road. Please obey all posted signs and be sure to use the left side of the groomed ski track, designated for backcountry skiers, snowshoers, and hikers, on the way in and out of this area. The road climbs gently for approximately 1 mile toward Lake Mary. Once you reach Lake Mary, the routes to the near or far terrain of the Mammoth Crest split.

Near routes: For the Red Cone or TJ Bowl, head west across the north end of Lake Mary and past Lake Mamie, then continue west up the hill to Lake George, about 0.5 mile from the trail junction at Lake Mary. From Lake George, your objectives will be clearly visible rising up above the Lake George headwall on either side of Crystal Crag, with the Red Cone area to the southwest and the TJ Bowl area farther to the south. Depending on your objective the route splits here.

Red Cone: To get to Red Cone from Lake George, head west and climb past a number of small summer cabins to gain the ridge, then climb this forested ridge to the southwest until you reach the crest, about 1 mile from the trail junction at Lake George. From here you have several options: immediately north of Red Cone is a moderate north-facing bowl known as the Red Cone Bowl; the short, steep Hollywood Chute is just a short distance north along the ridge beyond that. At the bottom of either of these routes, traverse east around the end of the Red Cone ridge to return to Lake Mary. You can also drop the east-facing slopes of Red Cone down to Crystal Lake.

Jaws: Traverse south along the top of the crest to reach the steep rollover of the Jaws area. A number of steep, short, chutelike entrances line the ridge on either

Dropping into the east face of Red Cone with the Mammoth Crest stretching for miles

side of the main Jaws rollover. From Crystal Lake, you can head north and follow the outlet creek back down to Lake George, or do a short hike up to ski a line down the Lake George headwall.

TJ Bowl: To get to TJ Bowl from Lake George, go to the south end of Lake George and continue south up the drainage that leads to TJ Lake. Once at TJ Lake, continue south across it and up into the large bowl above you, about 1.5 miles from the Lake George trail junction. A few short, steep chutes lead to the ridge crest above the open slopes of the bowl.

Far route options: Access to the far terrain of the Mammoth Crest involves a little more distance, an additional 1–2 miles each way. From the trail junction on the east shore of Lake Mary, continue southeast along the lakeshore to the south end of the lake at the Cold Water campground. Continue southeast, paralleling Cold Water Creek on the summer campground road. When the road ends, follow the path of the drainage as it heads south toward the crest. When the drainage splits near Emerald Lake, so do the routes to Hammil Bowl, Ships Prow, and Blue Crag.

Top of Hammil Bowl option: At the fork in the creek drainage by Emerald Lake, head southwest following the creek drainage, then bear west toward Hammil Lake.

Once at Hammil Lake, the Hammil Chute will be above you to the southwest; it drops down into Hammil Bowl, which is a run directly south that follows your ascent line.

Ships Prow option: Head east of Hammil Bowl along the ridge crest to the rocky outcrop named for its resemblance to its namesake when viewed from the north. This high point has skiable runs down either side.

Blue Crag option: This prominent rock feature at the eastern end of Mammoth Crest has skiable routes on both sides—Blue Couloir on the east, Crag Couloir on the west. At the fork in the creek drainage by Emerald Lake, continue south all the way up to the col on the east side of Blue Crag, the top of the Blue Couloir.

Pick a run that best suits your abilities and conditions. For all the routes on the Mammoth Crest, return to the trailhead by retracing your approach route.

64 Bloody Mountain

Starting Points	Sherwin Creek Road, 7325 feet;
	second switchback on Laurel Lakes Road, about 9500 feet
High Point	12,558 feet
Distances	From lower Laurel Lakes Road, 12 miles;
	from upper Laurel Lakes Road, 4.8 miles
Elevation Gains	Sherwin Creek Road approach, 5260 feet;
	Laurel Lakes Road approach, 3075 feet
Times	Sherwin Creek Road approach, 6 hours;
	Laurel Lakes Road approach, 3 hours
Difficulty Level	Sherwin Creek Road approach, very strenuous;
	Laurel Lakes Road approach, moderate
Terrain Rating	4
Aspect	North
Seasons	Winter, spring
Map	USGS Bloody Mountain

The impressive north face and couloir of Bloody Mountain dominate the skyline as you drive south on US Highway 395 between June Lake and Mammoth Lakes. Looming high above the town of Mammoth Lakes, the Bloody Couloir is a beautiful line and an eastern Sierra classic just inside John Muir Wilderness. The couloir and descents that drop off the east ridge from Bloody Mountain's summit are popular among local backcountry skiers and visitors alike, and for good reason. From a distance, the upper part of the Bloody Couloir looks nearly vertical, but in reality it tops out around 45 degrees for the top 500 vertical feet or so. A Sierra rite of passage, this is an absolute must-ski for experts with an affinity for steep turns. Bear in mind when you plan to ski Bloody Mountain that Sherwin Creek Road is not cleared of snow in winter, so the length of this route varies wildly from season to season based on snow coverage. The farther you can get by vehicle, the easier and shorter this route becomes, obviously, so take that into consideration based on the season's coverage. In a heavy snow year, you may have to park as far as 6 miles from the base of the Bloody Couloir, making for a very long approach. When there is snow coverage this low, many approach this zone with snowmobiles. Early and late in the season or when the snow line is high, however, you can often drive a good part of the way toward Bloody Mountain.

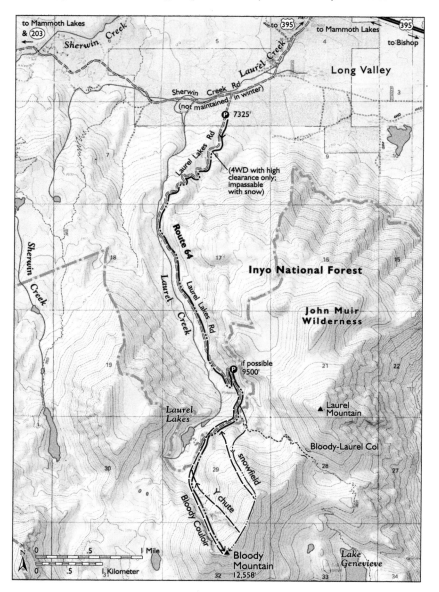

GETTING THERE

From US 395, approximately 1 mile south of the Mammoth Lakes exit, turn right onto the east end of Sherwin Creek Road, which is not maintained in winter. **Sherwin Creek Road:** In a heavy snow year, this road may be snowbound. I would not recommend attempting this route when that is the case unless you have a snowmobile to get you closer to the bottom of this route since it is a 15-mile round trip from here. If Sherwin Creek Road is clear of snow, follow it southwest for 1.5 miles to the junction with Laurel Lakes Road and turn left. High-clearance four-wheel-drive vehicles are mandatory for this steep, rocky dirt road—seriously—so if your vehicle can't handle this rugged road or if the road is snowbound from here up, park here (7325 feet). **Laurel Lakes Road:** If there is no snow on the switchbacks of Laurel Lakes Road, you can generally drive 3.6 miles farther south on this rugged road, climbing up the moraine and back into the Laurel Lakes drainage, closer to the bottom of Bloody Mountain; I recommend driving as far as the second switchback on the upper portion of the road (roughly 9500 feet); after that, the road becomes a very narrow, steep sidehill with nowhere to turn your vehicle around. Just be aware of the potential for rockfall where you leave your vehicle.

THE ROUTE

Sherwin Creek Road: From the junction of Sherwin Creek Road and Laurel Lakes Road, if you can't drive up Laurel Lakes Road, follow it on foot for 1.6 miles and 1160 vertical feet as it switchbacks up this northeast-facing slope into the Laurel Creek drainage. Even with snow coverage, the road and its switchbacks should be visible, at least up from Sherwin Creek Road to the top of the moraine. Once in the Laurel Creek drainage, follow the path of the road south for 2 miles and continue from the directions below.

Laurel Lakes Road: From the second switchback on Laurel Lakes Road, the road turns into little more than a trail that wraps above Laurel Lakes and underneath the north face of Bloody Mountain. The road's path is easy to follow as it leads you about 1 mile right to the bottom of the Bloody Couloir. If there is poor snow coverage, you may even be able to see the remnants of an old mining road that switchbacks nearly into the walls of the couloir.

The lower slope of the Bloody Couloir climbs gradually at first but steepens steadily as it enters the walls of the couloir, about 1000 vertical feet above. Within the walled confines of the couloir, the pitch becomes steep enough to require most people to switch to boot-packing with crampons and/or and an ice axe for the duration of the climb. Two distinct rock islands split the couloir, one near the top and one in the middle. Staying to climber's left of both of them makes for a slightly more moderate climb, but make no mistake: the pitch is still impressively steep for the top several hundred feet.

Those looking for a slightly mellower ascent may opt to climb the broad snowfield at the east end of the Bloody ridge. Instead of contouring above the Laurel Lakes and under the couloir, follow the summer trail toward the Bloody-Laurel Col. Once

Finishing the boot-pack near the top of the Bloody Couloir with early-season coverage

you've gained a couple hundred feet of elevation, contour around to the south onto the large snowfield, then climb it to the ridge. Walk southwest along the ridge to the descent of your choice.

Once you top out on the ridge of Bloody Mountain, be sure to take in the impressive views of the surrounding mountains, including Red Slate (Route 67), Baldwin, and Morrison (Route 65) to the south and Valentine and Pyramid to the west.

The classic entrance to the Bloody Couloir drops in off the west summit, far to skier's left, and is narrower and steeper than the skier's-right line that drops in off the true summit. These entrances to the Bloody Couloir join together about 500 feet from the top. Alternate descent routes farther northeast down the ridge include the Y chute and the large snowfield at the east end (the south-facing slopes drop off the back of the mountain into Convict Creek Canyon).

The easiest way out from Bloody Mountain is generally to return the way you came on the path of the road paralleling Laurel Creek.

65 Mount Morrison

Starting Point : Convict Lake (southeast shore), 7620 feet
High Points : North summit, 12,277 feet; Old Man Bowl, 10,850 feet
Distances : North summit, 7 miles; Old Man Bowl, 4.5 miles
Elevation Gains : North summit, 4657 feet; Old Man Bowl, 3200 feet
Times : North summit, 4.5 hours; Old Man Bowl, 3 hours
Difficulty Level : Strenuous
Terrain Ratings : North summit 4, Old Man Bowl 2
Aspects : East, north
Seasons : Winter, spring
Map : USGS Convict Lake

The sheer cliff face of Mount Morrison, one of the most prominent and visible peaks on the entire east side of the Sierra, towers above Convict Lake. It is hard to imagine that there is any skiing on this imposing tower of a peak, but Mount Morrison and Little Morrison (11,155 feet) combine for a vast array of skiable terrain in very close

Dropping down Mount Morrison's east face from the mountain's lofty summit (Oscar Havens)

proximity to the parking area at Convict Lake, just a few miles south of Mammoth Lakes off US Highway 395 and within John Muir Wilderness. There is a variety of descent options suitable for a broad range of ability levels on both the east face of Mount Morrison and the east and north flanks of Little Morrison. The route to all of the descents in this area climbs the moraine from Convict Lake and heads south into the valley between Mount Morrison and the Mount McGee–Mount Aggie ridge. The short and relatively straightforward approach and myriad descent options make this zone great for doing a mellow morning lap or exploring the steeper complex runs in this beautiful drainage. Mount Morrison's summit offers one of the greatest views available in this part of the range, and that, coupled with the amazing skiing on the east face, makes for a truly incredible eastern Sierra experience.

GETTING THERE

From US 395, 4.4 miles south of the Mammoth Lakes exit and 34 miles north of Bishop, turn southwest onto Convict Lake Road, which is cleared of snow year-round, making this a popular and easy spot for midwinter access. Follow it uphill for 2.2 miles to Convict Lake. When you reach the lake, turn left and follow the road another 0.5 mile around the lake to the parking area at the road's end on the lake's southeast side.

THE ROUTE

From the end of the parking area on the southeast shore of Convict Lake, head southeast up the obvious drainage to the top of the moraine, 600 feet or so above. Then head south along the bottom of the drainage. You have many objectives to choose from.

Little Morrison option: Continue south, contouring along the bottom of Little Morrison's east face. There are a number of great east-northeast-facing gully descents down the flanks of Little Morrison between Convict Lake and the Old Man Bowl that are perfect for a quick lap.

Old Man Bowl: This obvious, mellow, east-facing bowl's bottom is about 1.5 miles and 1900 vertical feet from the parking area. If this is your objective, simply skin west up it another 1300 or so feet to the top.

Hippy Chutes option: Continue south up the drainage to get to the short north-facing Hippy Chutes on the back side of Mount Aggie. The Hippy Chutes zone comprises a collection of 500-foot runs that are great for a shorter tour. If you have extra time after skiing Old Man Bowl or the east face of Mount Morrison, check them out.

North summit: From the bottom of Old Man Bowl, continue south for about another mile to the bottom of the impressive east face of Mount Morrison; the route up will mostly be in view. The upper part of the face is easy to see, although the narrow exit chute below the upper face won't be visible until you are right underneath it. As you begin to climb the mellow lower slope of the east face, look for the south-facing exit chute where the gray and red rocks meet. Climb up this short, narrow chute to where it tops out in the east face; from here the route up to the north summit will

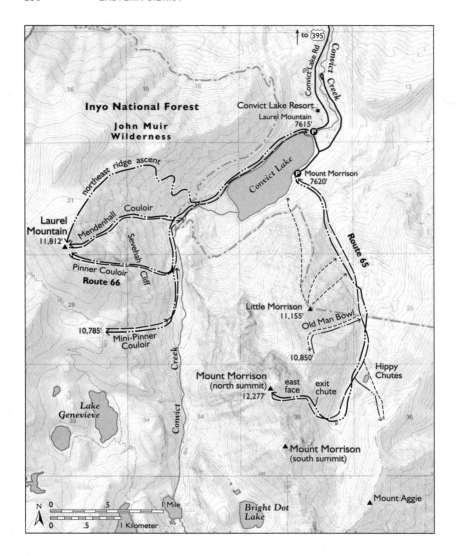

be quite obvious, but it is important to note that you are exposed above a cliff for the duration of the climb and descent back to this point. Simply head up this steep gully—boot-packing will probably be necessary—until you reach a bench below the more moderate ramp that makes up the top of the face. Head up this wide-open face by whatever means suit the conditions; it may be possible to skin up to the ridgeline and onto the lofty north summit of Mount Morrison.

Take in the amazing view from this spot, especially of neighboring Laurel Mountain (Route 66) and the upper reaches of the Convict Creek drainage up to Red Slate

Mountain (Route 67). Drop in for a fun and interesting run back down the way you came to the top of the exit chute, and then ski that down onto the apron. Enjoy the long, mellow cruise north back down the drainage and over the moraine down to the parking area.

66 Laurel Mountain

Starting Point	Convict Lake (north shore), 7615 feet
High Points	Laurel Mountain, 11,812 feet;
	top of Mini-Pinner, 10,785 feet
Distances	Mendenhall Couloir, 5 miles;
	Pinner and Mini-Pinner Couloirs, 6 miles
Elevation Gains	Mendenhall and Pinner, 4197 feet; Mini-Pinner, 3300 feet
Time	4 hours for each route
Difficulty Level	Strenuous
Terrain Rating	4
Aspect	East-northeast
Seasons	Winter, spring
Map	USGS Convict Lake

Laurel Mountain rises above the western shore of Convict Lake at the mouth of Convict Creek Canyon. The distinctive multicolored Sevehah Cliff rocks of Laurel Mountain's east face that catch the first morning light are also home to several beautiful ski routes in John Muir Wilderness. The most obvious line on this face is the Mendenhall Couloir, a gorgeous chute clearly visible from the parking area that drops from the summit down toward Convict Lake. Despite being a highly visible and sought-after ski run, the Mendenhall Couloir gets skied less than you might imagine. A certain snow level is required to cover a couple of cruxes; the upper one is sometimes an ice bulge, and advanced rope skills may be necessary. Scope this route from afar with binoculars to see if it is in condition before attempting it. Slightly farther south into Convict Creek Canyon are the Pinner and Mini-Pinner couloirs, a couple of narrow chutes hidden behind the steep, colorful cliffs until you are directly beneath them. The Pinner Couloir drops in from near the summit and cuts a winding, narrow pathway through towering rock walls. The Mini-Pinner is a shorter version of the Pinner located slightly farther up into the Convict Creek Canyon drainage. All these east-facing lines are surrounded by large rock walls, so solar radiation is a big factor for snow and avalanche conditions. Time your ascent and descent accordingly, and be aware that these chutes may catch snow and rockfall debris that sloughs from the walls throughout the day's warming. It is important to start and finish these routes early, since these east-facing lines lose sunlight by the early afternoon and refreeze.

The view of Laurel Mountain from the summit of Mount Morrison

GETTING THERE

On US Highway 395, 4.4 miles south of the Mammoth Lakes exit and 34 miles north of Bishop, turn southwest onto Convict Lake Road, which is cleared of snow year-round, making this a popular and easy spot for midwinter access. Follow it uphill for 2.2 miles to Convict Lake. Turn right and park near the boat ramp and Convict Creek Trail. Later in the spring, during fishing season, this parking lot may be full of anglers' vehicles and you may have to park in the overnight hiking lot just east of the Convict Lake Resort.

THE ROUTE

Depending on the winter, Convict Lake may or may not be frozen. Fortunately, a summer trail that skirts along the north edge of the lake leads directly beneath the east face of Laurel Mountain and into Convict Creek Canyon. From the parking area, follow this trail southwest for nearly 1 mile until you reach the western end of the lake.

Mendenhall Couloir: From here, you have two ways to get to the top of the Mendenhall Couloir: you can climb straight up it, or you can climb the northeast ridge of the mountain. The more direct route straight up the couloir is straightforward: simply skin as far as possible before switching to boot-packing plus crampons and/or ice axe for the duration. When climbing this route, be sure to keep your eyes peeled for rock- or icefall as the day warms.

Those looking to minimize their exposure may opt for the northeast ridge route to the top. From the west end of Convict Lake, climb north up to the northeast ridge.

Follow this windswept ridge southwest to the summit. The upper portion of this route may be scoured down to rock, so be prepared to do some talus or trail walking before you reach the summit.

From the summit, there are incredible views of the eastern slope of the Sierra to the north, Mammoth Crest (Route 63), the Convict Creek Canyon and Red Slate Mountain (Route 67), and neighboring Mount Morrison (Route 65).

On the descent of the Mendenhall Couloir, the upper pitch is a broad bowl before it chokes down to a narrower chute several hundred feet down. The chute then maintains its narrow confines and steep pitch for a couple thousand vertical feet before moderating toward the bottom.

Pinner Couloir: From the bottom of the Mendenhall Couloir, just head south into Convict Creek Canyon. As soon as you begin to enter the narrower confines of the canyon, the Pinner Couloir should come into view to the west (climber's right). It is easiest to boot-pack this route to the top, but stay alert for rockfall or snow shedding from the steep rock walls. The Pinner Couloir can also be accessed from the top via an ascent of the northeast ridge since the entrance lies just south of the summit.

Mini-Pinner Couloir: From the bottom of the Pinner Couloir, continue just a short distance farther south into Convict Creek Canyon, staying on the west side of the creek, and as you enter a massive grove of aspen trees, look for the bottom of the couloir up and to your right just under 0.5 mile beyond the bottom of Pinner. Boot-pack up Mini-Pinner until you top out on the ridge several hundred feet lower than the other lines on Laurel Mountain, at around 10,785 feet. Enjoy beautifully walled-in, steep turns down this narrow chute back down to Convict Creek.

For all of these lines on Laurel Mountain, retrace your route back to Convict Lake when you're finished with your descent.

67 Red Slate Mountain

Starting Point	Convict Lake (north shore), 7615 feet
High Point	13,163 feet
Distance	16 miles
Elevation Gain	5573 feet
Time	7 hours to 2 days
Difficulty Level	Very strenuous
Terrain Ratings	4–5 (depending on exposure of entrance)
Aspect	North
Seasons	Winter, spring
Map	USGS Convict Lake

If there's such a thing as a perfect run, the north couloir of Red Slate Mountain might just be it. Clearly visible from nearby summits to the north, this wide, steep couloir catches the eye with its split of the north face of Red Slate Mountain. But because it

Red Slate Mountain and its north couloir

is deep within John Muir Wilderness, 8 miles and 5573 vertical feet from the nearest parking, laying tracks down this beauty is certainly no easy task. A run on Red Slate can be completed by fast hikers in a day in the right conditions, but those with an aversion to suffering will probably enjoy this tour more as an overnight mission. One of the Sierra's classic routes, the north couloir of Red Slate should be on everyone's list. Despite the impressive distance of this route, it is relatively straightforward because it stays in Convict Creek Canyon on the way both in and out.

GETTING THERE

On US Highway 395, 4.4 miles south of the Mammoth Lakes exit and 34 miles north of Bishop, and directly across from the airport, turn southwest on Convict Lake Road, which is cleared of snow year-round, making this a popular and easy spot for midwinter access. Follow it uphill for 2.2 miles to Convict Lake. Turn right and park near the boat ramp and Convict Creek Trail. Later in the spring, during fishing season, this parking lot may be full of anglers' vehicles and you may have to park in the overnight hiking lot just east of the Convict Lake Resort.

THE ROUTE

Depending on the winter, Convict Lake may or may not be frozen. Fortunately, a summer trail skirts along the north edge of the lake and leads into Convict Creek Canyon. From the parking area, hike along the trail to the west end of the lake in

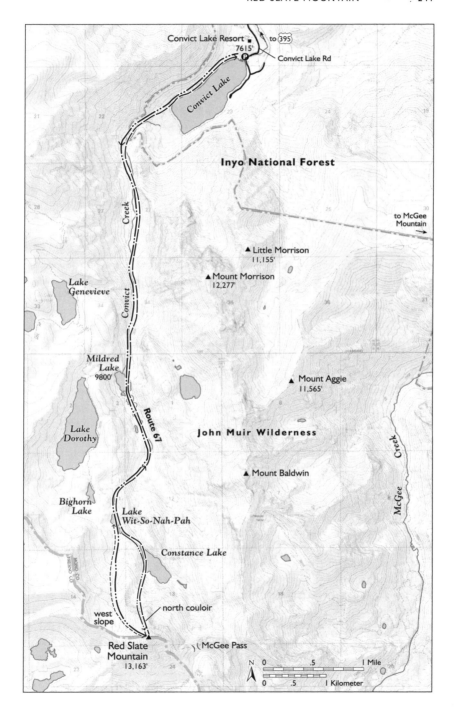

about 1 mile. Head underneath the east face of Laurel Mountain (Route 66) and the beautiful Mendenhall Couloir, then continue south into the Convict Creek Canyon. The trail continues up this creek drainage, which is invaluable for traveling back here in low snow years or late spring and early summer. As you make your way south, you pass beneath the Pinner and Mini-Pinner couloirs that drop down from Laurel Mountain; take a good look and add them to your list for future exploration.

Continuing south along the creek, you may need to switch sides of the drainage occasionally based on snow conditions and coverage. Depending on the season's snowpack, crossing the creek may be extremely easy or challenging; either way, use caution. About 2 miles from the parking area, the drainage widens into a large, flat area full of aspen trees. The east (climber's-left) edge of this area is more likely to hold snow, where the west slope of Mount Morrison meets the canyon floor, which provides easy passage when snow-covered. Be sure to take a good look around; the contrasting rock layers and geology of this area are some of the most beautiful and interesting in the entire Sierra.

After roughly 4 miles and 2200 vertical feet from the parking area, you exit the somewhat narrow confines of Convict Creek Canyon as you reach Mildred Lake (9800 feet). From here you'll have a direct view of Red Slate Mountain and its impressive north couloir as well as the ascent route up the west slope of the peak. At this point, you are basically half the distance and a third of the effort into the route.

Continue south along the flat valley bottom for about 1 mile beyond Mildred Lake, then head southwest up a small drainage for 600 vertical feet to Lake Wit-So-Na-Pah. Anyone opting to spend the night out here will find plenty of flat camping options in the valley just south of Mildred Lake or by Lake Wit-So-Na-Pah. Those who prefer to climb the couloir will want to make a direct line to the base of the couloir.

From Wit-So-Na-Pah, continue south up the large bowl that leads to the saddle on the west side of Red Slate Mountain. From the saddle, the route becomes steeper as you proceed up the slope toward the summit. The pitch of this slope increases dramatically near the top; boot-packing for a few hundred feet may be necessary. As with most summits in the Sierra, the view from the top of Red Slate is outrageous.

Those looking for a mellower ski route may opt to descend the west slope the way you came, but most people venturing out to Red Slate come to ski the north couloir. Entering the north couloir from the summit is extremely exposed and dangerous. The route drops onto the northeast face from the east side of the summit, then immediately traverses across a series of three fins, all while you are exposed above several hundred vertical feet of cliffs. To fall during this traverse would almost certainly be fatal, and in my opinion, entering the couloir this way is unnecessarily dangerous. For that reason, I generally recommend that anyone who wishes to ski the north couloir either climb up it or enter from the alternate entrance near the top of the west slope; both options reduce the deadly exposure significantly. The alternate, or gentleman's, entrance (as I like to call it) drops into the top of the couloir from 150 feet or so down the west slope in a notch in the north ridge. This entrance is visible from a distance on the approach, and you should be able to look down it from the top to make sure it has adequate coverage.

However you get there, the north couloir of Red Slate is one of the best and most sought-after runs in the entire Sierra. This wide couloir holds a sustained steep pitch for 1200 vertical feet within its walls. Once you exit the couloir, enjoy wide-open turns in the apron down to Constance Lake, 2300 feet below the summit. Reverse the route of your approach to return to the car.

Options: An alternate route down the southeast face of Red Slate from the summit is also said to be well worth the effort. This route returns to the Convict Creek drainage through a pass on the east side of the mountain. Other notable descents in the Convict Creek drainage include Mount Baldwin, the south face of Bloody Mountain (Route 64), and the various couloirs on Laurel Mountain (Route 66).

68 Esha Peak

Starting Point : McGee Creek Pack Station, 7800 feet
High Point : 12,221 feet
Distance : 6 miles
Elevation Gain : 4421 feet
Time : 4 hours
Difficulty Level : Strenuous
Terrain Rating : 3
Aspects : Northeast, north-northwest
Seasons : Winter, spring
Map : USGS Convict Lake

The steep north-facing headwall of Esha Peak inside John Muir Wilderness is clearly visible while you drive south on US Highway 395 near McGee Creek. The chutes of the Esha Peak headwall look tantalizingly close from the road, but the bottom of this face is actually a couple miles and 2700 vertical feet from the nearest parking. McGee Creek Road, the access to Esha Peak, is not cleared of snow during the winter, and the road can often be snowbound to the highway. In midwinter, snowmobiles are often used to access this area. If you can't drive all the way to the end of the road, try to drive to the snow line to shorten the extra 3.5 miles of walking (which keeps foot traffic to a minimum) until snow recedes. Fortunately, Esha Canyon is a beautiful, moderately pitched climb and a long, fun descent on the way out. Once you are at the base of the upper face, climb and descend up to 1700 vertical feet in the chute of your choice, then enjoy the surfy cruise back down the canyon. The fittest skiers can be done with a lap on Esha by lunchtime, while others may take most of the day to complete this tour. Either way, a trip up Esha Canyon to Esha Peak should not be missed.

GETTING THERE
On US 395 approximately 8.6 miles south of Mammoth Lakes and 30 miles north of downtown Bishop, turn west onto McGee Creek Road and follow it uphill, over the

The gullies of Esha Peak's northeast-facing headwall

moraine, and into McGee Creek Canyon for approximately 3.5 miles and park in the gravel lot immediately past the McGee Creek Pack Station buildings. If you can't drive this far, follow the path of the road to this point.

THE ROUTE

From the McGee Creek Pack Station, find a good spot to cross the creek to the mouth of Esha Canyon, a short distance directly south across the creek. This crossing may be tricky during high flows, but there are usually some logs or a board across the creek near the pack station. Walk through the sagebrush and up into Esha Canyon. The mouth of the canyon is narrow, but once you get up the first couple hundred feet, it widens for the duration. Follow the canyon south and uphill; be aware of the large avalanche paths that line the canyon on both sides.

The canyon continues south, skirting the back side of Nevahbe Ridge on Mount Morgan North (Route 69). As you climb the canyon, you go up and over several short, steeper rollovers. After almost 2 miles and 2700 vertical feet, you reach the top of the canyon and the frozen pond at the base of the Esha Peak headwall.

From here you can easily evaluate the snow conditions and coverage on the chutes that lead to the summit of Esha Peak. Bear in mind that some slightly challenging scrambling is in store for anyone trying to summit from the chutes that don't top out nearest the summit. With good snow conditions, you can generally skin a good portion of the way up this face, but most people finish the climb with skis on their backs, boot-packing for the top several hundred vertical feet.

From the summit be sure to take in the expansive 360-degree view that includes Mount Morgan (Routes 69–70), Red Slate Mountain (Route 67), Mount Morrison (Route 65), Mount Baldwin, and Lake Crowley far in the valley below. Pick the line with the best snow or the least tracks and savor the steep turns back down to the top of Esha Canyon. When conditions are right, descending the canyon can be the most fun part of your day, so enjoy the long, mellow cruise back down to McGee Creek. Retrace your route back over the creek and to your vehicle.

Wineglass Chute option: An alternate run off of Esha Peak, the Wineglass Chute, is named for its resemblance to a wineglass with a narrow stem and a larger bowl above. This line drops northwest from the north end of the ridge that extends from the summit and into the McGee Creek drainage. Because this route starts quite a way from Esha's

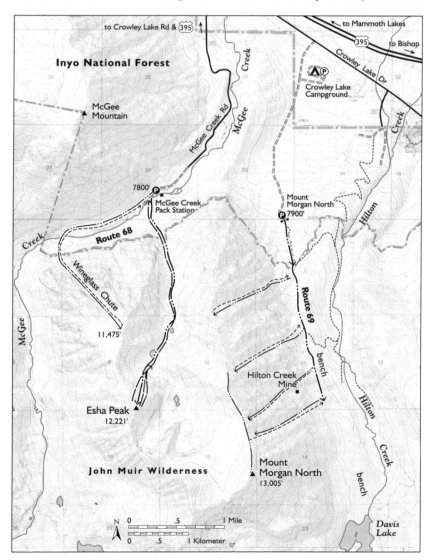

summit, it is best approached from the bottom. Instead of crossing McGee Creek, follow it upstream for just over 1 mile from the pack station until you can see up Wineglass Chute from the bottom. Then head south and southeast to climb the narrow confines of the lower chute to the large bowl above (11,475 feet). Descend the way you came.

69 Mount Morgan North: Nevahbe Ridge

Starting Points	Crowley Lake campground, 7000 feet; upper gate, 7900 feet
High Point	13,005 feet
Distances	From gate, up to 8 miles; from campground, up to 12 miles
Elevation Gains	From gate, up to 5105 feet; from campground, up to 6005 feet
Time	4 hours from gate
Difficulty Level	Strenuous
Terrain Rating	3
Aspect	East-northeast
Seasons	Winter, spring
Map	USGS Convict Lake

Mount Morgan North and the Nevahbe Ridge are among the most distracting pieces of eye candy when you are driving US Highway 395 near Crowley Lake. This east-northeast-facing ridgeline stretches for more than 2 miles in John Muir Wilderness, with a collection of massive 2500-plus-foot gully descents to choose from between Mount Morgan's summit and the north end of the ridge above McGee Creek. Simply hike along the base of this broad face until you find the gully of your choice before starting the long ascent up to the ridge. Anyone wishing to reach the summit of Mount Morgan North will be better off climbing one of the gullies that tops out on the ridge at or near the summit since it is a long and potentially arduous ridge walk from the gullies that top out farther north. In the middle of winter, or anytime the valley floor is blanketed in snow, there will be a bit of flat travel both to and from the base of the face. Come spring, or anytime there is a higher snow line, you may be able to drive a good portion of the approach, shaving as much as 2 miles off each way.

GETTING THERE

From US 395, 8.6 miles south of Mammoth Lakes and 30 miles north of downtown Bishop, turn west onto McGee Creek Road, then take the first left, onto Crowley Lake Drive. Follow Crowley Lake Drive southeast for 1 mile and take a right at Crowley Lake campground. This road is not plowed in winter, so you may have to start the hike from here. In the spring, or depending on snow coverage, you may be able to drive almost 2 miles farther on the dirt road up toward the base of Nevahbe Ridge until eventually a locked gate blocks your path. Park here.

Looking back up after skiing one of the numerous gullies of Nevahbe Ridge on Mount Morgan North (Kendra Nardi)

THE ROUTE

From the campground: Make your way on the snow-covered dirt road that continues past Crowley Lake campground to the gate, nearly 2 miles and a very gradual 900 vertical feet from Crowley Lake Drive.

From the gate: Head south up the drainage, following an old mining road 0.75 mile until it turns northeast (see Option, below), then continue south along the base of Nevahbe Ridge. The south end of this massive ridgeline is 2.5 miles away from here, with enticing skiable gullies the entire way.

Approaching and climbing any of these gullies is relatively straightforward; however, choosing the one you want to ski can be a challenge. The gullies are all relatively similar in length and pitch, all getting slightly steeper near the ridgetop, with aspects ranging primarily between east and north. The farther south you go before ascending a gully, the higher you'll be when you top out on the ridge, and the closer you'll be to the summit of Mount Morgan. If you are hiking along the ridge to the summit, be prepared for a potentially long ridgetop walk to reach it.

Climb the gully of your choosing, but be aware that most of them are 2500 vertical feet or so from the bench to the ridge, so settle in for a long ascent. Top out on the ridge, and once you've enjoyed the view and caught your breath, drop back down the way you came, to the bench far below. Once you hit the bench, head north, making sure to stay high and not get drawn down into the Hilton Creek drainage since it leads you away from where you started. Instead, continue north along the bench, dropping back down the drainage you hiked up initially to the gate and the road you came in on.

Option: If the low-elevation snow coverage is poor, when the old mining road takes a northeasterly turn at 0.75 mile from the gate, you can follow it for a more circuitous but potentially less bushwhacking approach. It cuts into the Hilton Creek drainage, where it continues south for a little more than 0.5 mile and then turns west, up onto the bench at the base of Nevahbe Ridge.

70 Mount Morgan South

Starting Points	Sno-Park, 8800 feet; Rock Creek Lake, 9700 feet
High Points	Summit, 13,748 feet; top of gullies, 13,330 feet
Distances	Sno-Park, 15 miles; Rock Creek Lake, 9 miles
Elevation Gains	Sno-Park, up to 4948 feet; Rock Creek Lake, up to 4048 feet
Times	Sno-Park, 8 hours; Rock Creek Lake, 5 hours
Difficulty Level	Strenuous
Terrain Rating	3
Aspect	North-northeast
Seasons	Winter, spring
Map	USGS Mount Morgan

Just 252 feet shy of 14,000 feet, Mount Morgan South is the highest peak in the Rock Creek region in John Muir Wilderness and the tallest in the Sierra north of the town of Bishop. A long approach in winter keeps traffic in this area to a minimum, but the Rock Creek Lodge, located 1 mile past the Sno-Park, operates year-round and grooms the road for cross-country skiing from the closure to Mosquito Flat, making for relatively easy travel on the road. As the snowpack recedes in the spring and Rock Creek Road opens up, the peaks in this area see a dramatic increase in skier traffic. Visible only for moments from Rock Creek Road, the Francis Gullies on Mount Morgan South offer one of the highest concentrations of interesting ski terrain in the Rock Creek zone. Depending on the snowpack, as many as ten north-facing chutes and gullies drop 1000-plus vertical feet from Mount Morgan South's summit plateau. Hike an extra 500 vertical feet to stand atop the summit and spend the rest of your day doing laps on the gullies.

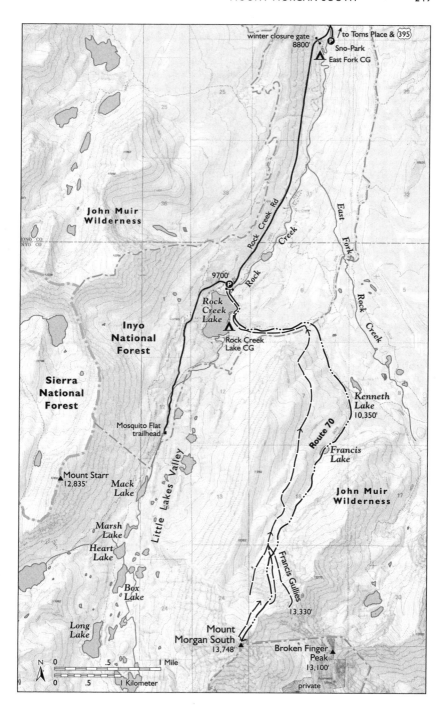

to Toms Place & 395

winter closure gate
8800'

Sno-Park
East Fork CG

John Muir
Wilderness

Rock Creek Rd

Rock Creek

East Fork Rock Creek

9700'

Rock
Creek
Lake

Inyo
National
Forest

Rock Creek
Lake CG

Kenneth
Lake
10,350'

Sierra
National
Forest

Route 70

Francis
Lake

Mosquito Flat
trailhead

John Muir
Wilderness

Little Lakes Valley

Mount Starr
12,835'

Mack
Lake

Marsh
Lake

Heart
Lake

Box
Lake

Francis Gullies

13,330'

Long
Lake

Mount
Morgan South
13,748'

Broken Finger
Peak
13,100'

private

N

0   .5   1 Mile

0   .5   1 Kilometer

Breaking trail before switching to boot-packing on the way up Mount Morgan South

GETTING THERE

From US Highway 395 at the top of the Sherwin Grade, at Toms Place, turn south-west onto Rock Creek Road and follow it south as it climbs into Rock Creek Canyon. **Sno-Park:** In winter, the road is plowed for only 6 miles, to the winter closure gate at East Fork campground (8800 feet), the only Sno-Park in the entire eastern Sierra (fee required; see Resources). **Rock Creek Lake:** Once the road has been plowed, it may be possible to start this route at the lake, 3 miles closer.

THE ROUTE

From the Sno-Park: Follow the road 3 miles to the north end of Rock Creek Lake.

From the lake: Turn off of Rock Creek Road at a sign for Rock Creek Lake campground (it is pretty hard to miss) and head south past the locked gate for a couple hundred feet to the northern shore of Rock Creek Lake. Head left, southeast, across the dam and follow the campground road along the shore to the east side of the lake and the Dorothy Lake trailhead. Here the route begins to follow the Dorothy Lake Trail, which heads east, contouring around the northern end of the massive ridge that extends northeast from the shoulder of Mount Morgan South. After climbing 500 vertical feet to the east over 0.75 mile, the route contours along the base of the slope, gaining only 150 vertical feet over the next 1.25 miles to Kenneth Lake (10,350 feet).

From Kenneth Lake, the route now turns to the south and climbs into the valley created by the two large ridges that extend north from Mount Morgan South. After 0.75 mile you reach Francis Lake; continue south up the drainage as the beautiful Francis Gullies slowly come into view. About 0.5 mile past Francis Lake, the route heads into a jumbled mess of boulders and talus. In a big snow year, you may not even notice, but during low snow years this 0.75-mile stretch can be somewhat treacherous and frustrating; take your time and watch your step. Follow the path of least resistance and most snow to the base of the north-facing gullies and climb whichever one looks to provide easiest passage to the top.

If you're planning on summiting, continue south-southwest from the top of the gullies up the broad, mellow slope for another 0.5 mile. While the ski terrain between the summit and the gullies isn't great, the view from the top is well worth the extra effort.

Hopefully you scoped out the various gullies on your way up, so now pick your favorite. The lines get progressively longer and slightly steeper the farther skier's right you go, and there are plenty to choose from, depending on snow conditions and the size of your group. The gullies range from around 1000 to 1300 vertical feet long, so doing a couple of laps, depending on energy levels, is not out of the question once you're all the way back here.

After you're done skiing the gullies, head north back down the drainage you hiked up. Instead of following the exact path you came in on, though, contour as high as you can along the west (skier's-left) side of the valley so you can grab a few more turns from the north end of the ridge as you drop back down toward your route from Rock Creek Lake. From here, head back to your vehicle the way you came.

71 Mount Dade

Starting Point : Mosquito Flat trailhead, 10,230 feet
High Points : Mount Dade, 13,615 feet; Cat Ears Couloir, 13,500 feet;
: Hourglass, 12,600 feet
Distance : 9 miles
Elevation Gains : Hourglass, 2370 feet; Cat Ears Couloir, 3270 feet
Time : 6 hours to 2 days
Difficulty Level : Strenuous
Terrain Ratings : Hourglass 2; Cat Ears 4
Aspect : North-northeast
Season : Spring
Maps : USGS Mount Abbott; Mount Morgan

Mount Dade is home to what is the steepest, and recently the most sought-after, descent in the Rock Creek area: the Cat Ears Couloir. On the other end of the spectrum, the moderately pitched Hourglass gully is probably the most popular and frequently skied route in the entire zone. These fine north- and northeast-facing descents deep in John Muir Wilderness hold snow well into the late spring and early summer. During the winter, the very long approach to Mount Dade lends itself well to an overnight trip and skiing some of the other fabulous terrain in the area. Once the road has been cleared for the spring, the approach gets much shorter and day trips out here become much more reasonable. This route description starts from the Mosquito Flat trailhead, so please bear in mind the added distance if you start from the pack station or the Sno-Park when the road is closed below the trailhead. The Cat Ears Couloir doesn't always fill in, depending on the season's snowpack, but when it does, it provides the steepest turns you can find back here. The Hourglass, on the other hand, is a wide, moderate, 1200-foot gully that sits between Mount Dade and Pipsqueak Spire. No matter your ability level, there is great terrain to be found on Mount Dade and the surrounding peaks in the Rock Creek drainage.

GETTING THERE

From US Highway 395 at the top of the Sherwin Grade, at Toms Place, turn south-west onto Rock Creek Road and follow it south as it climbs into Rock Creek Canyon. In winter, the road is plowed only for 6 miles, to the winter closure gate at East Fork campground (8800 feet), the only Sno-Park in the entire eastern Sierra (fee required; see Resources). The Rock Creek Lodge, located 1 mile past the Sno-Park, operates year-round and grooms the road for cross-country skiing from the closure to Mosquito Flat, making for relatively easy travel on the road. Once the road has been plowed, it may be possible to start this route from the pack station above Rock Creek Lake, 3.5 miles closer, or the Mosquito Flat trailhead, 4.7 miles closer. This route is described from the trailhead, assuming spring conditions.

Bear Creek Spire (far left), the Hourglass framed by Pipsqueak Spire (center), and Mount Dade (right)

THE ROUTE

From the Mosquito Flat trailhead, head south into the Little Lakes Valley, following the drainage, or using the summer trail if snow coverage is poor, on a relatively flat path toward Mount Dade. As you head south, you hike along a string of lakes, and when frozen, these lakes make a very easy surface to travel on in this area. Simply follow the drainage as you hike past Mack Lake, Marsh Lake, Heart Lake, and eventually Long Lake (10,558 feet), 2.2 miles from the trailhead. All the while the Hourglass gully should be visible in the distance, although the Cat Ears Couloir on Mount Dade remains relatively hidden from view behind Treasure Peak until you reach the Treasure Lakes.

After hiking past Long Lake, the route begins to gain elevation steadily, although the pitch of the slope remains quite moderate until you cross the Treasure Lakes. Over the course of the next mile or so, you gain 600 vertical feet from Long Lake to the Treasure Lakes. Be sure to check out the east face of Treasure Peak as you hike beneath it, as this is an excellent corn descent in the right conditions. From the Treasure Lakes (11,175 feet), you'll finally have a good view up toward the summit of Mount Dade and the Cat Ears Couloir, which lie up to the west. At this point, you head directly southwest toward the Hourglass gully, and near the base of the Hourglass the routes to either the Cat Ears Couloir or the Hourglass split.

At the bottom of the Hourglass gully (11,500 feet), you can either continue to climb up it for a moderate ascent and descent or head west up toward the base of the steep Cat Ears Couloir.

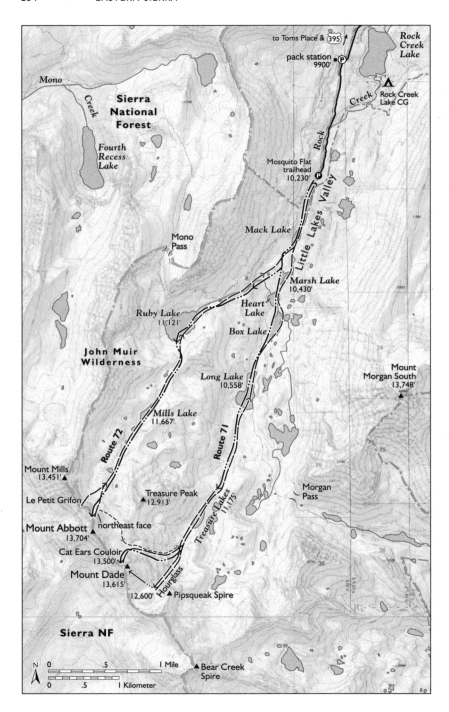

Mono Creek

Sierra
National
Forest

Fourth
Recess
Lake

Mono

to Toms Place & 395

pack station
9900'

Rock
Creek
Lake

Rock Creek
Lake CG

Rock Creek

Mosquito Flat
trailhead
10,230'

Little Lakes Valley

Mack Lake

Mono
Pass

Marsh Lake
10,430'

Heart
Lake

Ruby Lake
11,121'

Box Lake

John Muir
Wilderness

Long Lake
10,558'

Mount
Morgan South
13,748'

Mills Lake
11,667'

Route 72

Route 71

Mount Mills
13,451'

Le Petit Grifon

Treasure Peak
12,913'

Morgan
Pass

Mount Abbott
13,704'

northeast face

Cat Ears Couloir
13,500'

Treasure Lakes
11,175'

Mount Dade
13,615'

Hourglass

12,600'

Pipsqueak Spire

Sierra NF

N

0 .5 1 Mile

0 .5 1 Kilometer

Bear Creek
Spire

Hourglass: If you are headed up the Hourglass, simply skin up it and and top out at about 12,600 feet, then ski back down; it is straightforward from here. The summit of Mount Dade is also best approached from the top of the Hourglass via a large southeast ramp, which may or may not be scoured of snow, so be prepared for some rock walking if you have your heart set on summiting this peak.

Cat Ears Couloir: If you're headed to the steeper Cat Ears Couloir, from the base of the Hourglass climb west to the bottom of the couloir at about 12,800 feet. At this point you'll have a good view of the line and conditions. If coverage and conditions look good, skin as high as you can before switching to boot-packing for the duration of this somewhat short but steep line; an ice axe and/or crampons may be useful. This line tops out on the ridge at around 13,500 feet. Drop back in for some steep turns.

Then from either the Cat Ears or the Hourglass, return the way you came; the very moderate approach is every bit as long on the way back out. If you have extra energy or time, or you are camping out in this zone, be sure to check out the terrain on neighboring peaks like Mount Abbott (Route 72), Bear Creek Spire, and Treasure Peak.

72   Mount Abbott

Starting Point	Mosquito Flat trailhead, 10,230 feet
High Point	13,704 feet
Distance	9 miles
Elevation Gain	3600 feet
Time	6 hours to 2 days
Difficulty Level	Strenuous
Terrain Rating	3
Aspect	Northeast
Season	Spring
Maps	USGS Mount Abbott; Mount Morgan

The northeast face of Mount Abbott is one of the finest objectives deep out in the Rock Creek drainage in John Muir Wilderness. This short, steep face tops out in a rock headwall a couple hundred feet shy of the mountain's difficult-to-reach summit. In fact, the beautiful ridgeline formed by Mount Abbott and Mount Mills features only a couple of skiable routes in the northeast couloir and Le Petit Grifon just to the west, neither of which come all that close to either mountain's summit, although those with an affinity for fifth-class rock climbing may find a way. This route, and most in Rock Creek for that matter, involves a long but relatively moderate approach across many lovely alpine lakes surrounded by the majestic multicolored rocky peaks of the region. Once you finally make it to the base of Mount Abbott, the face rises steeply above you, starting wide and moderate but getting progressively narrower and steeper the higher you get before cliffs block passage to the ridge above. After skiing the northeast couloir, it is easy to link up with nearby routes like Le Petit Grifon or the Hourglass or the Cat Ears Couloir on neighboring Mount Dade (Route 71). Until the road is cleared of snow in the spring, the distance associated with accessing this area lends itself well to an overnight trip, as does the wealth of great skiing out in this area. This route description starts from the Mosquito Flat trailhead, so bear in mind the added distance if you start from the pack station or the Sno-Park when the road is closed below the trailhead.

GETTING THERE

From US Highway 395 at the top of the Sherwin Grade, at Toms Place, turn southwest onto Rock Creek Road and follow it south as it climbs into the Rock Creek Canyon. In winter, the road is plowed for only 6 miles, to the East Fork campground (8800 feet), the only Sno-Park in the entire eastern Sierra (fee required; see Resources). The Rock Creek Lodge, located 1 mile past the Sno-Park, operates year-round and grooms the road for cross-country skiing from the closure to Mosquito Flat, making for relatively easy travel on the road. Once the road has been plowed, it may be possible to start this route from the pack station above Rock Creek Lake, 3.5 miles closer, or the Mosquito Flat trailhead, 4.7 miles closer. This route is described from the trailhead, assuming spring conditions.

THE ROUTE

From the Mosquito Flat trailhead, head south into the Little Lakes Valley, following the Rock Creek drainage or the summer trail when there is no snow, to Mack Lake in 0.5 mile. Continue up the drainage or on the summer trail for another 0.4 mile to Marsh Lake (10,430 feet).

From here you begin to climb southwest up the obvious drainage that leads to Ruby Lake. Ideally there is adequate snow coverage in this narrow drainage, and there is a summer trail that leads up to Ruby Lake, although it follows a more circuitous route. Over the course of the next mile you gain 700 vertical feet as you climb up to Ruby Lake (11,121 feet). Ruby Lake is an impressive spot, with jagged cliffs and ridges rising above it in virtually all directions, and while it is incredibly beautiful, there isn't much in the way of skiable terrain.

The route continues southwest up the obvious drainage for about another mile and 500 vertical feet of gain to Mills Lake (11,667 feet). At Mills Lake the skiable objectives of Mount Abbott's northeast couloir and Le Petit Grifon loom above you, now only a short distance away.

Continue southwest from Mills Lake as the pitch of the ascent becomes steadier; you gain 800 vertical feet over the course of the next mile as you climb to the apron below the northeast couloir. Skin as high up the face as possible before inevitably switching to boot-packing if you are interested in making it to the top. The top of this face, around 13,300 feet, is really quite steep; be prepared to make your switchover for the descent on the slope since this line tops out in the near-vertical rock headwall below the summit ridge. Supposedly you can scramble to the summit from here, but that is well beyond my climbing abilities so I can't attest to that.

The northeast face of Mount Abbott from a flat perch at the top

Drop in for steep turns back down to the moraine below, and if you have time and energy, do a lap on the Le Petit Grifon before you return the way you came to get back to the trailhead.

Options: From the base of Abbot's northeast face, you can contour around to the east to do the Cat Ears Couloir or the Hourglass on neighboring Mount Dade (Route 71). From there, you can enter the Little Lakes Basin and make this a loop by returning on the Mount Dade route. The Mount Abbott approach can also serve as the route to do a simpler loop tour around Treasure Peak.

BISHOP AREA

Bishop sits on US Highway 395 sandwiched between the Sierra Nevada to the west and the White Mountains to the east, at the northern end of the Owens Valley just south of the Sherwin Grade, at an elevation of 4150 feet. This small city has a diverse population of just under 4000 permanent residents (as of the 2010 census), with a mix of ranchers, retirees, Native Americans, rock climbers, and backcountry enthusiasts of all kinds. World-class bouldering in the Buttermilk zone and climbing in the Owens River Gorge are just a short distance from town. The view of the Sierra from Bishop is amazing, with many classic summits and routes visible, and the backcountry access to this part of the range is unbelievable. High concentrations of excellent ski terrain sit above this area's access roads, and consequently a high percentage of routes in this region are described in this guidebook. Many more descents and tours exist than are described in detail here, and I suggest spending as much time as you can exploring the wealth of terrain that lies in these mountains.

Bishop has the least-expensive gas on the east side of the Sierra, as well as grocery stores, restaurants, and shops of all kinds. For the purposes of this guidebook, the Bishop region extends from the dramatic Wheeler Crest above Pine Creek Road in the north to the South Fork of Bishop Creek and South Lake in the south. Several roads head west from Bishop toward the mountains, with Pine Creek Road, Buttermilk Road, North Lake Road, and South Lake Road providing access to this backcountry bounty.

Paved roads offering midwinter access are limited to Pine Creek Road and CA 168 to the small town of Aspendell. Depending on the season's coverage, as snows recede or are cleared for the fishing season, the options open up and you can more easily reach the outstanding and plentiful peaks and routes of this region. Both South Lake Road and CA 168 to Lake Sabrina and North Lake are typically cleared of snow for "Fishmas," the opening weekend of fishing season: the last Saturday in April. Until then, accessing these areas involves road approaches and a significant amount of additional distance.

Buttermilk Road is a rough dirt road that requires a high-clearance vehicle to negotiate a creek crossing in its upper reaches. This road provides amazing access to the mountains above it, but it can be snowbound for miles. Depending on the season's coverage you may be able to get up it all winter long or have to wait until late spring to access this zone. Prior to the road melting out, people often hike into this area from the snow line.

The Eastern Sierra Avalanche Center provides a regular avalanche advisory for the mountains of this region (see Resources).

73 Wheeler Crest: Scheelite Chute

Starting Point : Pine Creek Road, 7000 feet
High Point : 13,000 feet
Distance : 4 miles
Elevation Gain : 6000 feet
Time : 5 hours
Difficulty Level : Very strenuous
Terrain Rating : 4
Aspect : South-southeast
Seasons : Winter, spring
Maps : USGS Mount Morgan; Rovana

The Wheeler Crest is one of the most impressive features on the eastern escarpment of the Sierra. Situated northwest of Bishop and just west of US Highway 395 near the Sherwin Grade, this broad southeast face stretches for several miles from the top of Pine Creek Canyon to the north, creating the eastern edge of the Rock Creek drainage in John Muir Wilderness. With dramatic vertical relief, the Wheeler Crest is impressive. Accessible all winter from Pine Creek Road, the Scheelite Chute rises 6000 vertical feet from the road to the top of the crest at 13,000 feet near Broken Finger Peak. This massive chute is challenging to find in good condition, and often the crux of this route is simply having adequate coverage on the lower couple thousand feet. Despite looking nearly vertical from a distance, the lower half of the Scheelite Chute is quite moderately pitched, especially when compared to the steep, narrow confines within the walls of the upper chute. Even when there is coverage to the road, some parties are often turned around within the first 1000 vertical feet at a short, rocky "waterfall" or wall-to-wall bowling ball–shaped avalanche debris. Get an early start on this one.

GETTING THERE

From Bishop, drive north on US 395 for 10 miles to the bottom of the Sherwin Grade, then turn west onto Pine Creek Road. After 3 miles you pass through the small town of Rovana; continue on Pine Creek Road for 4.5 more miles and park near the bottom of the Scheelite Chute, at 7000 feet.

THE ROUTE

From where you park on the road, you can look straight up this route and see almost the entire way to the top, but despite looking deceptively close, it is every bit of 6000 vertical feet away. The only part of the route you can't see is near the bottom, where the chute goes around a small bend. The short but tricky waterfall hides behind this bend, and a brief section of bushwhack scrambling may be necessary to get around this crux if it isn't snow-covered. Ideally, there will be snow to the bottom of the chute, which makes for much easier travel both up and down.

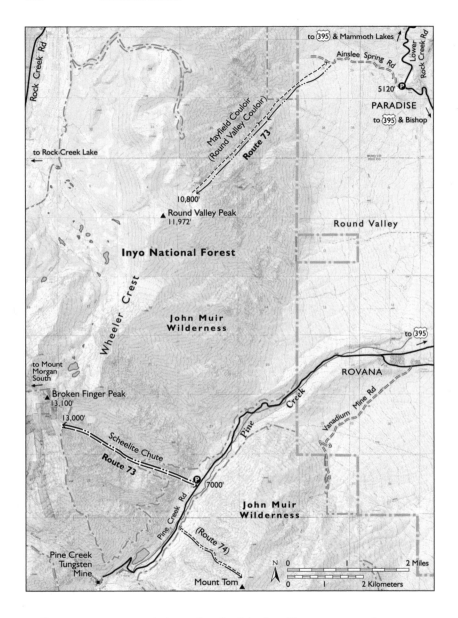

Few routes are as straightforward as the Scheelite Chute, assuming that coverage and conditions are lined up in your favor. In the right snow conditions, it may be possible to skin as much as half the way up before the pitch gets steep enough to require boot-packing for the duration. After you switch over, simply climb straight up and be sure to stay to climber's left into the upper chute to make it to the very top.

The top half of the Scheelite Chute (right) as seen from Mount Tom

It's an interesting view from the top: the beautiful north wall of Mount Tom (Route 74) to the southeast, northwest into Rock Creek, out west deep into the range, and south down toward the old mines. It looks as though at some point it may have even been possible to drive a vehicle on the old mining roads to within a few hundred feet of where you stand. Depending where you parked, you might even be able make out your vehicle on Pine Creek Road far below.

The top thousand feet of this line are by far the steepest, from the top until you exit the narrow, walled-in upper chute; after that, the pitch gets progressively mellower as you descend. This is a very long run, possibly the longest walled-in chute in the entire Sierra. Timing is important on this beast due to its southeastern exposure; the chute itself catches lots of debris from the massive flanks adjacent to it, so be sure to start early in the day and be out of harm's way early, especially if there has been recent snowfall.

Option: The Mayfield, or Round Valley, Couloir is a moderately pitched northeast-facing chute a few miles northeast of the Scheelite Chute. From Bishop, drive north on US 395 for 10 miles to Pine Creek Road and turn west. Take the first right onto Lower Rock Creek Road and follow it north. After 5.5 miles, just after the small town of Paradise, go around a couple of sweeping turns and turn left (west) onto Ainslee Spring Road. This dirt road has a small loop parking area (5120 feet) that is cleared in winter, but if conditions allow, follow the road uphill to its end near Ainslee Spring. Head southwest up the very obvious gully-chute that tops out on the ridge just below Round Valley Peak at around 10,800 feet. This route is 9.25 miles and 5700 vertical feet round-trip from the parking area, made shorter if you can make it farther up the dirt road to park. This unique canyon-like chute is walled in for nearly 5000 vertical feet but requires a decent low-elevation snowpack due to the relatively low starting point.

74　Mount Tom

Starting Point : Vanadium Mine Road, 6350 feet
High Point : 13,652 feet
Distance : 7 miles
Elevation Gain : 7300 feet
Time : 8 hours
Difficulty Level : Very strenuous
Terrain Rating : 4
Aspect : East-northeast
Seasons : Winter, spring
Maps : USGS Mount Tom; Mount Morgan; Rovana

If you've ever driven south on US Highway 395 between Mammoth Lakes and Bishop, you have definitely seen Mount Tom. This massive, eye-catching mountain in John Muir Wilderness lies just northeast of all the major peaks of the Buttermilk climbing area, creating the imposing southern wall of Pine Creek Canyon. Mount Tom was named after Thomas Clark, who is credited with its first ascent in 1860. More recently, a descent of Mount Tom has become considered an eastern Sierra backcountry classic, and rightly so. While there is a nearly limitless supply of skiable terrain on Mount Tom, a large, moderate, northeast-facing gully called Elderberry Canyon that rises more than 4600 vertical feet to the base of a massive headwall and the site of the Lambert Mine (10,900 feet) is the most popular route on the mountain. The impressive east-northeast-facing headwall climbs another 1700 vertical feet or so up to the summit ridge. From the top of the headwall (around 12,600 feet), the summit is still about 0.75 mile and 1000 vertical feet to the south along the north ridge; you can decide for yourself if the long scramble both ways is worth the effort. This route via Elderberry Canyon starts from the end of Vanadium Mine Road, and timing and snow coverage are important since you want to get as close to the end

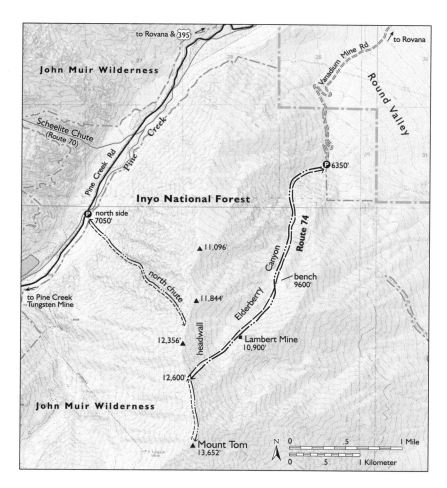

of Vanadium Mine Road and the base of Elderberry Canyon as possible to start this already massive route. There is a lifetime of skiing to be done on Mount Tom; the Elderberry Canyon route to the headwall is only the obvious starting point. This mountain is basically a mountain range in and of itself, and there is no limit to the exploration and descents that can be had on its flanks.

GETTING THERE

From Bishop, drive US 395 north for 10 miles, then turn left (west) onto Pine Creek Road and follow it for 3 miles to the town of Rovana. Turn left on Virginia Avenue, then left again on Vanadium Ranch Road, and make a right turn onto Vanadium Mine Road. Follow this dirt four-wheel-drive road uphill for as far as you possibly can, hopefully to the base of Elderberry Canyon at 6350 feet. Even from here, be prepared for a long hike since it is well over 4000 vertical feet just to reach the base of the headwall.

Booting up near the top of one of the couloirs on the north side of Mount Tom

THE ROUTE

From the end of the road, head west, climbing gradually up the lowest reaches of the canyon. After about 0.4 mile, follow the contours of the canyon as it turns and heads south, gaining elevation more steadily for just over a mile up to a bench around 9600 feet. Continue climbing Elderberry Canyon for 0.8 mile as it heads southwest up to a moraine and the site of the Lambert Mine (10,900 feet) at the base of the infamous headwall, approximately 2.3 miles from the top of the road.

A vast array of complex chutes and gullies descend the nearly mile-wide headwall, ranging in length from 2000 feet at the south (skier's-right) end to 1200 feet on the north (skier's-left) end. Climb one of these fine lines to the ridge, but just know that when you get there, you are still a fair amount of distance and vertical away from Mount Tom's summit. The farther south you are when you crest the ridge, the closer you are to the summit. Either way, it is a long scramble to reach the summit from here.

Pick a line in the headwall zone and drop back down to the moraine at the base of the face before cruising the 4000-plus feet back down Elderberry Canyon to your starting location at Vanadium Mine Road.

Option: There is also a rarely skied north-facing couloir that fills in on good snow years on the northwest flank of the mountain. From Bishop, drive north on US 395 for 10 miles to the bottom of the Sherwin Grade, then turn west onto Pine Creek Road. After 3 miles you pass through the small town of Rovana; continue on Pine Creek Road for about 5.2 more miles and park near the tailing ponds. The ascent up this north chute heads southeast and tops out on the ridge above the headwall.

75 Basin Mountain

Starting Points	Horton Lakes Road, 7940 feet; Buttermilk Road spur, 7800 feet
High Point	13,187 feet
Distances	From Horton Lakes Road, 5 miles; from Buttermilk Road spur, 5.4 miles
Elevation Gain	5400 feet
Time	5 hours
Difficulty Level	Strenuous
Terrain Rating	3
Aspect	East-northeast
Seasons	Winter, spring
Maps	USGS Mount Tom; Tungsten Hills

Clearly visible from the town of Bishop, the peaks of the Buttermilk region in John Muir Wilderness offer one of the highest concentrations of incredible ski terrain in the entire Sierra. When viewed from Bishop, Basin Mountain stands proudly in front of the Buttermilk peaks. Situated just south of Mount Tom (Route 74) and just east of Mount Humphreys (Route 76), Basin Mountain is the closest and most clearly visible objective in the area. The mountain's impressive east face is split by the classic east couloir, a huge, moderately pitched chute that tops out a couple hundred feet below the rocky summit and stares at you from town. It can be somewhat difficult, but not impossible, to reach the summit from the top of the east couloir, as it involves wrapping around the top of the south couloir and scrambling to the top. In good snow years, several other lines may fill in on Basin Mountain, including a narrow chute on the south face and several skinny options farther north down the craggy east face. As usual, the starting location for this route depends on snow coverage.

GETTING THERE

From downtown Bishop on US Highway 395, turn west onto West Line Street (CA 168) and follow it uphill for 7 miles to the junction with Buttermilk Road. Turn right

Basin Mountain, with its classic east couloir, is one of the most prominent peaks of the Buttermilk region when viewed from Bishop

onto Buttermilk Road and follow it uphill past climbing boulders and campsites. Once you pass the climbing campsites, the road gets significantly rougher, and a high-clearance four-wheel-drive vehicle is preferred. Continue on Buttermilk Road for 5.9 miles from CA 168 to the junction with Horton Lakes Road. From here, you have two approach options. **Horton Lakes Road:** Turn right onto Horton Lakes Road and continue for another mile or so, depending on snow coverage and your vehicle's clearance, to the end of the road. **Buttermilk Road:** From the junction with Horton Lakes Road, stay on Buttermilk Road another 0.1 mile and turn right onto a short spur road, then park at its end.

THE ROUTE

From Buttermilk Road spur: At the end of this road, walk in a straight line west-northwest toward the large, fan-shaped moraine that is the route's base. This 0.2-mile option goes through a little sagebrush before joining the main route.

From Horton Lakes Road: From the end of this road, head west up the broad, fan-shaped moraine that has a gully down the middle. The climb starts gradually and gets progressively steeper as it approaches the bench at around 10,200 feet at the bottom of the east couloir bowl. Continue climbing this broad, mellow bowl to the west-southwest up to the next bench, at 11,400 feet.

The remainder of the climb is a bit steeper and the couloir somewhat narrower until it tops out at a col in the ridge at just over 12,800 feet. Depending on the snow coverage, wrapping around the south side to climb to the summit (still nearly 400 feet above) may be a challenging, rocky scramble that offers little to no additional skiing.

From the top of the east couloir to the bottom is 5000 or so vertical feet. While it starts out moderately steep for the first 1400 feet, the rest is fun, cruisey terrain all the way back to the bottom.

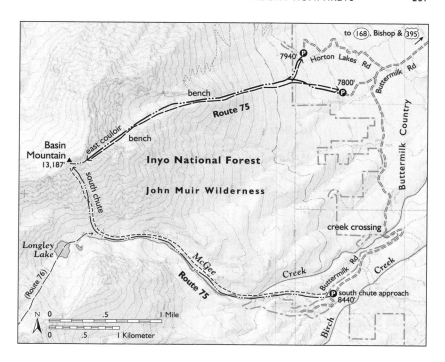

Option: A skinny south-facing chute that tops out very near Basin Mountain's summit may also fill in. This line is accessed from the McGee Creek drainage via the end of Buttermilk Road (see Getting There for Route 76) and follows the Mount Humphreys route toward Longley Lake. Just east of the lake, turn north and head straight up this moderately pitched chute for 2500 vertical feet, topping out just west of the summit. This is a great option for extended periods of high pressure when you are searching for corn skiing terrain.

76 Mount Humphreys

Starting Point : Buttermilk Road, 8600 feet
High Points : Summit, 13,986 feet; north couloir, 13,550 feet
Distance : 8.25 miles
Elevation Gain : 4900 feet
Time : 5 hours
Difficulty Level : Strenuous
Terrain Rating : 4
Aspect : Northeast-north
Seasons : Spring, early summer
Maps : USGS Mount Tom; Tungsten Hills

Mount Humphreys and its stunning north couloir as seen from the top of Basin Mountain's south chute

Mount Humphreys is the tallest peak in the greater Bishop area and the fourteenth-highest peak in California. At just a few feet shy of 14,000 feet, the sheer cliff walls of Mount Humphreys' rocky summit block tower above most of the surrounding peaks of the Buttermilk region in John Muir Wilderness, dominating the skyline when viewed from nearby Bishop. As with most routes in the Buttermilk area, how far you can drive up Buttermilk Road varies greatly depending on the season's snowpack and the snow line when you make your attempt. This route is described from near the end of Buttermilk Road, so starting lower than this adds distance and elevation gain. When conditions allow, drive past McGee Creek and up to roughly 8600 feet. The beautiful north couloir on Mount Humphreys is by far the most popular descent on the mountain, topping out on the ridge a few hundred feet below the summit. Those looking to stand atop the mountain have a challenging fourth-class scramble up and down and may consider bringing climbing shoes and a rope. This steep ski descent, with or without the summit scramble, is considered a Sierra classic.

GETTING THERE

From Bishop on US Highway 395, turn west onto West Line Street (CA 168) and follow it uphill for 7 miles to the junction with Buttermilk Road. Turn right onto Buttermilk Road and follow it uphill, past the climbing boulders and campsites as far as you can, 7 more miles if possible. Once you pass the climbing campsites, the road gets significantly rougher, and a high-clearance four-wheel-drive vehicle is necessary

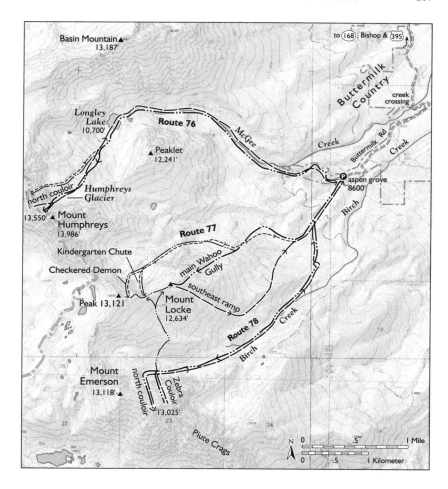

if you plan to make it through McGee Creek. Continue past the junction with Horton Lakes Road and eventually into the aspen grove and across McGee Creek. Because of snow coverage, the crux of this road is often driving from the creek up the north-facing slope of the moraine. Continue uphill, taking a right turn at every intersection you come to. Park at the very end of the road if possible; otherwise, park as far as you can get by vehicle, then walk or skin up the road to its end or follow the path of McGee Creek to just beyond the road's end.

THE ROUTE

From the end of Buttermilk Road, continue west, climbing gently up into the McGee Creek drainage formed by Basin Mountain to the north and the Peaklet—the prominent rock outcrop at the east end of the ridge that extends from Mount Humphreys' summit. Follow this drainage for a couple miles; you can follow a summer trail when there is no snow, because it climbs gradually to the west toward Longley Lake. Continue until you reach Longley Lake (10,700 feet); at this point, you've climbed roughly 2000 vertical feet, and the top of the Humphreys couloirs, clearly visible from here, are still 3000 feet above.

From Longley Lake, the route turns southwest and then climbs the broad, open slopes up to the Humphreys Glacier. If the north couloir is too steep for you or the conditions in it are poor, consider doing some laps in this prime ski terrain above Longley Lake. Otherwise, climb directly toward the chute and switch over to boot-packing, crampons, and an ice axe when necessary. The couloir splits about a third of the way up; stay climber's left for a steeper and narrower ascent and descent, or head climber's right for a slightly less steep and wider route.

Occasionally, a bergschrund may form where the couloir and glacier meet, at roughly 12,400 feet, which is usually negotiable on one side or the other. Climb the chute until it tops out on the ridge. The view in all directions is amazing, especially to the west into the heart of the range. A couple other chutes farther north along the ridge are also generally skiable in a good year, so be sure to take a good look around.

Enjoy the consistent, steep turns of the north couloir down to the glacier, then savor the wide-open slopes back down to Longley Lake. Retrace your route down along the drainage to return to your vehicle.

77 Mount Locke: Wahoo Gullies

Starting Point	Buttermilk Road, 8600 feet
High Point	12,634 feet
Distance	4 miles
Elevation Gain	4034 feet
Time	3.5 hours
Difficulty Level	Strenuous
Terrain Rating	2
Aspects	Northeast, southeast
Seasons	Winter, spring, early summer
Maps	USGS Mount Tom; Tungsten Hills

While it isn't named on maps of the Buttermilk region, Mount Locke was named by friends in memory of Bob Locke, a late Bishop-area climber and skier. Mount Locke is known mostly for the Wahoo Gullies, a collection of fun runs on its northeast face, and a spring descent here has long been considered a rite of passage for Sierra skiers. The closest and shortest objective from the end of Buttermilk Road, the mountain has lightly colored granite that glows in the early morning sunlight. Mount Locke and the Wahoo Gullies, the perfect introduction to the impressive terrain in the Buttermilk area of John Muir Wilderness, are ideally situated to be combined with nearby descents for a big ski day.

Hiking past the pale rock of Mount Locke shortly after sunrise

GETTING THERE

From downtown Bishop on US Highway 395, turn west onto West Line Street (CA 168) and follow it uphill for 7 miles to the junction with Buttermilk Road. Turn right onto Buttermilk Road and follow it uphill, past the climbing boulders and campsites as far as you can. Once you pass the climbing campsites, the road gets significantly rougher, and a high-clearance four-wheel-drive vehicle is necessary if you plan to make it through McGee Creek. Continue 7 more miles past CA 168, if possible, past the junction with Horton Lakes Road, and eventually into the aspen grove and across McGee Creek. Because of snow coverage, the crux of this road is often driving from the creek up the north-facing slope of the moraine. Continue uphill, taking a right turn at every intersection you come to. Park in the aspen grove by the drainage that empties out from the face of Mount Locke and Wahoo Gullies. If you can drive this far, don't be surprised to encounter some dirt walking at the beginning of this route. If you can't drive this far, generally follow Buttermilk Road to this same starting point.

THE ROUTE

From the aspen grove, head south through the dense aspens and into the creek drainage. Follow this drainage southwest, climbing gently for about 0.75 mile to the broad bench below the Wahoo Gullies. Head west on this bench, contouring underneath the gullies to get to your route of choice. Of the five gullies on the northeast face of Mount Locke, the one in the middle is the most straightforward and the best way up to the summit. I recommend climbing the gully that you intend to ski to make the routefinding easier.

This route is within rock walls for around 2000 vertical feet up to where it tops out on the ridge just a few hundred vertical feet shy of the summit. Skin up this main gully as high as you can before switching to boot-packing if necessary. Once you hit the ridge, you'll have a great view down Locke's massive southeast ramp as well as of the few hundred vertical feet left to reach the summit. Boot-pack or skin up to the top and prepare to have your jaw dropped by the incredible view of Mount Emerson (Route 78), Peak 13,121, Basin Mountain (Route 75), and the east face of Mount Humphreys (Route 76).

From the summit you've got a few options for descending. The central Wahoo gully that you climbed is the primary descent route for most visitors to Mount Locke. The other gullies to skier's right of the central line also offer incredible skiing but aren't easily accessible from the ridge.

The southeast-facing ramp off the summit is another fine run on Mount Locke that is often ignored due to the higher-profile Wahoo Gullies next door. You can drop into this slope right off the summit and enjoy the long, wide-open slope for 2000 vertical feet. At the bottom of the southeast ramp, contour north over the ridge and eventually drop back down to the large bench you hiked across at the beginning of your ascent. From this flat bench, all routes drop into the drainage and head northeast to return to the road where you parked.

Options: Sharing the ridgeline with Mount Locke is Peak 13,121, about 0.5 mile to the west. The Kindergarten Chute drops in from the low saddle in the ridge between the summits of Locke and 13,121. Despite its name, the Kindergarten Chute isn't exactly child's play: the wide, north-facing chute is actually quite steep. The infamous Checkered Demon lives right next door. Its steep, narrow, off-camber entrance is considered one of the more intimidating and committing lines in the Sierra. Just a couple hundred feet shy and east of the summit of Peak 13,121, the Demon drops steeply to the north. Once these two lines converge in the peak's northeast bowl, descend to the northeast and wrap around to rejoin the ascent route at the bench below the Wahoo Gullies.

78 Mount Emerson

Starting Point	Buttermilk Road, 8600 feet
High Point	13,025 feet
Distance	6.5 miles
Elevation Gain	4425 feet
Time	6 hours
Difficulty Level	Strenuous
Terrain Rating	4
Aspects	North, northeast
Seasons	Winter, spring
Maps	USGS Mount Tom; Mount Darwin; Tungsten Hills; Mount Thompson

Topping out on Mount Locke after skiing the north couloir of Mount Emerson

The north couloir and the Zebra Couloir cut parallel lines down the steep north face of Mount Emerson (see map in Route 76). Both classic Sierra descents, the Zebra and north couloirs are almost as beautiful to look at as they are to ski: striking, clean white lines down the multicolored rock face of Mount Emerson. The Zebra Couloir is a narrow, steep, 1500-vertical-foot chute that tops out in the cliffs just shy of the summit ridge. The north couloir climbs 1800 vertical feet, holding its 40-plus-degree pitch within walls for its entire length to a saddle in the ridge just east of Mount Emerson's summit. Emerson's couloirs are worth the trip on their own, but they can also be combined with nearby descents on Mount Locke (Route 77) or Peak 13,121 for an even bigger day. With such a wealth of ski terrain in the immediate area in John Muir Wilderness, many people choose to spend a night or two back here, especially when the approach is longer.

GETTING THERE

From downtown Bishop on US Highway 395, turn west onto West Line Street (CA 168) and follow it uphill for 7 miles to the junction with Buttermilk Road. Turn right onto Buttermilk Road and follow it uphill, past the climbing boulders and campsites as far as you can. Once you pass the climbing campsites, the road gets significantly rougher, and a high-clearance four-wheel-drive vehicle is necessary if you plan to make it through McGee Creek. Continue 7 miles from CA 186, if possible, past the junction with Horton Lakes Road and eventually into the aspen grove and across McGee Creek. Continue uphill, taking right turns at every intersection you come to. Park about 0.25 mile shy of the actual end of the road, just beyond a left-to-right S-turn. If you can't drive all the way to the end of Buttermilk Road, hike to this point to start the route.

THE ROUTE

From near the end of Buttermilk Road, head southwest, through the aspen trees and across the creek drainage. Continue southwest and up the drainage that comes down from the base of Mount Locke's Wahoo Gullies—this is the same approach as for Route 77. After about 0.75 mile, leave the Mount Locke approach and begin to head south to contour around the east end of Mount Locke's east ridge and into the Birch Creek drainage. Follow Birch Creek southwest toward the Piute Crags and Mount Emerson. Continue southwest along the bottom of the drainage, past the basin below the Piute Crags, eventually heading west and underneath the north face of Mount Emerson. This route gains elevation quite gradually, about 1000 feet per mile, but that changes dramatically once you start to climb the couloirs.

Zebra Couloir: The first couloir that you come to as you skin west along the bottom of the basin is the Zebra: the colorful, vertically striped rock is a dead giveaway. Skin the couple hundred feet up to the bottom of the walls, then switch over to boot-packing for the duration of the climb. After about 1500 vertical feet, the line ends among the sheer rock walls a few hundred feet shy of the ridge. Be prepared for the difficult task of switching into downhill mode on the 45-degree slope at the top of the couloir. Enjoy the consistently steep pitch and narrow confines of the Zebra Couloir all the way back down to the bottom of the north face.

North couloir: About 0.25 mile west of the Zebra is the bottom of the north couloir. Skin up to the bottom of the cliff walls, then prepare for a long boot-pack to the top. As you near the top, be ready for some rocks that typically protrude from the snow for the last 50 vertical feet or so. These rocks can often make it difficult to top out on this line or to reenter the couloir once you make it past them. If you're able to top out on the ridge, you'll find a nice flat spot for a break and for switching back to skis for the ride down. Be sure to take in the outstanding view of the Evolution Basin to the south. Carefully make your way back down over the rocks into the top of the couloir, then enjoy one of the finest runs in the Sierra back down to the bottom of the north face.

From here, you can head back out the Birch Creek drainage the way you came, or extend your tour on one of many nearby lines in the area.

Options: Ascend a couple thousand vertical feet on the south slope of Mount Locke to the Wahoo Gullies (Route 77), along with the Kindergarten and Checkered Demon chutes that drop off of Peak 13,121. The Piute Crags also have a couple of fun, steep chutes that are reasonably close by.

79 Mount Goethe

Starting Point	North Lake, 9255 feet
High Point	13,264 feet
Distance	15 miles
Elevation Gain	4500 feet
Time	One very long day or 2 days
Difficulty Level	Very strenuous
Terrain Rating	4
Aspect	North-northeast
Season	Late spring
Maps	USGS Mount Thompson; Mount Darwin

Mount Goethe (pronounced GOO-ta) features a bounty of skiable terrain that drops down from the ridge known as the Goethe Cirque to what remains of the Goethe Glacier above Goethe Lake. These short, steep couloirs and gullies vary in length

Dropping into some chalky snow on Mount Goethe in the Goethe Cirque

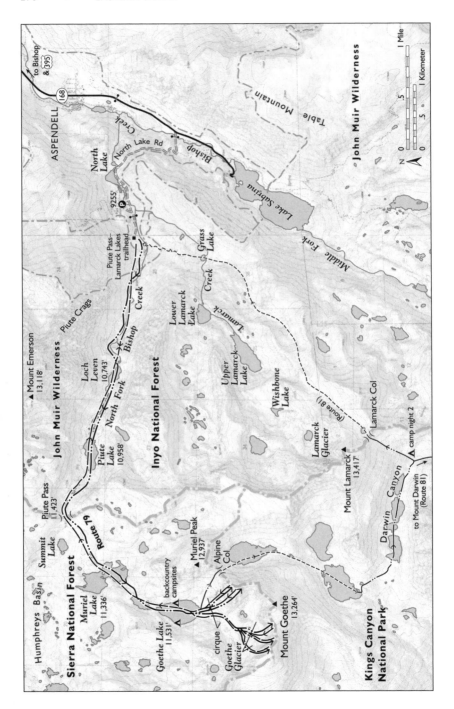

from 800 to 1000 vertical feet and split clean, aesthetic lines down the otherwise sheer cliff face of the Goethe Cirque. The cirque sits just north of Kings Canyon National Park on the Sierra crest, a relatively long walk from the nearest trailhead (7.5 miles one way and 4500 vertical feet), which makes getting to the Goethe Cirque far from easy—but it is well worth the effort. Access to this area in John Muir Wilderness becomes much easier in the late spring when the road above Aspendell to North Lake is opened for fishing season. By the time the road is opened in the spring, however, snow may be burned off of some of the approach, but fortunately there is a summer trail to follow up the North Fork of Bishop Creek to Piute Pass. Due to the distance associated with accessing this area, spending a night or two out in this zone skiing the various lines of the Goethe Cirque or nearby Muriel Peak is recommended. This route can also be combined with other nearby routes, such as Mount Darwin (Route 81), for a longer tour deep into the heart of the range.

GETTING THERE

From downtown Bishop on US Highway 395, head west on West Line Street (CA 168) for 17.8 miles to the small town of Aspendell. In winter, CA 168 is closed just beyond Aspendell and typically reopens to Lake Sabrina and North Lake for the fishing season in late April. Just after you pass through Aspendell, turn right onto North Lake Road. Follow this narrow dirt road uphill for 1.6 miles. Turn right at the gate and continue for 0.2 mile to the Piute Pass–Lamarck Lakes trailhead parking area, by the pack station a short distance from the actual trailhead. Accessing this area before the road opens is by no means impossible; it just adds roughly 2.5 miles of easy road travel to the trailhead at the beginning of this route.

THE ROUTE

From the trailhead parking area, head west along the dirt road for 0.5 mile, past the locked gate to the campground and the trailhead sign at the Piute Pass–Lamarck Lakes trailhead. Follow the summer trail west toward Piute Pass. If there is adequate snow coverage, you can make a more direct line west up the North Fork of Bishop Creek drainage; otherwise, hike along the summer trail until there is adequate snow coverage to start skinning. The trail climbs gradually for 1 mile, where you encounter a short, steep headwall. Once you negotiate this steeper section, you reach Loch Leven Lake (10,743 feet), and the route becomes quite gradual to Piute Pass.

Continue west from Loch Leven Lake, following the drainage for another mile up to Piute Lake (10,958 feet). Keep heading west for another mile until you reach Piute Pass (11,423 feet). Here the route turns southwest as you descend gradually over 0.75 mile to Muriel Lake (11,336 feet). After crossing Muriel Lake, you gain a couple hundred vertical feet over the next mile while contouring around the northwest ridge of Muriel Peak and south into the Goethe Cirque at Goethe Lake. From Goethe Lake, the impressive rock walls of the Goethe Cirque will be clearly visible above you as will the several skiable lines that split attractive diagonal chutes down the sheer face.

Goethe Lake is a great place to set up camp if you are overnighting in this area. From here you are in easy striking distance of the numerous lines in the Goethe Cirque. With a good snowpack, there may be as many as six or more lines to choose from in the Goethe Cirque. From Goethe Lake you can eye up the line of your choice before continuing south and heading up to the moraine below the Goethe Glacier (12,080 feet). Head directly for the line of your choice. You may encounter a small bergschrund near the base of the cliff walls, so skin as high as you can and switch to boot-packing as necessary to make it to the top of your line. If you have the time and the snow is good, take as many laps as you can muster; it's a long way back here, after all.

Once you've had your fill of the amazing terrain in the Goethe Cirque, head back out the way you came.

Options: Alpine Col is the low saddle southeast of Goethe Lake between the northeast ridge of Mount Goethe and Muriel Peak (12,937 feet), which has numerous lines as well. If you are doing a longer overnight tour out toward Mount Darwin (Route 81), this is the col you would pass over to head south to Darwin Canyon.

80 Mount Lamarck

Starting Point	North Lake, 9255 feet
High Point	13,417 feet
Distance	10 miles
Elevation Gain	4500 feet
Time	6 hours
Difficulty Level	Strenuous
Terrain Ratings	Col route 2; north couloir 4
Aspects	North-northeast, east
Seasons	Winter, spring
Maps	USGS Mount Thompson; Mount Darwin

Mount Lamarck is one of the closest ski objectives out of North Lake, and once the road to North Lake opens for the spring, access to this area in John Muir Wilderness becomes much easier. But at 5 miles one way and 4500 vertical feet, it is still a big effort. Mount Lamarck's north couloir remains largely hidden from view until you are either in the basin beneath it or looking down it from above. The top of this sheltered north-facing couloir gets scoured by the wind above its steep rock walls that drop onto the Lamarck Glacier below. Another more moderately pitched and wider chute lies just east of the summit, as does the much mellower east face and Lamarck Col route. The variety of terrain on Mount Lamarck means that you can find descents suitable for a variety of ability levels and have the opportunity to find good snow conditions somewhere. The view from the summit is hard to beat as Mount Lamarck is situated in one of the most spectacular parts of the range just outside Kings Canyon

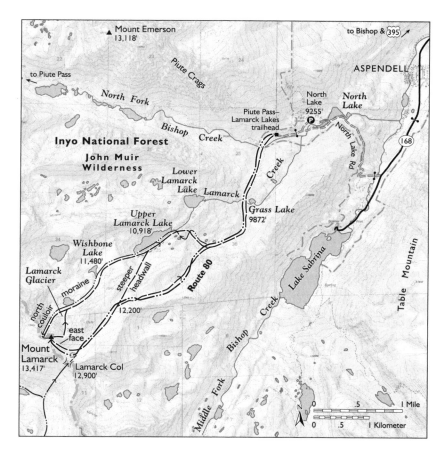

National Park. The Lamarck Col is also used as access for longer overnight tours and to get into and out of the Darwin Canyon from nearby routes on Mount Darwin (Route 81) or Mount Mendel.

GETTING THERE

From downtown Bishop on US Highway 395, head west on West Line Street (CA 168) for 17.8 miles to the small town of Aspendell. CA 168 is closed in winter just beyond Aspendell; the road typically reopens to Lake Sabrina and North Lake for the fishing season in late April. Just after you pass through Aspendell, turn right onto North Lake Road. Follow this narrow dirt road uphill for 1.6 miles. Turn right at the gate and continue for 0.2 mile to the trailhead parking area by the pack station a short distance from the actual trailhead. Accessing this area before the road opens is by no means impossible; it just adds roughly 2.5 miles of easy road travel to the trailhead at the beginning of this route.

Nearing the top of Mount Lamarck with Mount Darwin and the peaks of the Evolution region in the background

THE ROUTE

From the parking area at North Lake, head west for 0.5 mile, past the gate, to the Piute Pass–Lamarck Lakes trailhead by the walk-in campground. Follow the trail west for a short distance until it splits: the trail to Piute Pass continues west, and the Lamarck Lakes Trail heads south. Follow the Lamarck Lakes Trail south up the forested slope for 500 vertical feet. Continue south over this hump and downhill to Grass Lake (9872 feet). Continue south across the flat expanse of Grass Lake and continue up the drainage as it climbs and begins to head southwest. At this point, you can decide whether to ascend via the easier Lamarck Col route or head up to Upper Lamarck Lake and into the basin below the north couloir of Mount Lamarck. I recommend the easier route via the col.

Lamarck Col to east face: Keep following the drainage above Grass Lake as it continues to climb gently southwest toward Lamarck Col. About 3.5 miles from the trailhead, you reach 12,200 feet and the point at which the Lamarck Col descent route splits. You can also descend the moderate route you have been using for the ascent, but skiing the steeper headwall that drops down toward Lamarck Lakes is a fun option for the way down. Continue heading southwest up this drainage toward Lamarck Col for another mile, and at 12,720 feet you are just below Lamarck Col. The broad and moderate southeast face of Mount Lamarck rises above you with the summit approximately 700 feet away. Head up this face to the summit for one of the most amazing views in the Sierra. Off the summit, you have several descent options.

Head down the east face and continue back down the moderate Lamarck Col route that you ascended. There is also the option to drop down the steeper headwall above Lamarck Lake, but otherwise basically retrace your route to return to the trailhead.

North couloir direct approach: From where the approach routes split above Grass Lake, veer northwest from the main route and climb to Upper Lamarck Lake (10,918 feet). Head west across Upper Lamarck Lake and climb 600 vertical feet or so to Wishbone Lake (11,480 feet). In lower snow years, this area is prone to being a jumbled mess of moraine boulders. From here you head southwest and up the moraine to the Lamarck Glacier, then climb one of the two steeper north-facing chutes that drop down from near the summit.

If you approached the summit via the Lamarck Col and east face route, hike a short distance west from the summit and down to the saddle in the ridge that marks the top of the north couloir. The entrance of this line is often wind scoured down to rocks, but the coverage improves just a short distance down from the ridge. Drop down this relatively steep couloir to the Lamarck Glacier. Or from the summit, drop down the east ridge a bit to the top of another steep, north-facing gully and drop down it to the Lamarck Glacier.

From the glacier, both these gullies link up, allowing you to stay high and cross over the moraine before continuing northeast and dropping down to Wishbone Lake, then down to Upper Lamarck Lake. At the east end of Upper Lamarck Lake, head due east and over the small rise to drop back down into the drainage you ascended. Make your way to Grass Lake and follow your approach route back down to the trailhead.

Option: Lamarck Col is where you would head over to the southeast for a longer overnight tour out toward Mount Darwin (Route 81).

81   Mount Darwin

Starting Point	North Lake, 9255 feet
High Point	13,831 feet
Distance	14 miles
Elevation Gain	7100 feet
Time	One very long day or 2 days
Difficulty Level	Very strenuous
Terrain Rating	3
Aspects	North-northeast, southwest
Season	Late spring
Maps	USGS Mount Thompson; Mount Darwin

Named for famed naturalist Charles Darwin, Mount Darwin is one of a group of mountains named after the theory of evolution by the US Geological Survey. All the peaks in the Evolution Basin region lie in close proximity to Mount Darwin, which sits just west of the Sierra crest in Kings Canyon National Park. The impressive north face of Mount Darwin is the primary skiing attraction, with a broad face that narrows to a steep chute topping out on the mountain's flat summit. Mount Darwin's location lends itself to a more casual overnight mission deep into the heart of the range, but

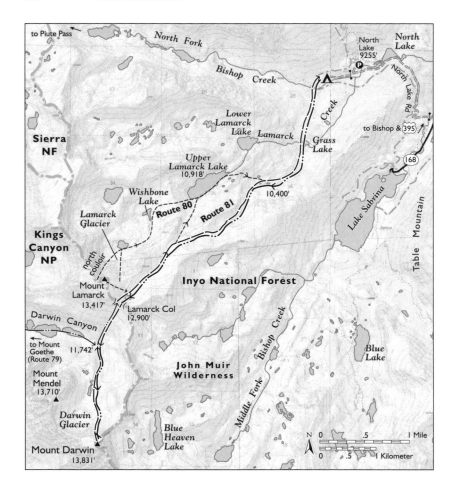

masochistic skiers may be able to complete this route in a very long day. The route involves a long approach through John Muir Wilderness up and over Lamarck Col before dropping down into Darwin Canyon and climbing Mount Darwin via the Darwin Glacier, then climbing back up and over Lamarck Col for a long and moderate return back to the trailhead. A trip out to Mount Darwin is best attempted once the road to North Lake has been opened for the spring, typically in late April, as this approach is incredibly long when the road is closed.

GETTING THERE

From downtown Bishop on US HIghway 395, head west on West Line Street (CA 168) for 17.8 miles to the small town of Aspendell. CA 168 is closed in winter just beyond Aspendell, and the road typically reopens to Lake Sabrina and North Lake for the fishing season in late April. Just after you pass through Aspendell, turn right onto North Lake Road. Follow this narrow dirt road uphill for 1.6 miles. Turn right at the gate and continue for 0.2 mile to the trailhead parking area by the pack station a short distance from the actual trailhead. Accessing this area before the road opens is by no means impossible; it just adds roughly 2.5 miles of easy road travel to the trailhead at the beginning of the route.

THE ROUTE

The start of this route follows the somewhat long but mellow approach to Lamarck Col detailed in Route 80, Mount Lamarck. Over the course of 4.5 miles and 3800 vertical feet of elevation gain, you reach Lamarck Col (12,900 feet). Once you are there, the rest of the route will be obvious and in plain sight.

Drop southwest from the col down the moderately pitched slope to the uppermost lake on the eastern end of Darwin Canyon (11,742 feet). This lake is a prime camping location if you are spending the night out in this beautiful area, and it sets you up for a short hike to Mount Darwin the following day or for an approach to the multitude of other skiable lines on nearby Mount Mendel's ridge.

From the lake, head south, climbing the drainage directly toward Mount Darwin for 0.4 mile and 400 vertical feet. At this point you are on a small bench (12,135 feet) where the remainder of the route up Mount Darwin will be in plain view. Continue south and across the flats toward the moraine below the Darwin Glacier for 0.25 mile, then turn southeast and onto the broad apron of Mount Darwin's north face. Skin up this broad face as high as you can before eventually switching to boot-packing when it becomes too steep to skin.

As you get higher on the face, it narrows into more of a chute and splits climber's right into an even narrower and steeper chute that tops out on the mountain's large, flat-topped summit. In a low snow year, this narrow chute may not be filled in all that well, in which case you can top out to climber's left a couple hundred feet shy of the summit, also a good option for those who don't want to tackle the steep, narrow confines of the upper chute. For those willing and able to make it here, the view from the top of Mount Darwin is not to be missed, with the Evolution Basin and the other peaks of the Evolution region in full view.

From wherever you decide to top out on Mount Darwin, drop back down the way you came for 1300 vertical feet or so of sustained fall-line pitch. At the bottom of the apron, follow the drainage back down to the upper lake of Darwin Canyon. Switch back over to skins and ascend back up the southwest-facing slope to Lamarck Col, about 1200 vertical feet, making sure to pass back up and over the same spot you crossed over on the approach. Once at the col, you have the option of descending the moderately pitched Lamarck Col route or bumping 500 vertical feet up to the summit of Mount Lamarck (Route 80) to tackle its steeper north couloir. Either way, eventually make your way down past Grass Lake and to the trailhead at North Lake.

Options: A wonderful tour starting from North Lake involves two nights of camping while exploring the Goethe Cirque (Route 79), Mount Darwin (Route 81), and Mount Lamarck (Route 80). From North Lake, the route follows the North Fork of

Heading from Darwin Canyon toward the north face of Mount Darwin

Bishop Creek up to Piute Pass before turning southwest toward the Goethe Cirque. Set up camp below the Goethe Cirque, and the next morning get up and tackle a couple of the couloirs. Then head over Alpine Col and south to the mouth of Darwin Canyon. Continue east into Darwin Canyon and set up camp for the night. The next morning, get up and tackle Mount Darwin's north face or one of the many couloirs on Mount Mendel's west ridge before climbing up to Lamarck Col and the summit of Mount Lamarck, eventually dropping back down to the trailhead at North Lake. This tour is a big loop with lots of options for amazing descents.

82 Hurd Peak

Starting Point	South Lake trailhead, 9850 feet
High Point	12,218 feet
Distance	5 miles
Elevation Gain	2368 feet
Time	3 hours
Difficulty Level	Moderate
Terrain Rating	3
Aspect	North
Seasons	Late spring, early summer
Map	USGS Mount Thompson

The pointy rock summit and face of Hurd Peak are clearly visible from the South Lake parking area. The closest and shortest objective above South Lake, the peak has a steep, short, north-facing headwall that is easily accessible relative to other peaks in the area. Hurd Peak is perfect for a quick lap or two or a side trip on the way back from one of the deeper routes nearby. Come fishing season, you'll get to enjoy not only easy access to this beautiful zone in John Muir Wilderness, but also the bewilderment and confusion of the hordes of beer-swilling fishermen who line the shores of this alpine lake as you come and go from your route.

GETTING THERE

From downtown Bishop on US Highway 395, turn west onto West Line Street (CA 168) and follow it uphill into Bishop Creek Canyon for 15 miles to the junction with South Lake Road. Turn left onto South Lake Road and follow the South Fork of Bishop Creek for 7 miles up to South Lake. In winter, this road is cleared of snow only to the Four Jeffreys campground, about 1 mile up South Lake Road, roughly 6 miles from South Lake. For that reason, winter traffic in the South Lake area is relatively limited, and people sometimes use snowmobiles to access this area until later in the spring. Once fishing season has begun, the last weekend of April, the road is cleared up to the parking area at the north end of South Lake. Lately, the road has been getting plowed only to Parcher's Resort, about 1 mile from the lake, making for a slightly longer but completely manageable approach. Wherever you park, make your way to the trailhead parking area at the north end of South Lake, with pit toilets and ample parking—but be warned: weekends during fishing season may see hundreds of fishermen dropping lines through the ice or from the lakeshore.

THE ROUTE

From the trailhead parking area at the north end of South Lake, make your way to the south end of the lake. Ideally, the frozen lake affords you the flattest and easiest

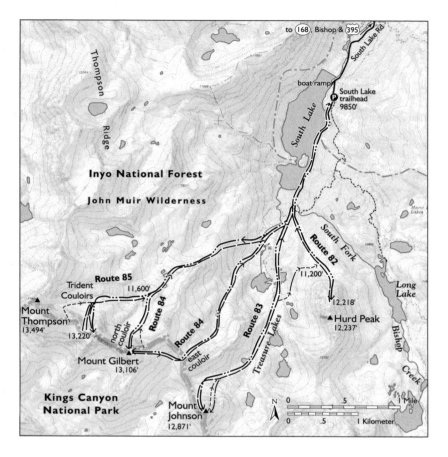

passage to the far end about 0.9 mile away. Otherwise, contour along the eastern bank on intermittent snow and ice patches, a slightly less pleasant start to the tour.

Once you reach the south end of the lake, the face of Hurd Peak will loom above you, little more than a mile farther south. At this point, the route heads south up the small drainage of the South Fork of Bishop Creek on the eastern edge of the south end of the lake. Continue south, climbing a couple hundred vertical feet before the slope levels off. About 0.25 mile from the lakeshore, the approach splits from that for Mount Johnson (Route 83) as you head southeast directly toward the base of Hurd Peak. It's about a mile of casual uphill from the end of the lake to the bottom of the face. As you get closer, bear slightly east up onto the apron below the face (11,200 feet).

Skin as high as you can up into the gullies, but you'll likely have to switch to boot-packing soon after entering the rocks. This face may be short, but these gullies hold their steep pitch for their 1000-vertical-foot drop. It may be the shortest peak in the area, but the view from the top of Hurd Peak is pretty hard to beat. Be sure to check out the neighboring peaks, including Mounts Thompson (Route 85), Gilbert

Skinning across the frozen surface of South Lake (Oscar Havens)

(Route 84), Johnson (Route 83), Goode, Agassiz, and Cloudripper, and make plans to eventually ski all of them.

In a good year, the entire face will fill in with as many as five separate lines with varying degrees of exposure and difficulty. The main gully in the middle is the most likely to hold snow, even into early summer, and is generally the easiest route up and down. Pick your line and enjoy consistent, steep turns down to the apron below. From the bottom of the face, eye your next line and head back up for more, or head back the way you came to return to the parking area at the lake.

83 Mount Johnson

Starting Point	South Lake trailhead, 9850 feet
High Point	12,871 feet
Distance	6.75 miles
Elevation Gain	3021 feet
Time	5 hours
Difficulty Level	Strenuous
Terrain Rating	4
Aspect	North-northeast
Season	Late spring
Map	USGS Mount Thompson

Mount Johnson sits hidden from view in John Muir Wilderness behind the east ridge of Mount Gilbert. For that reason, it sees much less traffic than its more prominent and visible neighbors. With only a slightly longer approach than that for Mount Gilbert (Route 84) or Mount Thompson (Route 85), Mount Johnson has a more

Booting to the top of Mount Johnson's north couloir

remote feel with equally good skiing on the edge of Kings Canyon National Park. Two 1000-foot couloirs that split the north face of Mount Johnson are hard to ignore once you know they're back there. A descent of Mount Johnson is worth the trip in its own right, and it is conveniently situated for a lap on nearby Hurd Peak (Route 82) on the way out.

GETTING THERE

From downtown Bishop on US Highway 395, turn west onto West Line Street (CA 168) and follow it uphill into Bishop Creek Canyon for 15 miles to the junction with South Lake Road. Turn left onto South Lake Road and follow the South Fork of Bishop Creek for 7 miles as it makes its way up to South Lake. In winter, this road is cleared of snow only to the Four Jeffreys campground, about a mile up South Lake Road, roughly 6 miles from South Lake. For that reason, winter traffic in the South Lake area is relatively limited, and people often use snowmobiles access this area until later in the spring. Once fishing season has begun, the last weekend of April, the road is cleared up to the parking area at the north end of South Lake. Lately, the road gets plowed only to Parcher's Resort, about 1 mile from the lake, making for a slightly longer but completely manageable approach. Wherever you park, make your way to the trailhead parking area at the north end of South Lake, with pit toilets and ample parking—but be warned: weekends during fishing season may see hundreds of fishermen dropping lines through the ice or from the lakeshore.

THE ROUTE

From the trailhead, follow the Hurd Peak (Route 82) approach to the south end of the lake (about a mile) and head south up the small South Fork of Bishop Creek drainage on this end of the lake. Continue south, climbing a couple hundred vertical feet before the slope levels off. About 0.25 mile from the lakeshore, the approach splits from that for Hurd Peak as you continue south into the Treasure Lakes drainage between Hurd Peak and the east ridge of Mount Gilbert (Route 84).

Follow the drainage under the west slope of Hurd Peak for a little over a mile. After you reach the first two of the Treasure Lakes, head southwest into the valley below the east ridge of Mount Gilbert. As you head into this valley, the north face of Mount Johnson and its couloirs slowly come into view. Continue to the couloir of your choice and skin as high as you can before switching over to boot-packing for the duration.

Anyone wishing to reach the summit of Mount Johnson can do so from the couloir on climber's right. This wide and more moderately pitched couloir climbs to the ridge just west of the summit. From the ridge it is a short, but exposed and challenging, snow and rock scramble to the summit. In a big snow year, it is possible to ski off the summit, but you'll notice as you climb that the upper hanging snowfield from the summit to the top of the couloir has a convex roll and is very exposed.

While you can't reach the summit from the climber's-left couloir, that chute is slightly steeper and narrower. You may also have to negotiate a narrow rock-choke crux near the bottom of the chute and transition from climbing to skiing in the steep upper couloir below the exposed rocks and small cornice that forms at the top.

Regardless of your chosen line, buckle down for exciting late-season turns back to the bottom. From the bottom of Johnson's north face, retrace your route out via the Treasure Lakes drainage back to South Lake—or wrap around the north ridge of Hurd Peak (Route 82) for an extra-credit lap on the way out.

84 Mount Gilbert

Starting Point	South Lake trailhead, 9850 feet
High Point	13,106 feet
Distance	6.5 miles
Elevation Gain	3256 feet
Time	5 hours
Difficulty Level	Strenuous
Terrain Ratings	East couloir 3; north couloir 4
Aspects	North-northeast, east-northeast
Seasons	Late spring, early summer
Map	USGS Mount Thompson

Mount Gilbert offers a wide variety of skiing on the slopes that drop off its 13,106-foot summit. Those looking for some legitimately steep turns need look no farther than the north couloir. One of the Sierra's classic ice climbs, the north couloir fills in nicely for some seriously pucker-inducing steep skiing. Those looking for a more moderate route should check out the east couloir, a short chute that drops off the summit plateau on the other side of the mountain. Those hoping to summit Mount Gilbert can do so from this side, dipping into Kings Canyon National Park, and the broad, rolling terrain below the east couloir is great skiing in its own right. Mount Gilbert is conveniently situated close to the other fine skiing objectives in John Muir Wilderness in the South Lake region, making this a great spot to hit a few lines in the same day or spend a few days skiing the abundance of terrain back in this zone.

GETTING THERE
From downtown Bishop on US Highway 395, turn west onto West Line Street (CA 168) and follow it uphill into Bishop Creek Canyon for 15 miles to the junction with South Lake Road. Turn left onto South Lake Road and follow the South Fork of Bishop Creek for 7 miles as it makes its way up to South Lake. In winter, this road is cleared of snow only to the Four Jeffreys campground, about a mile up South Lake Road, roughly 6 miles from South Lake. For that reason, winter traffic in the South Lake area is relatively limited, and people occasionally use snowmobiles to access this area until later in the spring. Once fishing season has begun, the last weekend of April, the road is cleared up to the parking area at the north end of South Lake. Lately, the road has been getting plowed only to Parcher's Resort, about 1 mile from the lake, making for a slightly longer but completely manageable approach. Wherever you park, make your way to the trailhead parking area at the north end of South Lake, with pit toilets and ample parking—but be warned: weekends during fishing season may see hundreds of fishermen dropping lines through the ice or from the lakeshore.

THE ROUTE
From the trailhead, follow the Hurd Peak (Route 82) approach to the south end of the lake (about a mile) and head up the small South Fork of Bishop Creek drainage on this end of the lake. Continue south, climbing a couple hundred vertical feet before the slope levels off in pretty dense forest on a tree-covered bench. As you head toward Mount Gilbert there is typically some tricky, convoluted routefinding as well as some awkward skinning moves to get up and over some short, steep rolls. Here, about 0.25 mile from the lakeshore, the approach splits from those for Hurd and Mount Johnson (Route 83) as you head southwest toward the ridge that extends north from Mount Gilbert's summit. At the base of this ridge, choose your approach: the east couloir or the north couloir.

North couloir: Skin southwest to the open slopes of the ridge and follow it uphill toward the base of the rocky prow of the north ridge of Mount Gilbert; as you climb, the trees open up and you can follow a pretty direct route up to the ridgetop. Once you've gained the ridge (around 11,400 feet), cross over it, contouring west, up and across a large bowl, to a bench (11,600 feet) in the basin created by the ridges of Mount Gilbert and Mount Thompson. From this bench, the chutes of Mount Thompson

The imposing north face of Mount Gilbert on the approach to Mount Thompson

(Route 85) are just a short skin to the west, and the north couloir of Mount Gilbert will be clearly visible almost directly south. Skin up to the bottom of Gilbert's north couloir and switch to boot-packing when it gets too steep. The north couloir is very steep, so have an ice axe handy for the climb.

Near the top of the slope, be prepared to switch back to skis or snowboard on slope as it may be difficult to top out on this line due to a small wind-pillow feature that forms at the top. The top of the north couloir is roughly 100 vertical feet shy of the summit, and unless you brought climbing shoes, don't expect to reach it from here. Instead, drop in for some of the steepest turns in the South Lake area. A couple of other lines that drop down the north side of Mount Gilbert are located just down the ridge east of the summit. These short chutes are generally guarded by cornices but can typically be accessed from the summit plateau.

East couloir: This moderate feature of Mount Gilbert is clearly visible from the South Lake parking area. When the approach routes split, continue south and up into the huge basin on the east side of Mount Gilbert's north ridge. Head up this wide-open, rolling terrain to the head of the basin formed by the north and east ridges of Mount Gilbert, and skin up to the base of the east couloir. Though it is only about 250 vertical feet, the east couloir does get quite steep as you climb up onto the ridgetop. From here, your straightforward descent follows your ascent route.

You can also contour the summit ridge to the west for about 0.5 mile and 600 vertical feet to the summit of Mount Gilbert and the optional north-facing runs that drop off the summit ridge.

Whether you climbed the north or east couloir of Mount Gilbert, reverse your route to return to the trailhead parking area. Those with time and energy to spare may want to do a lap on nearby Mount Thompson (Route 85) or Hurd Peak (Route 82).

85 Mount Thompson

Starting Point	South Lake trailhead, 9850 feet
High Points	Summit, 13,494 feet; Trident Couloirs, 13,220 feet
Distance	6.5 miles
Elevation Gain	3650 feet
Time	4 hours
Difficulty Level	Strenuous
Terrain Ratings	3–4
Aspect	North-northeast
Season	Spring
Map	USGS Mount Thompson

The ridges that extend from the 13,494-foot summit of Mount Thompson create the western border between the South Lake area and Kings Canyon National Park. With Table Mountain, Mount Thompson also serves as the divide between the Middle and South forks of Bishop Creek. In addition to dictating which fork of Bishop Creek the snowmelt drains into, Mount Thompson offers some outstanding ski terrain in John Muir Wilderness. The ridge that extends east from the summit is home to a trio of steep, north-facing chutes, known as the Trident Couloirs, which remain almost completely hidden from view until you are right underneath them. From the trail-head parking area at South Lake, you should just be able to see the top of Mount Thompson and its summit ridge. If you know what you're looking for, you can catch a glimpse of the chutes from here. That's about the best view that you'll have of the Thompson chutes until you get just beneath them. These high-elevation 1000-foot north-facing shots hide cold snow after storms and hold snow well into early summer. Any of the chutes can be skied in a half-day tour or combined with some of the nearby routes for an all-day affair.

GETTING THERE

From downtown Bishop on US Highway 395, turn west onto West Line Street (CA 168) and follow it uphill into Bishop Creek Canyon 15 miles to the junction with South Lake Road. Turn left onto South Lake Road and follow the South Fork of Bishop Creek for 7 miles up to the parking area at South Lake. In winter, this road is cleared of snow only to the Four Jeffreys campground, about a mile up South Lake Road, roughly 6 miles from South Lake. For that reason, winter traffic in the South Lake area is relatively limited, and people occasionally use snowmobiles access this area until later in the spring. Once fishing season has begun, the last week of April, the road

Making turns down the skier's-left chute on Mount Thompson (Oscar Havens)

is cleared up the parking area at the north end of South Lake. Lately, the road gets plowed only to Parcher's Resort, about 1 mile from the lake, making for a slightly longer but completely manageable approach. Wherever you park, make your way to the trailhead parking area at the north end of South Lake, with pit toilets and ample parking—but be warned: weekends during fishing season may see hundreds of fishermen dropping lines through the ice or from the lakeshore.

THE ROUTE:

From the trailhead, follow the Hurd Peak (Route 82) approach to the south end of the lake (about a mile) and then follow the approach for Mount Gilbert (Route 84) to the bench (11,600 feet) below Mount Gilbert and Mount Thompson. From here you'll have a great view of the north couloir of Mount Gilbert to the south, but the Thompson chutes will still be just out of view to the west.

Continue south to the end of the bench, then head west up the mellow, rolling terrain and shortly leave the Mount Gilbert route to continue west to the base of the Thompson chutes (12,200 feet). The climber's-left chute typically offers the easiest passage to the ridge and is also the mellowest of the three chutes to ski down. Skin up as high as you can, then switch to boot-packing as it becomes narrower and steeper. Once you're on the ridge, the summit is about 0.5 mile and a few hundred vertical feet to the west. Other than standing on the summit and checking out the amazing view of the Evolution group and Sabrina basin to the north, there is no real benefit for skiers to summit Mount Thompson.

The other two chutes drop in off the ridge just a couple hundred feet west of the one you climbed. While all the chutes on Thompson have steep entrances, both the middle and the skier's-left chutes have special considerations, so scout them from the bottom and the top before attempting them. The middle chute occasionally doesn't fill in completely, often leaving a small but mandatory cliff to negotiate about 100 feet down. The skier's-left chute is frequently guarded by a cornice, making entry from the top extremely difficult, sometimes impossible. When that is the case, those looking to ski it may want to climb up it as high as they can.

All three of these lines are about 1000 vertical feet long, so after your descent, head back up for another lap, or simply reverse your route to return to the parking area. South Lake may be less frozen in the afternoon than it was in the morning, so choose your return route accordingly.

Options: An alternate chute drops in farther west along the ridge toward Mount Thompson's summit, hidden in a cleft in the peak's massive cliff face. To reach it, continue west under the Trident Couloirs for another 0.25 mile until you can see up this challenging line, then boot up it to the top. Those with a little extra energy may want to consider doing multiple laps or checking out the steep north couloir of Mount Gilbert (Route 84) right next door.

Opposite: *Dropping into 3000 vertical feet of perfect corn snow on Mount Keith*

PART V
SOUTHERN SIERRA

AS YOU MAKE YOUR WAY SOUTH of Bishop via US Highway 395, the mountains get progressively taller and the vertical relief from summit to valley increases in kind. The scale of the mountains can be hard to grasp, as many of the summits tower some 10,000 vertical feet above Owens Valley. With the exception of Mount Shasta in the southern Cascades and White Mountain to the east of Bishop, all of California's 14,000-plus-foot peaks are located in this part of the range, including Mount Whitney, the highest summit in the contiguous forty-eight states. South of Mount Langley, the southernmost fourteen-thousand-footer in the Sierra, the range begins to taper off dramatically down to its southern end.

By now you've probably noticed that this book lacks descriptions of routes on the western slope of the Sierra. While there is an endless sea of mountains and fabulous descents waiting for adventurous backcountry travelers out there, getting to them is far from easy or convenient. In contrast to the precipitous eastern slope of the range and the relative ease of access on that side, the western slope rises quite gradually from the Central Valley, and very few roads are open in the winter to get you anywhere near the incredible bounty of skiable terrain. Most of the roads that do climb into the western slope are closed in winter and typically don't reopen until very late in the spring or early summer, and even then most of the objectives are still quite far from the trailheads and often require overnight trips to reach them. Due to the difficult access on this side of the Sierra, it is generally off the radar for most backcountry skiers in the state.

In Sequoia National Park, however, the Pear Lake Ski Hut is one spot in the southwestern Sierra that is accessible all winter long and a fabulous place to stay and explore this unique and wonderful part of the range. Day trips are possible into this zone, but the long approach lends itself well to spending the night at the hut and enjoying the wealth of intermediate to advanced terrain in the area. The hut is available by reservation only, and details are listed in the route's description.

While it is not described in this guidebook, Yosemite National Park's Ostrander Hut is another way to experience backcountry skiing on the western slope of the Sierra, although the ski terrain is relatively limited in comparison to that of the Pear Lake Hut. There are also rare occasions when a number of lines may become skiable within the Yosemite Valley, though they are quite steep and challenging, and the window to experience them is quite short due to their low elevation.

SOUTHERN SIERRA

Backcountry adventures in the southern stretch of the Sierra often involve a significant amount of mileage and vertical gain. While most of the routes described in this section can be completed in a day, quite often they are well suited to an overnight trip, potentially involving numerous peaks and descents. How long it takes to complete these routes varies wildly based on snow coverage, conditions, weather, and the fitness of you and your group.

Three small towns dot US Highway 395 in the Owens Valley to the east far below these majestic mountains. From north to south, Big Pine, Independence, and Lone Pine sit a short distance apart at the foot of the southeastern slope of the Sierra. Each town has basic necessities, including gas, general stores, and a small restaurant or two. Each town also serves as an access point to some of the biggest and least crowded backcountry in the state.

From the town of Big Pine, Glacier Lodge Road heads west, climbing more than 4000 vertical feet to Glacier Lodge and Big Pine Creek trailhead (7825 feet), which is used to access routes on and around the Palisade Crest. This road is cleared of snow all year, although sometimes a bit shy of the road end, providing some of the best midwinter and spring access in the southern part of the range. McMurry Meadows Road, accessed from Glacier Lodge Road, runs north-south along the base of the mountains. McMurry Meadows Road is not maintained in winter but opens up as snow coverage allows to get to the starting points of routes such as Birch Mountain and Mount Tinemaha.

From Independence, Onion Valley Road cuts west into the mountains and whisks backcountry users as high as Onion Valley and the Kearsarge Pass trailhead (9200 feet) when it is clear of snow in the spring. Onion Valley Road is not maintained in winter, although you can usually drive to the snow line throughout the winter, cutting down on the approach significantly. Foothill Road, accessed from Onion Valley Road, is a dirt road that runs north-south along the base of the eastern slope and accesses the Shepherd Pass trailhead and Bairs Creek farther south.

From Lone Pine, Whitney Portal Road climbs west to the Whitney Portal trailhead (approximately 8000 feet). In winter this road is not maintained and has a soft closure quite far from the trailhead, at 6500 feet. Most of the time you can drive as far up this road as snow allows, often getting quite close to the trailhead. Once the road is clear of snow in spring, it provides easy access to Mount Whitney and a number of other excellent routes in this spectacular part of the range. Horseshoe Meadows Road, which is accessed from Whitney Portal Road just west of the Alabama Hills, heads south to reach the trailhead for Mount Langley.

Visalia and Fresno are the two nearest cities used to access the southwestern Sierra. Both cities are situated on CA 99, which runs north-south through California's Central Valley. You can find everything you could ever possibly need in either city on your way to or from a trip in this region, and a number of smaller towns as you head east along the way also have necessities like food and fuel.

In the late spring, the Kings Canyon Highway (CA 180) to Cedar Grove and Roads End in Kings Canyon National Park and Mineral King Road off CA 198 into Sequoia National Park are cleared of snow and provide access to a number of remote peaks. Although none of these routes are described in detail in this section, a great amount of terrain, and especially overnight tours, can be accessed from these roads when conditions allow.

There is no regular avalanche advisory for the mountains in the southern Sierra or on the western slope of the Sierra—for general weather conditions, visit the website of the National Weather Service (see Resources). Road conditions within Yosemite and Kings Canyon–Sequoia national parks can be checked on the National Park Service website (see Resources).

86   Kid Mountain

Starting Point	Glacier Lodge, 7825 feet
High Point	11,834 feet
Distance	4 miles
Elevation Gain	4314 feet
Time	4 hours
Difficulty Level	Strenuous
Terrain Rating	3
Aspects	North, northwest
Seasons	Winter, spring
Maps	USGS Split Mountain; Coyote Flat

Glacier Lodge Road offers some of the easiest winter access to skiing in the Sierra south of Bishop. Just west of Big Pine, Glacier Lodge Road whisks skiers 4000 vertical feet above the Owens Valley up into the Big Pine Creek drainage. One of the most easily accessed peaks from the top of this road is Kid Mountain. Sitting just east of the Sierra crest and some of the biggest peaks in the John Muir Wilderness range, Kid Mountain is often passed by for more sought-after descents in the area, but its north face holds a number of excellent 4000-vertical-foot gullies that rise up right from the

The massive north-facing gullies of Kid Mountain (center) rise 4000 vertical feet above Glacier Lodge Road.

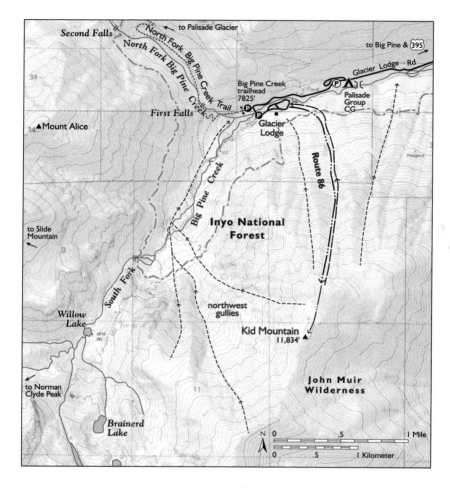

road. Simply pick the one you want to ski and climb up it. These moderately pitched gullies are prime ski terrain and one of the easiest midwinter and spring objectives in the southern Sierra. This is a great "short" descent, relative to nearby mountains, a great place to familiarize yourself with the rest of the bigger descents in this area. Kid Mountain also hides a number of other northwest-facing gullies just around the corner above the South Fork of Big Pine Creek.

GETTING THERE

From Big Pine on US Highway 395, turn west onto West Crocker Avenue and follow it for 0.5 mile until it turns into Glacier Lodge Road. Continue heading west on Glacier Lodge Road, uphill, for 9.9 miles to the Big Pine Creek trailhead, then turn left toward Glacier Lodge, cross the creek, and park as far east as you can to get closer to the bottom of the face. If you can't make it all the way to the trailhead by vehicle, follow the road to this point. If you plan to ski any of the gullies farther east than the main route described here, park at the Palisade Group campground about 0.9 mile east of Glacier Lodge, where a footbridge crosses the creek.

THE ROUTE

All you really need to do is find and climb the gully that suits your fancy. The first gully east of the parking area is one of the finest, and it tops out the highest on the summit ridge; it is also the easiest and fastest way to the top of Kid Mountain. This gully is the main ascent route described here. From the parking area, head east, contouring as you climb for less than 0.25 mile. Soon you will be in the bottom of this massive gully. From here it is about 4000 vertical feet straight up the gully to the top, and the slope gets progressively steeper as you ascend, so it may be necessary to switch from skinning to boot-packing as you near the top. At the top of the gully, you are a short distance south of the summit, which is a relatively flat, optional out-and-back for those hoping to reach the highest point.

Take in the amazing views of some of the biggest and most impressive peaks in the range: Birch Mountain (Route 91), Middle Palisade, Mount Sill, and the Palisade Crest are all nearby. Head back down the gully of your choice for 4000 vertical feet of fall-line skiing back to the parking area.

Options: From the alternate parking at the campground, cross the creek on the footbridge and head up- or downstream to access the bottom of any of the gullies on Kid Mountain's north face. A handful of northwest-facing gullies are also located on the flanks of Kid Mountain a short distance up the South Fork of Big Pine Creek. To access them, park at the Big Pine Creek trailhead, then head southwest along the South Fork of Big Pine Creek for about 1.25 miles to the bottom of the northwest gullies, which top out in various places, including near the summit and up to around 12,500 feet.

87 North Palisade: U-notch; Polemonium Peak: V-notch

Starting Point	Big Pine Creek trailhead, 7825 feet
High Point	14,000 feet
Distance	16 miles
Elevation Gain	6200 feet
Time	One very long day to 2 days
Difficulty Level	Very strenuous
Terrain Rating	4
Aspect	North-northwest
Seasons	Winter, spring, early summer
Maps	USGS Coyote Flat; Split Mountain; Mount Thompson; North Palisade

Hiking over the moraine toward the Palisade Glacier and the U-notch (right) and the V-notch (left)

The Palisades region is home to several of California's 14,000-plus-foot peaks and a number of super classic ski routes. Situated on the Sierra crest north of Kings Canyon National Park, about midway between Mount Sill and Thunderbolt Peak, and framing Polemonium Peak, the U-notch and the V-notch are two such lines that have drawn backcountry skiers and snowboarders to this area for decades. Named for the distinctive shapes of the notches in the ridge at the top of each couloir, both offer some legitimately steep north-facing skiing from the ridge of the Palisade Crest down to the Palisade Glacier. The V-notch is considered to be located on Polemonium Peak, while depending which guidebook you look at, the U-notch is said to be located on either the North Palisade or Polemonium Peak. Since the top of the U-notch creates the low spot in the ridge between the two summits, I choose to say that it is on both peaks. The V-notch is known for being the steeper of the two couloirs and one of the classic extreme descents of the Sierra. The U-notch is tamer than the V-notch, but at only a few degrees less steep in pitch, it is still plenty challenging. Both couloirs are also prone to having exposed ice and may also have a gaping bergschrund that opens up in the spring. Single-day trips into this area deep in John Muir Wilderness are possible, but the distance to get here and the wealth of terrain in the North Fork of Big Pine Creek drainage makes this zone worthy of an overnight trip.

GETTING THERE

From Big Pine on US Highway 395, turn west onto West Crocker Avenue and follow it for 0.5 mile until it turns into Glacier Lodge Road. Continue heading west on

Glacier Lodge Road, uphill, for 9.9 miles until it ends at a locked gate and the Big Pine Creek trailhead; park here. If you can't make it all the way to the trailhead by vehicle, follow the road to this point.

THE ROUTE

From the trailhead, follow the summer trail west past the summer cabins and take the first right, onto the North Fork Big Pine Creek Trail. The route from the trailhead up to First Lake may vary slightly based on snow coverage, but fortunately, this trail is quite pleasant to hike when coverage is poor below 10,000 feet. If there is snow, generally follow the trail as it parallels the North Fork of Big Pine Creek; if there isn't snow, simply take the trail. Follow this trail north as it switchbacks up the hill past First Falls. Where the trail intersects an old road, go right on this road and cross the creek on a bridge. Continue north up this old road for 0.75 mile, following signs for the North Fork trail.

The trail begins to climb more steadily toward the John Muir Wilderness boundary at Second Falls. Once you pass Second Falls, the trail mellows out and heads west, wrapping around the north side of Mount Alice. About 0.6 mile after Second Falls you pass the Big Pine Creek Ranger Station. Continue along the trail as it heads southwest on its gradual climb toward First Lake.

At a trail junction at 3.8 miles from the trailhead, turn left to head south to First Lake. First, Second, and Third lakes are all great places to camp if you are spending the night in this area. There is plenty of flat ground, and it is likely that you can even find some dry ground or rock for a comfortable campsite. If the lakes are frozen solid, it is easiest to hike across them, following the drainage from First Lake (9961 feet) up to Second Lake (10,089 feet) and then up to Third Lake (10,269 feet), about 5 miles from the start. If the lakes are not frozen solid, continue on the trail as it skirts above and west of First and Second lakes up to Third Lake.

At Third Lake, you leave the trail to head south up the massive gully at the base of Temple Crag's northwest face. Over the course of a mile, you gain 2000 vertical feet as you climb to the moraine at the toe of the Palisade Glacier below Mount Gayley. As you approach the moraine, head west and contour up along the top of the moraine toward Thunderbolt Peak, gaining nearly 400 vertical feet over the next 0.5 mile to the low spot in the moraine (12,231 feet). From here, head south, directly toward the line of your choice, while climbing gradually up the Palisade Glacier just west of Mount Gayley and Mount Sill. It is nearly a mile from the moraine to the base of the couloirs—an easy mile with about 1000 vertical feet of gain. Hike to the couloir of your choice and switch to boot-packing with crampons and an ice axe to climb either couloir to the ridge.

Take in the amazing views in all directions and gather yourself for the steep descent back down to the glacier; beware of the bergschrund near the bottom of either couloir during your ascent and descent. From the glacier, return over the moraine and down the large gully to Third Lake and eventually return the way you came to get back to the trailhead.

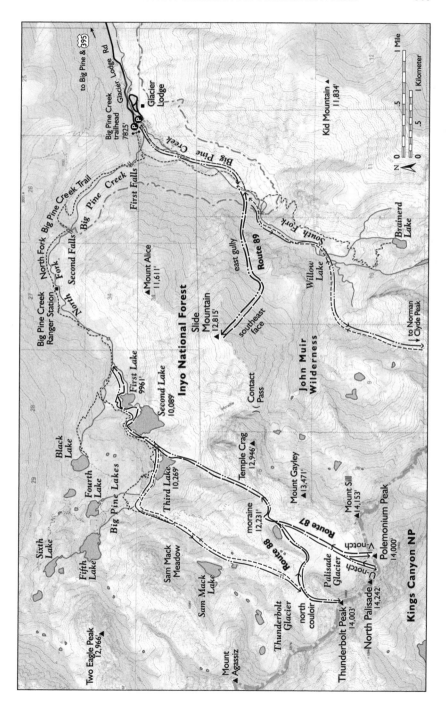

Options: Once you are up here, it is relatively quick to do multiple laps, and skiing both of the notches in a single day is quite possible. Also be sure to check out the northwest couloir on Mount Sill or the north couloir of Thunderbolt Peak (Route 88).

88 Thunderbolt Peak

Starting Point	Big Pine Creek trailhead, 7825 feet
High Point	14,003 feet
Distance	16 miles
Elevation Gain	6200 feet
Time	One very long day to 2 days
Difficulty Level	Very strenuous
Terrain Rating	4
Aspect	North-northwest
Seasons	Winter, spring, early summer
Maps	USGS Coyote Flat; Split Mountain; Mount Thompson; North Palisade

Thunderbolt Peak sits on the Sierra crest on the boundary of Kings Canyon National Park, just northwest of North Palisade, above the Thunderbolt and Palisade glaciers. Named for a close encounter with lightning on the first ascent of the mountain long ago, Thunderbolt Peak has a fine north-facing chute that tops out on the ridge near the hard-to-reach summit. The north face remains relatively hidden from view until you wrap around onto the Thunderbolt Glacier and are right beneath it. This 1000-vertical-foot chute is less steep than the neighboring U-notch and V-notch (Route 87), although it is more likely to fill in during a low snow year. This chute is one of many reasons to spend a few nights back in this area of John Muir Wilderness skiing the multitude of classic lines in this rugged and beautiful part of the range. Thunderbolt Peak can be skied in a day by those who like to suffer, but a more casual overnight approach to this area is definitely preferred.

GETTING THERE
From Big Pine on US Highway 395, turn west onto West Crocker Avenue and follow it for 0.5 mile until it turns into Glacier Lodge Road. Continue heading west on Glacier Lodge Road, uphill, for 9.9 miles until it ends at a locked gate and the Big Pine Creek trailhead; park here. If you can't get all the way to the trailhead by vehicle, follow the road to this point.

THE ROUTE
From the trailhead, follow the approach for North Palisade and Polemonium Peak (Route 87) to Third Lake, at about 5 miles from the start. From here you continue on the path of Route 87, but you also have an option.

Taking a break below the Thunderbolt Glacier and the north couloir of Thunderbolt Peak

Option: From Third Lake you can approach Thunderbolt Peak by heading west from the lake, then turn southwest and ascend the drainage up to Sam Mack Meadow, Sam Mack Lake, and eventually up to the Thunderbolt Glacier. (This alternate approach route is equally suitable on the way out of this zone.)

The main route continues from Third Lake to the low spot in the moraine below the Palisade Glacier at 12,231 feet. Head southwest from the moraine, eventually cutting over the far west side of the moraine and traversing around the northeast ridge of Thunderbolt Peak and onto the Thunderbolt Glacier. As you traverse onto the glacier, you'll begin to see up the north couloir. Skin as high as you can up the apron to the base of the chute. Be on the lookout for a bergschrund in this area that tends to open up in the spring. Eventually switch to boot-packing for the rest of the climb up to the ridge at the top of the chute. Take in the jaw-dropping views of nearby peaks: Mount Winchell, Mount Agassiz, Cloudripper to the north, and the sea of mountains to the west.

Depending on the season's snowpack, the upper part of the north face may have a variety of ways down it that all converge into one exit at the bottom of the face. From the bottom of the apron below the chute, make your way back up to the moraine below the Palisade Glacier, then wrap back around to the east and the large gully that drops north back down to Third Lake. From Third Lake head back down the way you came, following the trail paralleling the North Fork of Big Pine Creek back down to the trailhead.

89 Slide Mountain

Starting Point	Big Pine Creek trailhead, 7825 feet
High Point	12,815 feet
Distance	6.5 miles
Elevation Gain	5000 feet
Time	4 hours
Difficulty Level	Strenuous
Terrain Rating	3
Aspect	East-southeast
Seasons	Winter, spring
Maps	USGS Coyote Flat; Split Mountain

Slide Mountain, sometimes known as Contact Peak, sits on the ridgeline that separates the South and North forks of Big Pine Creek, between Mount Alice and Temple Crag and just east of Contact Pass. While it isn't officially named on maps of the area, Slide Mountain offers some prime southeast-facing ski terrain in one of the most beautiful parts of the range. At 5000 vertical feet of gain and only 3.25 miles one way, Slide Mountain is a short and easy day trip relative to the other objectives in the immediate area. Don't be discouraged if there is no snow at the parking area, as a trail makes for a nice approach with no bushwhacking to the base of this route. Slide Mountain's massive southeast-facing upper ramp is perfect corn harvesting terrain that leads to a wide and long east-facing gully, which drops down to the South Fork of Big Pine Creek. The views from the summit are hard to beat: Thunderbolt Peak, Polemonium Peak, North Palisade, and Mount Sill to the west; Norman Clyde Peak and Middle Palisade to the south; and Kid Mountain to the east. This is a great route for corn skiing on solar aspects, for those looking for a "short" day out of Glacier Lodge, or for familiarizing yourself with the amazing terrain in this part of John Muir Wilderness.

GETTING THERE

From Big Pine on US Highway 395, turn west onto West Crocker Avenue and follow it for 0.5 mile until it turns into Glacier Lodge Road. Continue heading west on Glacier Lodge Road, uphill, for 9.9 miles until it ends at a locked gate and the Big Pine Creek trailhead; park here. If you can't make it all the way to the trailhead by vehicle, follow the road to this point.

THE ROUTE

From the trailhead, head southwest into the drainage of the South Fork of Big Pine Creek. Take the summer trail if snow coverage is poor, following signs for the South Fork Trail (the North Fork Trail heads up into the Palisade Glacier area (Routes 87 and 88). In just over 1 mile you gain approximately 700 vertical feet and reach the bottom of the east-facing gully. Climb this gully for 2200 vertical feet, and when you top out you will be on the massive southeast face that leads to the summit of Slide Mountain.

Dropping into perfect corn snow from the summit of Slide Mountain (Oscar Havens)

Wrap around to the south and onto the main upper southeast face, then begin the long ascent to the summit, 2000 vertical feet above. In the right conditions it may be possible to skin all the way up this face. From the top, take in the expansive views of the Palisade Crest and surrounding area, and take note of all the incredible terrain and approaches to various other ski objectives.

Drop in for 2000 vertical feet of perfectly pitched open terrain, then be sure to wrap back to the north to the top of the large gully you ascended. Drop down the huge east-facing gully for 2200 vertical feet, ending back where you started your ascent. Head northeast down the South Fork of Big Pine Creek drainage to return to the parking area.

90 Norman Clyde Peak

Starting Point	Big Pine Creek trailhead, 7825 feet
High Points	Top of couloir, 13,376 feet
Distance	10 miles
Elevation Gains	Top of couloir, 5600 feet
Time	7 hours
Difficulty Level	Very strenuous
Terrain Rating	4
Aspect	North-northeast
Seasons	Winter, spring
Maps	USGS Coyote Flat; Split Mountain

Norman Clyde Peak is a stunning mountain that sits along the crest of the Sierra just north of Kings Canyon National Park and Middle Palisade, above both the Norman Clyde and Middle Palisade glaciers. It is named in honor of the famed Sierra mountaineer who in 1930 first climbed the peak and is credited with as many as 130 other first ascents. Norman Clyde Peak is an aesthetic summit in one of the most beautiful and rugged parts of the range, a fitting tribute to this pioneer of Sierra mountain climbing. The north couloir of Norman Clyde Peak remains relatively hidden from view on the mountain's north side, except from neighboring Slide Mountain (Route 89), until you are in the drainage directly beneath it. If snow coverage is poor, a summer trail makes for easy access with no bushwhacking to get into this area; if there is snow coverage at the trailhead, this route is significantly easier and quicker than when you have to walk on dirt to the snow line, but it is worth the effort either way. This beautiful 1000-vertical-foot couloir looks impressively steep from a distance but is less steep than it looks, and it empties onto a perfectly pitched apron for another 1300 vertical feet down to the moraine far below. The chute tops out at a col in the ridge well below the summit with amazing views into some of the most remote mountains in the range. There are much steeper runs to be taken in this part of John Muir Wilderness, but many who have skied this route consider it one of the most enjoyable.

The view of Norman Clyde Peak from halfway up neighboring Slide Mountain

GETTING THERE

From Big Pine on US Highway 395, turn west onto West Crocker Avenue and follow it for 0.5 mile until it turns into Glacier Lodge Road. Continue heading west on Glacier Lodge Road, uphill, for 9.9 miles until it ends at a locked gate and the Big Pine Creek trailhead; park here. If you can't make it all the way to the trailhead by vehicle, follow the road to this point.

THE ROUTE

From the trailhead, the approach routes differ slightly depending on low-elevation snow coverage, but both approaches converge at Willow Lake.

Good snow at the trailhead: If there is snow, head southwest from the parking area and parallel the South Fork of Big Pine Creek for 1.3 miles and around 800 feet of vertical gain. If there is good snow coverage on the lower southeast face of Slide Mountain, simply hike a direct line southwest up into the drainage that comes out from Willow Lake, reaching the lake in another 0.8 mile and 900 vertical feet of gain.

No snow at the trailhead: You may want to start this adventure in sneakers, as you will probably want them for the hike back down. Rather than following the direct line up the creek all the way to Willow Lake, take the summer trail southwest past the locked gate and summer cabins, following signs for the trail as it crosses the North Fork of Big Pine Creek, and continue heading southwest into the South Fork of Big Pine Creek drainage. Follow the trail southwest, switching to skis and skins if coverage allows, for 1.8 miles and 1000 vertical feet to the John Muir Wilderness boundary sign at the bottom of a steep headwall, just east of the drainage that comes out of Willow

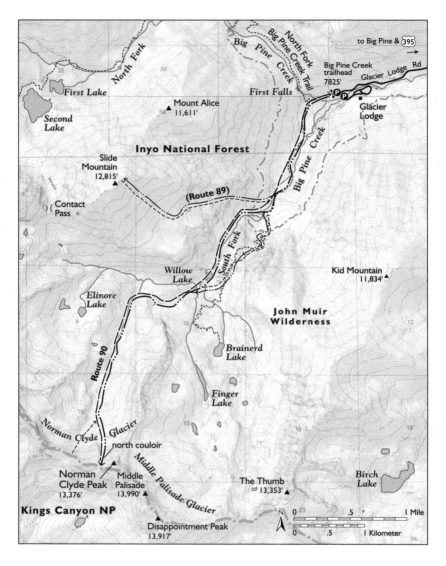

Lake. Head up this steep face on the west side of Kid Mountain, either on the trail or on snow, for 0.75 mile and 1000 vertical feet, to the crest of the ridge above Willow Lake. Make your way down to Willow Lake, losing about 300 vertical feet.

From Willow Lake (9554 feet), the two approaches converge and the route becomes more straightforward. Head west-southwest, gradually gaining elevation over the course of a mile as you wrap around the end of Norman Clyde Peak's north ridge and south into the Norman Clyde Glacier drainage. Once in this drainage, the route becomes incredibly obvious. As you ascend, the north couloir will come into view towering high above. Simply head south and up this drainage for another mile and approximately 1000 vertical feet to the moraine below the Norman Clyde Glacier (11,100 feet). From here the entirety of the run will be in view as will another short chute, a mellower alternative to the north couloir, that drops in from the lowest col just north along the ridge.

Continue south from the moraine, steadily gaining vertical as you climb the massive apron to the base of the north couloir. After 1200 vertical feet or so, near the base of the couloir, be on the lookout for a bergschrund that typically opens up in the spring. Switch to boot-packing and kick steps directly up the north couloir to the col at the top.

Take in the expansive views to the west, and prepare for one of the most fun descents in the Palisades region. Once you are out of the walled confines of the couloir, the apron offers more perfectly pitched turns down to the moraine below.

After your descent, head north down the drainage, wrapping around the ridge east down to Willow Lake. Depending on the coverage, you may be able to cruise out the creek drainage from Willow Lake, or you may have to hike back up and over the ridge and back down to the summer trail. Basically, return the way you came based on the current coverage and conditions.

91   Birch Mountain

Starting Point	McMurry Meadows, 6440 feet
High Point	13,685 feet
Distance	7 miles
Elevation Gain	7200 feet
Time	6 hours
Difficulty Level	Very strenuous
Terrain Rating	3
Aspects	Southeast, east
Seasons	Winter, spring
Maps	USGS Split Mountain; Fish Springs

My best description of Birch Mountain is that it is the Mount Shasta of the southern Sierra. This massive mountain stands relatively alone in front of the Sierra crest in John Muir Wilderness, its summit looming 9000-plus feet above the town of Big Pine. Birch's broad, moderate southeast face makes for one of the longest pitches in the range and an incredibly fun run. Timing is important on Birch Mountain, and being there with coverage to McMurry Meadows is ideal, but a short walk through sagebrush at the bottom can usually be expected when the road is clear enough to drive there. The southeast slope of Birch also has the perfect aspect for growing corn when other routes in the area may be firm or icy. Often overlooked due to its taller and more famous neighbors, like Split Mountain (Route 92) and North Palisade (Route 87), Birch Mountain has great views and excellent moderate ski terrain.

GETTING THERE

From Big Pine on US Highway 395, at the traffic light turn west onto West Crocker Avenue and follow it for 0.5 mile until it turns into Glacier Lodge Road. Continue west on Glacier Lodge Road, uphill, for approximately 2.6 miles to the junction with McMurry Meadows Road. Turn left (south) on McMurry Meadows Road; high-clearance our-wheel-drive recommended on this dirt road. At about 2.5 miles, at a four-way intersection, continue straight, uphill. The road switchbacks through Birch Creek, then heads south through McMurry Meadows to the south end of the meadows. Where McMurry Meadows Road begins to drop downhill to the southeast, there is a fork; follow the fork to the right and park, approximately 3 miles from Glacier Lodge Road. From here the summit of Birch Mountain towers 7200 feet above you to the west. If you can't drive to this point, get as close as you can by vehicle before parking. From the crossing of Birch Creek (6200 feet), you can hike generally southwest uphill through McMurry Meadows to start this route. This parking area can also be approached as for Split Mountain (Route 92) by following McMurry Meadows Road from the south.

THE ROUTE

From the parking area, head west through the meadow, following an old double track up a gentle hill. At the second meadow, get off the double track and continue heading west through the meadows and into the sagebrush. Continue west and aim for

Dropping into corn snow on one of Birch Mountain's south-facing ramps

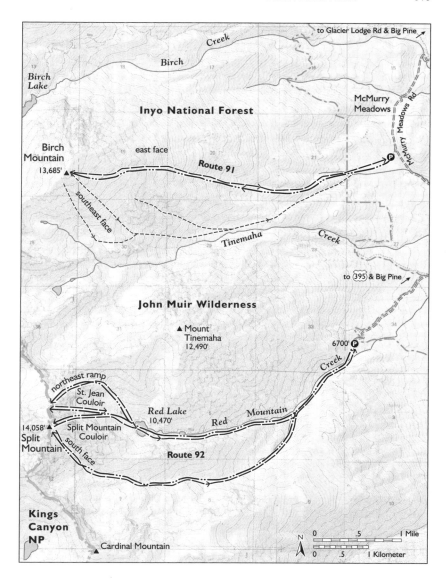

one of the prominent gullies at the base of the southeast slope. These gullies often hold snow, making for easier walking, on their north-facing (climber's-left) side. At about 8000 feet, the gullies open up to the east face, and your route to the top will be very apparent.

The top of the mountain looks deceptively close from here, but it still lies more than 5000 vertical feet above. Continue up the huge east face, aiming for the highest point that now connects to the ridge above you: the trio of short gullies at the top of the slope. As the slope steepens, it may be necessary to switch to boot-packing, but be sure to leave your skins on; you may want to skin the moderate slopes from the top of this ridge to the summit. Once you gain the southeast ridge, at around 12,000 feet, the moderate southeast ramp sits before you, your route to the summit.

Cross over onto the massive southeast-facing ramp and skin the mellow pitch up to the summit. While it is a pretty moderate slope, it's all above 12,000 feet, so it takes a bit more effort than you'd think to finish the climb. The summit of Birch is an incredible vantage point to take in the Palisades region to the northwest, Mount Bolton Brown and Split Mountain to the southwest, and Mount Tinemaha to the southeast.

Drop into the southeast slope, and follow it back down to the point where you crossed over the ridge from the east face. Wrap over the ridge and descend the east face all the way back down to McMurry Meadows.

Options: On a mountain as big as Birch, there are plenty of other ways down it. The broad upper southeast face leads down to a number of gullies below it that have the potential to go through, although due to their aspect and elevation they may not always fill in. Be sure to scope them before you summit to check out this adventurous route down into the Tinemaha Creek drainage. Those with a keen eye and great routefinding skills may enjoy doing some exploring on this eastern Sierra giant.

Mount Tinemaha, Birch's neighbor to the south, sits directly east of Split Mountain and also has a number of beautiful east-facing gullies that are worthy of exploration when coverage allows.

92　Split Mountain

Starting Point	Red Lake trailhead, 6700 feet
High Point	14,058 feet
Distance	9 miles
Elevation Gain	7358 feet
Time	One very long day to 2 days
Difficulty Level	Very strenuous
Terrain Ratings	St. Jean Couloir, northeast ramp, and south face 4; Split Mountain Couloir 5
Aspects	Northeast, east, southeast
Seasons	Winter, spring
Maps	USGS Split Mountain; Fish Springs

Split Mountain, the eighth-highest mountain in California, is home to several fine descents, the most well known and coveted being the classic northeast couloir, which drops from the saddle in the mountain's twin summits that split the northeast face above Red Lake. This aesthetic line tips the extreme scale with a large cliff at the bottom that must be negotiated on the way both up and down. Global ski icon and

Skiing corn snow at 14,000 feet from Split Mountain's south summit

Sierra skiing legend Glen Plake is credited with the first ski descent of the northeast couloir. Good coverage, as well as ice climbing and rappeling skills, is an absolute must for attempting this committing line. Fortunately for the less extreme skier, there are several other ways up and down this mountain in John Muir Wilderness on the edge of Kings Canyon National Park. The narrow St. Jean Couloir splits a clean line from the summit ridge down the cliffy face a short distance north of the northeast couloir, and the northeast ramp of the mountain rolls into a couple of short, steep chutes that wrap back around down toward Red Lake. A massive and beautiful southeast-facing ramp drops down from the mountain's south summit, a great option during extended periods of high pressure when there is good snow coverage. Getting to the Red Lake trailhead can often be a challenge for many people; while it looks relatively straightforward on a map, a number of somewhat confusing turns tend to lead people awry, so it is much easier to find your way here during daylight. While the distance from the nearest trailhead isn't all that daunting, with more than 7000 vertical feet of elevation gain an ascent of Split Mountain is by no means easy. Fit parties may be able to complete this route in a single day, while others may opt for a more casual overnight trip.

GETTING THERE

From Big Pine, head south on US Highway 395 for 4.6 miles. Turn right onto Fish Springs Road and continue south for 2.1 miles. Turn right onto Tinemaha Road and follow it south for 1.7 miles. At the Tinemaha campground, turn right onto Fuller Road and head west for 2.4 miles. At the gravel pit and old abandoned mine, take the first major right turn and follow this road for 1.1 miles as it wraps around north, skirting private land, and continues west to a junction with McMurry Meadows Road. Go around two old gates and take a hard left after the second gate.

You can also get to this point from Big Pine on US 395 by turning west at the traffic light onto West Crocker Avenue and following it for 0.5 mile until it turns into Glacier Lodge Road. Continue west on Glacier Lodge Road, uphill, for approximately 2.6 miles to the junction with McMurry Meadows Road and follow McMurry Meadows Road south for 8.9 miles. Turn left to continue head south on McMurry Meadows Road for 0.7 mile, then reach the junction with Tinemaha Road; turn right onto Tinemaha Road.

From either approach, follow Tinemaha Road west and uphill for 1.1 miles until it splits; bear left at the fork and continue uphill for another mile to the mouth of the Red Mountain Creek drainage and the Red Lake trailhead. At the end of the road it splits one more time, and which way you turn depends on the snow coverage. **Trail start:** If snow coverage is poor at this elevation, turn right and head to the top of the north parking area, where the Red Lake trailhead is actually located. **Creek start:** If there's decent snow coverage at this elevation, turn left and head down to the south parking area to start in the creek drainage. If there is snow before the trailhead, make your way along the road to this point.

THE ROUTE

Creek start: If there is decent snow coverage near the trailhead parking area, start from the south parking area and contour southwest into the Red Mountain Creek drainage. Cross the creek and follow it southwest for 0.8 mile until the drainage splits.

Trail start: If snow coverage is poor near the trailhead parking area, start from the north parking area and follow the summer trail as it climbs a bit, then descends to this same point where the drainage splits.

From here, the route up Split Mountain varies depending on your chosen descent: The Red Mountain Creek drainage up to Red Lake leads to the northeast couloir, the St. Jean Couloir, and the northeast ramp. The other (more southerly) drainage leads up to Cardinal Mountain and the south face of Split Mountain.

Red Mountain Creek approach: Continue heading west up the Red Mountain Creek drainage, gaining elevation much more steadily. The south (climber's-left) side of the drainage will likely hold more snow and provide for easier passage as you ascend. After another 1.75 miles and 2800 vertical feet or so, you arrive at Red Lake (10,470 feet). This is a great place to camp if you are doing this route as an overnight.

At the lake you'll be able to see the steep, narrow confines of the St. Jean Couloir, but the northeast couloir remains hidden behind rock walls. From Red Lake, head west-northwest for 2000 vertical feet to reach the bottom of both couloirs, which are relatively close together above what remains of the Split Mountain Glacier.

Split Mountain Couloir: From the bottom of the northeast couloir, climb a few hundred feet of mixed ice, rock, and snow to the crux: a cliff that guards this beautiful run at its base; as you both climb and descend, you are exposed above it the entire time. The couloir tops out in the saddle between the two summits of Split Mountain. This is the classic descent of Split Mountain, and the cliff must be negotiated with an ice climb on the way up and a mandatory rappel on the way down.

St. Jean Couloir: From the bottom of this couloir, ascending it is a bit more straightforward than for the northeast couloir. The St. Jean Couloir tops out on the ridge just north and a few hundred feet shy of the summit. Finding this couloir in good condition, however, can be a challenge. The couloir's east-facing aspect and rock walls leave a short time window for sun on this line; time it right, though, and you can have an amazing run down this gorgeous narrow, steep chute.

Northeast ramp: For the least committing and most circuitous route to the summit of Split Mountain, from Red Lake head north-northwest, climbing gradually toward the east end of the prominent ridge that extends down from Split's summit. Wrap around the end of this ridge and continue west, climbing up and over a moraine and up one of the northeast-facing chutes and gullies that head up to the massive, moderate, north-facing ramp leading up to the summit. This upper slope is subject to strong winds and may often be wind scoured, but there are likely to be large snow patches to connect between the open talus and rock. Head back the way you came from the summit to return to Red Lake.

After any of these descents in this Red Lake zone, retrace your route back down the Red Mountain Creek drainage to return to your starting point.

South face approach: To reach the south face, from the fork in the drainage near the bottom of the main route, go up the southerly drainage toward Cardinal Mountain. Follow this drainage, climbing gradually, as it initially heads south and then west toward the moraines at the base of Cardinal Mountain's north face and the bottom of Split Mountain's south face. As you ascend around 4000 vertical feet over nearly 3 miles from the fork in the drainage to the base of the south face, you climb a series of benches and eventually a large moraine as you begin to head northwest up the face. Climb this large gully face for 2500 vertical feet to the high point, Split Mountain's south summit. It takes good coverage for the south face to be skiable, and it may not fill in every year, but when it does, it affords the opportunity to ski corn snow from the top of this 14,000-foot peak. Retrace your route to return to your starting point.

Option: Neighboring Cardinal Mountain also has a number of excellent north- and northeast-facing chutes that are worthy of exploration, and an overnight trip to this zone can be a great way to experience them.

93 Independence Peak

Starting Point : Onion Valley Road, 8000 feet
High Point : 11,722 feet
Distance : 3 miles
Elevation Gain : 3722 feet
Time : 3 hours
Difficulty Level : Moderate
Terrain Rating : 3
Aspect : Northeast
Seasons : Winter, spring
Map : USGS Kearsarge Peak

Independence Peak towers above the town of Independence and US Highway 395 in the Owens Valley. One of the shorter mountains in the area, Independence Peak sits on the easternmost edge of the Sierra just outside John Muir Wilderness, and its long northeast gullies are some of the most obvious and eye-catching ski lines in the

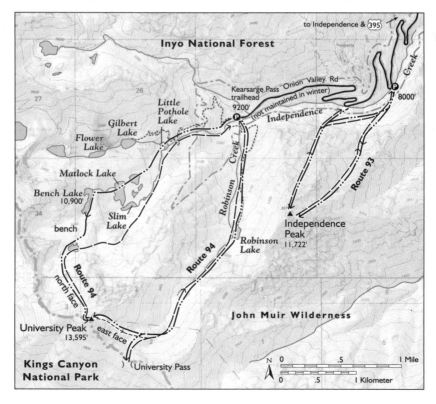

Topping out on the skier's-right gully on Independence Peak

area. Relatively speaking, this is a short and easy route, mainly because Independence Peak is situated in the land of the true southeastern Sierra giants; however, its moderately pitched gullies are more than 3000 vertical feet long. Two obvious north-northeast-facing gullies both drop from near the summit of Independence Peak, one on each side, offering great skiing. The northeast gully (skier's right) is slightly mellower in pitch while the more north-facing gully (skier's left) is just a little steeper. The gullies top out near the summit for a short scramble to the peak's highest point. This classic descent is relatively easy to access from Onion Valley Road, which rises as much as 5200 vertical feet from town. While this road is technically closed in winter (it is not maintained, but it isn't gated), it is passable to the snow line, so you can always drive as far up as snow coverage allows until the road is officially opened later in the spring. Quite often you can park right at the base of these incredible runs.

GETTING THERE

From downtown Independence on US 395, turn west onto West Market Street (Onion Valley Road). Follow the road uphill for 10 miles, watching for rocks and debris, to a switchback at 8000 feet (or higher up the road if it is clear) at the bottom of the northeast gullies of Independence Peak. Park out of harm's way from the frequent rockfall common in this area. Depending on snow coverage, you may not be able to drive to this point, so park lower down and follow the road or Independence Creek up to this point.

THE ROUTE

From the switchback in the road at 8000 feet, drop down and cross Independence Creek as soon as you can. If the snowpack is thin near the creek, it can be a mildly heinous bushwhack to start the route, but it is short lived.

After the crossing, begin to ascend gradually southwest to the line of your choice. The route up these gullies is quite straightforward. As you climb, the gullies get progressively steeper; skin as high as possible before switching to boot-packing if necessary near the top. It may be possible to skin all the way to the top in the right snow conditions.

At the top of either gully, it is a short scramble to reach the summit. Take in the amazing view of the surrounding peaks, some of which are among the highest in the range, and the dramatic relief down to the Owens Valley nearly 8000 vertical feet below. Drop in for 3000-plus vertical feet of goodness, then make your way back to your starting point.

94 University Peak

Starting Point	Kearsarge Pass trailhead, 9200 feet
High Point	13,595 feet
Distance	5.5 miles
Elevation Gain	4395 feet
Time	5 hours
Difficulty Level	Strenuous
Terrain Rating	3
Aspects	North-northeast, east
Seasons	Spring, early summer
Maps	USGS Kearsarge Peak; Mount Williamson

Mention the University of California (a.k.a. Cal) anywhere in the state of California and somebody within earshot is likely to say "Go Bears!" With as much Cal pride as there is in the state, it's no wonder that one of the peaks in the Sierra is named University Peak, after the University of California. The highest peak in the Kearsarge Pass area, University Peak sits just east of Kings Canyon National Park with a couple of excellent descents that drop either east or north from near its rocky summit. These routes both start in the same place but follow completely different drainages that are separated by a ridge extending northeast from University's summit. The large and moderately pitched north face, which remains almost entirely hidden from view until you are directly beneath it, is a Sierra classic, a great 2000-foot fall-line pitch in John Muir Wilderness. The Onion Valley Road is not maintained in winter, but it isn't gated either, so you can always drive to the snow line until the road melts out, which allows for good access to the numerous routes in the area. Once the road is cleared of snow and rocks in the spring (usually late April or May), however, you'll have even easier access to the wealth of terrain in the area.

Slashing into the top of University Peak's north face in late spring

GETTING THERE

From downtown Independence on US Highway 395, turn west onto West Market Street (Onion Valley Road). Settle in for the 13 miles of uphill driving and go easy on your car because you'll gain 5200 vertical feet of elevation. There is often rock debris on the road in the spring before it is maintained for the summer, so watch out as you drive up the switchbacks on the upper part of the road. Drive as far up Onion Valley Road as possible—ideally, all the way to the end of the road if snow conditions allow, and park at the Kearsarge Pass trailhead. Otherwise, drive up the road until it is blocked by snow or rockfall, and be sure to park off the road in a spot that isn't threatened by rockfall, then follow the road up to the trailhead.

THE ROUTE

North face: From the trailhead, head west and parallel Independence Creek, which drains the lakes between University Peak and Mount Gould. You climb 800 feet right out of the parking area and hit a small bench just below Little Pothole Lake. (If there isn't snow coverage at the trailhead, follow the summer trail as it switchbacks up to Little Pothole Lake.) From the lake, head southwest, climbing 500 vertical feet to Slim and Matlock lakes. Head west across the flats of the lakes and climb the short slope to Bench Lake (around 10,900 feet). Head southwest, climbing 500 vertical feet to the broad bench below the north face of University Peak.

Continue heading west until you are directly under the north face. As you climb the face, it starts out relatively mellow but gets steeper the higher you get, rising about 1800 vertical feet to connect with the ridge just west of the summit. Once you top out on the ridge, it's just a short scramble to the summit.

Head back down the way you came, but once you hit the bench at the bottom of the north face, traverse hard to the east (skier's right) for some short but fun shots through the cliffs above Slim Lake that were visible on the hike in.

East face: From the trailhead, head south into the Robinson Lake drainage. Hike along the path of Robinson Creek, paralleling the summer trail up to Robinson Lake, which sits below the steep western slope of Independence Peak. From here the route heads southwest up the creek drainage to the base of the east face. Head up the east face for about 1400 feet to the ridge just east of the peak. From here it is a short scramble to the summit. Reverse your route to return to the trailhead.

Options: Due to the east face route's exposure to the sun, it can often be burned off by the time the road is clear to the trailhead; if that is the case, this approach still offers some great skiing in the short chute that leads to University Pass, the low spot in the ridge at the head of the Robinson Creek drainage.

Other notable descents in the area are the northeast gullies of Independence Peak (Route 93), Mount Gould, and Sardine Canyon from the summit of Kearsarge Peak. Onion Valley is also a great starting point for multiday tours deeper into the range.

95   Mount Keith

Starting Point	Shepherd Pass trailhead, 6300 feet
High Point	13,977 feet
Distance	17 miles
Elevation Gain	8180 feet
Time	One very long day or 2 days
Difficulty Level	Very strenuous
Terrain Rating	3
Aspects	South
Seasons	Winter, spring
Maps	USGS Mount Williamson; Manzanar

Often overlooked due to the fact that it is a mere 23 feet shy of the 14,000-foot mark, Mount Keith nonetheless has south-facing gullies that offer some of the highest-quality skiing in the Shepherd Pass area of John Muir Wilderness. From the top of the climber's-right gully, it's a short scramble to this rocky summit overlooking the headwaters of the Kings and Kern rivers in Kings Canyon National Park, the Great Western Divide, the Owens Valley, and some of the most dramatic relief in the entire Sierra. The southern aspect of this slope is prone to melting off more quickly than other routes in the area, but you can find perfect high-altitude California corn growing here during extended periods of high pressure between storms in the winter and spring.

GETTING THERE

From downtown Independence on US Highway 395, turn west on West Market Street (Onion Valley Road) and follow it for 4.4 miles to the junction with Foothill Road. Turn left on Foothill Road and follow it south for about 2.5 miles, turn right, then stay right when the road forks as you drive up to the Shepherd Pass trailhead at the mouth of Symmes Creek.

THE ROUTE

From the trailhead, follow the Shepherd Creek Trail west up Symmes Creek for about a mile, crossing the creek several times. If there is snow this low, you may be able to skin the whole way, but more often than not the first part of the trail will be bare. At about 7000 feet, the trail crosses the creek for a fourth time and climbs southwest for 2100 vertical feet out of the Symmes Creek drainage. The trail switchbacks up this slope to a low spot in the ridge at 9100 feet. This north-facing slope is likely to hold snow, so you may be able to skin up through the trees rather than hiking along the trail switchbacks. Once you hit this saddle at 9100 feet, cross over the ridge onto the south-facing slopes of the Shepherd Creek drainage.

Climbing near the bottom of the south-facing gullies of Mount Keith with Shepherd Pass and Mount Tyndall in the background

Here you'll want to find the trail again, as the snow on this south-facing aspect is usually burned off or patchy. Over the next 1.5 miles, you lose roughly 500 vertical feet as the trail contours southwest slightly downhill into the Shepherd Creek drainage. While that may seem like a waste of precious energy, you're far better off following the trail than not, believe me—otherwise you'd be bushwhacking. Ideally, at the end of this slightly downhill section, there will be snow for the duration of your journey. Eventually you begin climbing the Shepherd Creek drainage.

Follow the drainage as it continues southwest, past Mahogany Flat (9400 feet) then Anvil Camp (10,040 feet), two summer camping areas along the trail. Make your way toward Shepherd Pass, but once you reach 11,000 feet or so in the basin below the pass, start to make your way northwest underneath the south face of Mount Keith.

Skin up as high as you can before switching to boot-packing for the duration. Both of the main gullies on this face offer equally good skiing; however, the climber's-left gully tops out on the ridge well below the summit. The slightly longer gully to climber's right tops out on the summit ridge just a short and easy scramble shy of the summit.

From just near the summit, drop into this uninterrupted pitch of roughly 2800 vertical feet to where it flattens out in the basin below Shepherd Pass. Descend the way you came back down to the Shepherd Creek drainage.

Options: Due to the massive distance associated with routes in this area, I recommend spending a night or two back here and skiing more than one route. The north face of Mount Tyndall (Route 96), the west gully of Mount Williamson, and the Super Bowl, among others, are all within striking distance for a multiday trip in this zone.

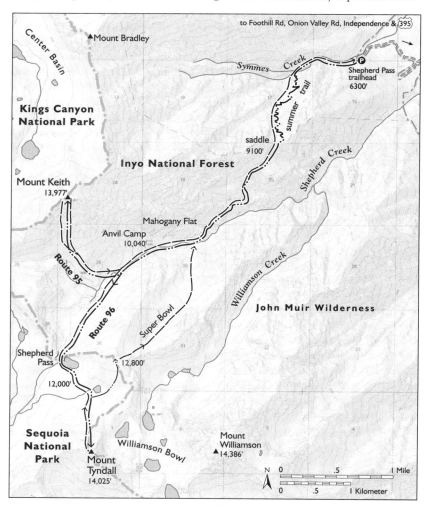

96 Mount Tyndall

Starting Point : Shepherd Pass trailhead, 6300 feet
High Point : 14,025 feet
Distance : 19 miles
Elevation Gain : 8300 feet
Time : One very long day or 2 days
Difficulty Level : Very strenuous
Terrain Rating : 3
Aspects : North, northeast
Seasons : Winter, spring
Maps : USGS Mount Williamson; Manzanar

Almost completely hidden from view on the west side of Mount Williamson, Mount Tyndall doesn't get a lot of attention. The tenth-highest mountain in the state, Tyndall is one of the least technically difficult California fourteeners to ski, but what it lacks in difficulty it more than makes up for in distance, as its summit sits roughly 9.5 miles and 7500 vertical feet from the nearest trailhead. Mount Tyndall and the Shepherd Pass area deep in John Muir Wilderness are about as remote as you can get in a day in the Sierra, and therefore it is an incredible spot to spend a night or two while exploring some of the neighboring peaks. The rugged terrain of the drainages at the base of Tyndall's eastern slope can be extremely challenging to navigate, but fortunately the start of this adventure follows the Shepherd Pass Trail into Sequoia National Park, which makes travel much easier and is a huge benefit for accessing this area in otherwise extremely difficult terrain, regardless of the season's snow coverage.

GETTING THERE

From downtown Independence on US Highway 395, turn west on West Market Street (Onion Valley Road) and follow it for 4.4 miles to the junction with Foothill Road. Turn left on Foothill Road and follow it south for about 2.5 miles, then turn right and stay right at the next fork as you drive up to the Shepherd Pass trailhead at the mouth of Symmes Creek.

THE ROUTE

From the trailhead, follow the route for Mount Keith (Route 95). As you cross over the saddle in the ridge at 9100 feet into the Shepherd Creek drainage, the impressive north face of Mount Williamson stares you in the face, and the Shepherd Pass Trail will likely become visible again on this south-facing slope. Follow the drainage west, but be sure to look up at the Super Bowl, immediately south across the creek. This massive, 4000-vertical-foot bowl that drops from the 12,800-foot high point just north of Mount Tyndall is a great way to ski back down to the trail on the way out.

Climbing up the north face of Mount Tyndall

As you make your way up the drainage, you eventually leave the route for Mount Keith and begin to head southwest, aiming for the low spot at the head of the drainage known as Shepherd Pass. Be sure to check out the two gullies that split the south side of Mount Keith (Route 95), one of the other objectives in the area as you may want to ski them too. People looking for a more protected place to camp might find it in the basin just below Shepherd Pass.

Make your way southwest up to Shepherd Pass; be ready, as the top couple hundred feet of the gully get pretty steep before cresting onto a massive plateau (12,000 feet). As you crest the pass, a sign indicates that you are entering Sequoia National Park. From here, the north face of Mount Tyndall lies a mile south. Take in the views of the Great Western Divide, including Milestone Mountain, across the head of the Kern River to the west. This massive flat area at the top of the pass is ideal terrain for camping as well, but at 12,000 feet it can be exposed to extreme winds and weather.

Head south to the flat area at the base of the north slope of Mount Tyndall, then skin as high as possible before switching to boot-packing to the top. Hike east along the ridge to reach the true summit and look down the sheer cliffs of the east face into the Williamson Bowl and the western slope of California's second-highest peak. As with most peaks in the Sierra, Mount Tyndall has views from the summit that are ridiculous. Check out the other routes in the area, including Mount Keith (Route 95), the west gully of Mount Williamson, and the Whitney area to the south (Route 97).

Enjoy moderately steep but wide-open turns for 1500 vertical feet back down to Shepherd Pass. Exit the Shepherd Creek drainage the same way you came. Following the summer trail back around into Symmes Creek is the easiest way back to the trailhead.

Option: From the flat area below the north face of Tyndall, it's only a 500-vertical-foot climb north to the top of the Super Bowl and its 4000 vertical feet of great turns back down to the Shepherd Pass Trail at Mahogany Flat. The Super Bowl itself might be worth the hike.

97   Mount Whitney

Starting Point	Whitney Portal trailhead, 8350 feet
High Point	14,505 feet
Distance	8.5 miles
Elevation Gain	6150 feet
Time	7 hours to 2 days
Difficulty Level	Very strenuous
Terrain Rating	4
Aspect	East
Seasons	Winter, spring
Maps	USGS Mount Whitney; Mount Langley

The impressive east face of the contiguous United States' highest peak, in John Muir Wilderness on the edge of Sequoia National Park, is clearly visible from US Highway 395 and the town of Lone Pine. Not only is Mount Whitney's summit the highest point in the Lower 48 (though the determination of its exact height varies), but the sheer spires of its east face are home to some of the finest alpine rock-climbing routes in the Sierra. The Mountaineers Route was first climbed by John Muir in 1873 but remained unskied until legendary photographer Galen Rowell laid the first tracks down it in 1974. These days, the Mountaineers Route sees regular winter traffic. The Whitney Portal Road is not maintained in winter, but you can usually drive up it to where it is blocked with snow. This point varies wildly from season to season, and the road may be blocked with snow miles from the trailhead, so keep that in mind when planning to attempt this route. The route can be done as a challenging single-day effort or a more casual overnight trip. Either way, climbing and skiing Mount Whitney is a unique and challenging experience that should be on everyone's list.

GETTING THERE

From the center of Lone Pine on US 395, turn west onto Whitney Portal Road and follow it uphill for 12 miles to the Whitney Portal trailhead. Park near the trailhead and put any food in the bear-proof food containers; bears have done damage to vehicles at this popular trailhead. If the road is not completely clear to the trailhead, drive up it as far as you can, then make your way up the road to the trailhead.

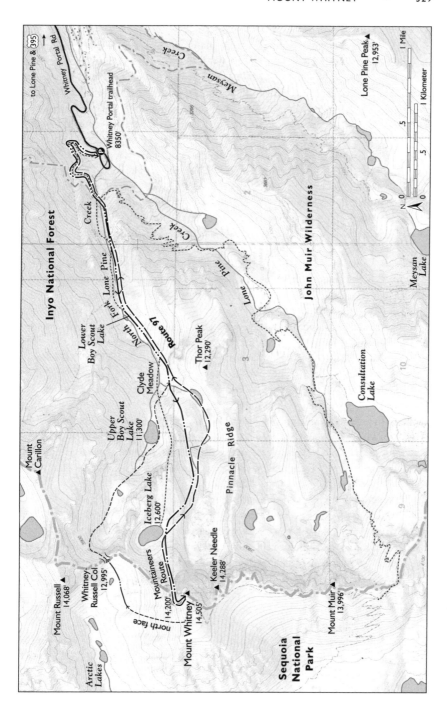

to Lone Pine & 395

Whitney Portal Rd

Whitney Portal trailhead
8350'

Inyo National Forest

Meysan Creek

Creek

North Fork Lone Pine Creek

Lower Boy Scout Lake

Clyde Meadow

Upper Boy Scout Lake
11,300'

Route 19

Thor Peak
12,290'

Iceberg Lake
12,600'

Pinnacle Ridge

Lone Pine Creek

John Muir Wilderness

Consultation Lake

Meysan Lake

Lone Pine Peak
12,953'

Mount Carillon

Mount Russell
14,068'

Whitney-Russell Col
12,995'

Mountaineers Route

north face

Keeler Needle
14,288'

Mount Whitney
14,505'
14,200'

Arctic Lakes

Mount Muir
13,996'

Sequoia National Park

N

0   .5   1 Mile

0   .5   1 Kilometer

THE ROUTE

From the Whitney Portal trailhead, follow the summer trail for approximately 0.75 mile. The second creek you come to, the North Fork of Lone Pine Creek, is the drainage you must climb to access the east face of Mount Whitney and the Mountaineers Route. Many would-be summiters of Mount Whitney have gone wrong here, just 15 minutes from the car, by continuing on the summer trail and going up the next drainage to the south, Lone Pine Creek, ending up on the wrong side of Pinnacle Ridge.

Ideally, there will be snow coverage on the south (climber's-left) side of the North Fork of Lone Pine Creek, making for a much easier start to your journey. If there isn't coverage this low, an unmaintained "climbers trail" should be readily apparent, as it is heavily used by rock climbers coming and going from routes on Mount Whitney and Mount Russell in the summer and fall. If there is snow, the better coverage will probably be on the south side of the creek, and travel will be relatively straightforward. The climbing trail crosses onto the north side of the creek along some rock ledges and stays on that side of the creek up to Lower Boy Scout Lake and Clyde Meadow.

From Clyde Meadow, continue following the drainage west toward Upper Boy Scout Lake. This lake is a good place to camp for those looking to do an overnight. Just before you reach Upper Boy Scout Lake (11,300 feet), head southwest into the drainage that leads toward the base of the east face of Mount Whitney. Continue west up the drainage while hugging the climber's-right side to about 12,400 feet. Here you head north up a steep slope for 200 vertical feet onto the shelf (12,600 feet) with Iceberg Lake, below the Mountaineers Route.

From here you should be able to see up the gully of the Mountaineers Route. This is a very popular mountaineering route, so as you climb the gully pay attention for rockfall since many climbers accidentally knock rocks loose near the top. The snow is often burned off for the top couple hundred vertical feet of this gully, so be careful while you walk on the loose rocks. Once you reach the top of the Mountaineers Route (14,200 feet), you still have some challenging and exposed rock and ice scrambling to get to the summit.

Drop over the ridge and head south up the main gully above you. Be aware that there is incredible exposure below you as you make your way up the often icy, steep rock ledges to the summit plateau. Bear in mind that you have to descend this same way back to the top of the Mountaineers Route, so take that into account before heading up, as this is by far the most dangerous and challenging part of the ascent and descent.

Once you reach the summit plateau, it's only a few hundred feet of relatively flat walking to the summit and the Smithsonian Institution Shelter. The view from Mount Whitney's summit is incredible since it is surrounded by many of the highest and most dramatic peaks in the Sierra.

Take your time and use extreme caution while descending back to the top of the Mountaineers Route, then enjoy the 1800 vertical feet down to Iceberg Lake. Retrace your route back down the North Fork of Lone Pine Creek to return to the Whitney Portal trailhead.

Catching the sunrise from the North Fork of Lone Pine Creek

Option: The north face of Mount Whitney is another descent option off the summit plateau. This face drops for 2000 vertical feet into the Arctic Lakes basin between Mount Whitney and Mount Russell. Routefinding can be tricky and snow coverage is often lacking on this slope, so it is important to do some reconnaissance if you hope to ski this route. From the bottom of the north face, head through the Whitney-Russell Col and descend southeast from the head of the Upper Boy Scout Lake drainage underneath Mount Russell's south face, past Upper Boy Scout Lake to Clyde Meadow, where you rejoin the main descent route.

98 Mount Langley

Starting Point	Tuttle Creek trailhead, 6950 feet
High Point	14,026 feet
Distance	11 miles
Elevation Gain	7076 feet
Time	8 hours to 2 days
Difficulty Level	Very strenuous
Terrain Rating	4
Aspect	Northeast
Seasons	Winter, spring
Map	USGS Mount Langley

Mount Langley is said to be one of the easiest California fourteener summits to reach in the summer, and while the winter route up Mount Langley is relatively straightforward, getting to the summit is by no means easy. At 5.5 miles one way with more than 7000 vertical feet of gain from the closest and highest starting point, a winter

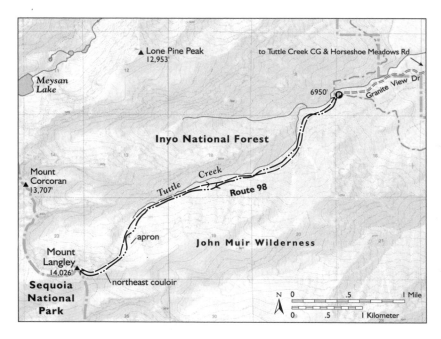

or spring jaunt to the summit is a massive effort. Just west of Lone Pine and only a few miles south of Mount Whitney, Mount Langley in John Muir Wilderness is the southernmost fourteener in the state. The route gains elevation gradually following Tuttle Creek west before ramping up steeply as it climbs the nearly 2000-vertical-foot northeast couloir up to the summit plateau on the border with Sequoia National Park. As with most objectives this far south in the range, snow coverage and conditions can be among the biggest challenges, but time it just right, and you can have an amazing ski descent from the ninth-highest summit in the state. Many people complete this route in a day, while others opt for an overnight, with numerous fine places to camp in the Tuttle Creek drainage.

GETTING THERE

From Lone Pine on US Highway 395, turn west onto Whitney Portal Road. Head uphill for just over 3 miles, and after you've passed through the Alabama Hills, turn left (south) onto Horseshoe Meadows Road. Follow this road south for 2 miles to Granite View Drive and turn right (west). Follow Granite View Drive uphill for 2.4 miles then bear right off the pavement onto a dirt road when you see a sign for the Tuttle Creek Trail. Follow this dirt road (high-clearance four-wheel-drive recommended) uphill for 2.5 miles to the Tuttle Creek trailhead at the end of the road or the snow line, whichever comes first. Snow coverage will likely dictate how far you can drive up this road, potentially adding a significant amount of distance to the already long approach.

THE ROUTE

From the Tuttle Creek trailhead, follow the summer hiking trail (or follow its path if there is snow) as it heads west, gaining elevation gradually for 0.8 mile to where it crosses Tuttle Creek. The trail continues for a short distance northwest to an old stone hut perched on the ridge. If there is good snow coverage at the creek crossing (7700 feet), head southwest up the drainage for another 2.25 miles until you reach the base of the massive apron below the northeast couloir. While heading up the lower reaches of the drainage, it is best to avoid being in the bottom near the creek. Being up a hundred feet or so on either side affords somewhat easier passage.

If there is no snow on the lower portion of this route, follow the summer trail to the old stone hut, then turn south-southwest to find a faint user trail that climbs and contours back into the Tuttle Creek drainage above Tuttle Creek. This south-facing side of the drainage is likely to be melted of snow, making for quick and easy travel to and from the snow line if necessary. Once you reach the snow line, follow the drainage up to the large apron below the northeast couloir.

At around 10,500 feet, you will be at the bottom of the huge apron, with the northeast couloir high above you. While you will be able to see the bottom of the couloir, most of it remains hidden behind a rock ridge until you are beneath it. Head

On the approach to Mount Langley in the Tuttle Creek drainage

southwest up the broad apron for roughly 1500 vertical feet to the base of the couloir. From here you should be able to see all the way to the top of the couloir. Switch over to boot-packing if you haven't already and settle in for the 2000-vertical-foot climb within the walls of the couloir to the summit plateau. You will likely want to use crampons and an ice axe here, especially if the snow is firm.

Once you reach the large and relatively flat plateau at the top of the couloir, the summit lies just a short distance northwest. Mount Langley's lofty summit sits atop the sheer cliffs of the mountain's north face with outstanding views in all directions, but especially of the Mount Whitney region to the north and Sequoia National Park and some of the most remote mountains in the Sierra to the west.

Retrace your route to the top of the northeast couloir and descend it to the apron far below. Enjoy the wide-open expanse of the large apron below the couloir, then follow the drainage east-northeast. Enjoy the mellow, rolling terrain of the Tuttle Creek drainage until you return to the forested lower slopes. Retrace your route out of the drainage to return to the parking area.

99   Pear Lake Hut

Starting Point	Wolverton trailhead, 7275 feet
High Point	9200 feet
Distance	11 miles
Elevation Gain	2000 feet
Time	6 hours
Difficulty Level	Strenuous
Terrain Rating	2
Aspects	Southeast, north, east, northeast; west, northwest
Seasons	Winter, spring
Map	USGS Lodgepole

Until the late spring, western access to the Sierra is extremely limited, with the exception of just a few places that offer relatively easy entry to the majestic mountains of the southwestern Sierra. The Pear Lake Hut is one such area that is accessible all winter long, starting from Wolverton Road in Sequoia National Park. (No matter how you approach this trailhead by car, you will enter either Sequoia or Kings Canyon National Park and must pay an entry fee or have an annual pass.) The historic Pear Lake Hut sits at an elevation of 9200 feet, just north of its namesake Pear Lake and Alta Peak (11,204 feet) and just west of the Tableland and the Kings-Kaweah Divide between Sequoia and Kings Canyon national parks. The route to Pear Lake is surprisingly straightforward and easy to follow, along a summer trail from Wolverton west past Heather Lake and Aster Lake and on to the Pear Lake Hut. A visit to the Pear Lake Hut is truly unique and unforgettable, and it is also one of the easiest ways to experience the terrain in this otherwise difficult-to-access part of the

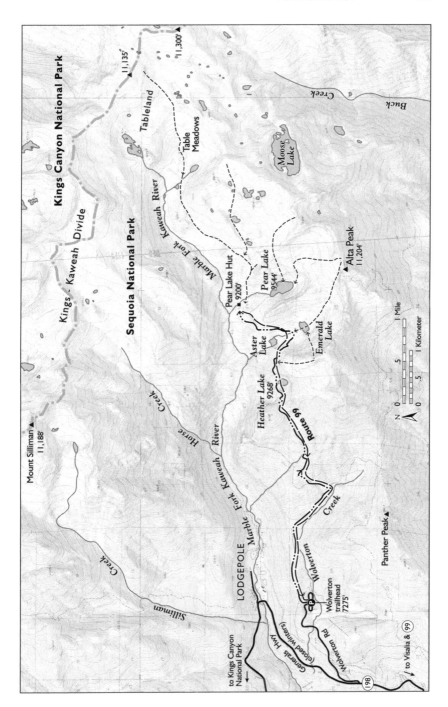

Sierra. The hut sleeps up to ten people and is available to the public from December through April; reservations are required (see Resources). People generally spend two nights at the hut, which allows them to explore the expansive intermediate terrain, with a sprinkling of expert terrain, surrounding it and the opportunity to view and explore some of the most remote country in the heart of the range. Day trips into this zone are also a possibility, with roundtrip distances of 11–13 miles and vertical gain of 4000-plus feet to ski the basins above both Emerald and Pear lakes. However, travel to and from the hut in stormy conditions may be very challenging due to limited visibility and travel through avalanche terrain.

GETTING THERE

In winter, the Generals Highway (CA 198) may be closed due to snow; when this is the case you must approach this area from the south. From Visalia, head east on CA 198 for 58 miles. Turn right on Wolverton Road and follow it east for 1.4 miles to the trailhead parking area. When the Generals Highway (CA 198) is open, you can also approach this trailhead from Fresno: Head east on CA 180 for 53 miles to the Kings Canyon National Park entrance. About 1 mile past the park entrance, turn right (south) on Generals Highway (CA 198). Follow CA 198 for 26.2 miles, and soon after passing through Lodgepole, turn left on Wolverton Road and follow it east for 1.4 miles. Turn left into the parking area and park by the trailhead.

THE ROUTE

From the trailhead parking area, head north for a few hundred feet, following the summer trail up onto the ridge crest. When snow coverage is poor down low by the parking area, using the trail to reach the snow line is an advantage. Take note of the yellow triangle blazes that mark the summer trail and route to the hut. Once on the ridge crest, head east for about a mile, staying on the ridge crest as it climbs very gradually.

The route then turns southeast, still following the summer trail, and begins to climb a bit more steeply for 0.6 mile before making a switchback and heading north for another 0.5 mile until you regain the ridge crest. Again the route turns southeast and follows the top of the ridge uphill for about 0.25 mile. The route then heads east, crossing a small drainage and again following the ridge crest uphill for another 0.75 mile to a saddle (9495 feet) just above and west of Heather Lake; this saddle is the high point of the route to the hut.

Continue east and drop down to Heather Lake (9268 feet), cross it, and head up the slope to a prominent bench on the other side. Follow this bench east as it wraps around the ridge and into the Emerald Lake basin. A wealth of moderate terrain, as well as some of the more challenging terrain in the area, lies in this zone above Emerald Lake. Contour south of and above Aster Lake and head north, eventually wrapping east around the end of the ridge that separates the Emerald and Pear lake basins. As you wrap around this ridge, be on the lookout for the hut nestled among a grove of trees just west of the creek that flows out of Pear Lake.

Pear Lake Hut in Sequoia National Park

From the hut, the best and easiest way to return to the trailhead is to retrace the route you used to approach the hut. Simply head back out exactly the way you came.

Options: Most people who head out to this area do so on an overnight trip to the hut so they have time to explore the various options, aspects, and terrain. A day trip into this zone is not out of the question for fit skiers, and cruising out here to see the zone and ski a peak is a long but very doable option. From the hut, the skiing options are generally all intermediate in difficulty, although expert skiers will sniff out some short, steeper terrain, which is plentiful in both the Pear Lake and Emerald Lake basins—including a summit of Alta Peak (11,204 feet). Endless options for long, mellow tours out toward the Tableland and Kings-Kaweah Divide (11,300 feet) are one of the main attractions in this unique part of the range.

Driving up Onion Valley Road en route to a descent of University Peak

RESOURCES

AVALANCHE ADVISORIES AND WEATHER INFORMATION

Eastern Sierra Avalanche Center, www.esavalanche.org
Howard Sheckter's Mammoth Weather, www.mammothweather.com
Lake Tahoe area snow forecast, www.opensnow.com/dailysnow/tahoe
Mount Shasta Avalanche Center, www.shastaavalanche.org
National Weather Service, www.weather.gov
Sierra Avalanche Center, www.sierraavalanchecenter.org

Avalanche Beacon Practice Parks

Kirkwood Beacon Training Park, Kirkwood Mountain Resort, (209) 258-6000
Mammoth Beacon Training Park, Mammoth Mountain ski area,
    (800) MAMMOTH
Mount Shasta Beacon Training Park, Mount Shasta Ski Park, (530) 926-8610
Squaw Valley Beacon Training, Squaw Valley Ski Patrol, (530) 581-7260

Avalanche Education

Alpenglow Expeditions, www.alpenglowexpeditions.com, (877) 873-5376
Alpine Skills International, www.alpineskills.com, (530) 582-9170
Donner Summit Avalanche Seminars, www.donnersummitavalancheseminars.com,
    (530) 412-3585
Expedition: Kirkwood, www.expedition.kirkwood.com, (209) 258-7360
High Sierra Snowcat and Yurt, www.highsierrasnowcat.com
Lake Tahoe Community College, www.ltcc.edu, (530) 541-4660
Mountain Adventure Seminars, www.mtadventure.com, (209) 753-6556
North American Ski Training Center, www.skinastc.com, (530) 582-4772
Safe as Clinics, www.safeasclinics.com
Shasta Mountain Guides, www.shastaguides.com, (530) 926-3117
Sierra Mountain Center, www.sierramountaincenter.com, (760) 873-8526
Sierra Mountain Guides, www.sierramtnguides.com, (760) 648-1122
Slide Snow School, www.slidesnowschool.com, (775) 849-0704
Tahoe Mountain School, www.tahoemountainschool.com, (530) 414-5295

Driving Information and Conditions

California Department of Transportation, www.dot.ca.gov/cgi-bin/roads.cgi,
    (800) 427-ROAD
Lassen Volcanic National Park, www.nps.gov/lavo/planyourvisit/conditions.htm
Nevada Department of Transportation, www.nevadadot.com/travel-info

Sequoia and Kings Canyon National Parks, www.nps.gov/seki/planyourvisit
/conditions.htm

Sno-Parks, $5 fee collected at self-pay stations; season passes available online or
at vendors; www.ohv.parks.ca.gov/snoparks

Yosemite National Park, www.nps.gov/yose/planyourvisit/conditions.htm

Guide and Other Services

Alpenglow Expeditions, www.alpenglowexpeditions.com, (877) 873-5376

Alpine Skills International, www.alpineskills.com, (530) 582-9170

Backcountry Adventure Center, Sugar Bowl Resort, www.sugarbowl.com
/backcountry, (530) 426-7005

International–California Alpine Guides, www.internationalalpineguides.com,
www.californiaalpineguides.com, (877) 686-2546

North American Ski Training Center, www.skinastc.com, (530) 582-4772

Saddlebag Lake Resort water taxi, www.saddlebaglakeresort.com/Boats.html

Shasta Mountain Guides, www.shastaguides.com, (530) 926-3117

Sierra Mountain Center, www.sierramountaincenter.com, (760) 873-8526

Sierra Mountain Guides, www.sierramtnguides.com, (760) 648-1122

SWS Mountain Guides: www.swsmtns.com, (888) 797-6867

Yurts and Huts

High Sierra Snowcat and Yurt, Virginia Lakes, www.highsierrasnowcat.com

Lost Trail Lodge, Truckee, www.losttraillodge.com, (530) 320-9268

Ostrander Hut, Yosemite National Park, www.yosemiteconservancy.org
/ostrander-ski-hut, (209) 379-5161

Pear Lake Ski Hut, Sequoia National Park, www.exploresequoiakingscanyon.com
/pear-lake-winter-hut.html, (559) 565-4251

Rock Creek Winter Lodge, www.rockcreeklodge.com/summer/winter,
(877) 935-4170

Sierra Club huts (Benson, Bradley, Ludlow, Peter Grubb huts), Lake Tahoe;
operated by Clair Tappaan Lodge by reservation, www.clairtappaanlodge.com
/backcountry-huts, (530) 426-3632

Ski and Winter Sports Resorts

Alpine Meadows (see Squaw Valley–Alpine Meadows)

Bear Valley Mountain, www.bearvalley.com, (209) 753-2301

Boreal Mountain Resort, www.rideboreal.com, (530) 426-3663

Diamond Peak Ski Resort, www.diamondpeak.com, (775) 832-1177

Heavenly Mountain Resort, www.skiheavenly.com, (775) 586-7000

Homewood Mountain Resort, www.skihomewood.com, (530) 584-6800

June Mountain ski area, www.junemountain.com, (888) 586-3686

Kirkwood Mountain Resort, www.kirkwood.com, (209) 258-6000

Mammoth Mountain ski area, www.mammothmountain.com, (800) MAMMOTH

Mount Rose Ski Tahoe, www.skirose.com, (775) 849-0704
Mount Shasta Ski Park, www.skipark.com, (530) 926-8610
Northstar-at-Tahoe, www.northstarcalifornia.com, (530) 562-2267
Sierra-at-Tahoe, www.sierraattahoe.com, (530) 659-7453
Squaw Valley–Alpine Meadows, www.squawalpine.com, (800) 403-0206
Sugar Bowl Resort, www.sugarbowl.com, (530) 426-9000

National and State Parks

Lassen Volcanic National Park
www.nps.gov/lavo
Plumas-Eureka State Park
310 Johnsville Road
Blairsden, CA 96103
(530) 836-2380
www.parks.ca.gov/?page_id=507
Sequoia and Kings Canyon
National Parks
www.nps.gov/seki
Yosemite National Park
www.nps.gov/yose

National Forests

Eldorado National Forest
100 Forni Road
Placerville, CA 95667
(530) 622-5061
www.fs.usda.gov/eldorado/
Humboldt-Toiyabe National Forest
1200 Franklin Way
Sparks, NV 89431
(775) 331-6444
www.fs.usda.gov/htnf
Inyo National Forest
351 Pacu Lane, Suite 200
Bishop, CA 93514-3101
(760) 873-2400
www.fs.usda.gov/inyo
Lake Tahoe Basin Management Unit
35 College Drive
South Lake Tahoe, CA 96150
(530) 543-2600
www.fs.usda.gov/ltbmu

Lassen National Forest
2550 Riverside Drive
Susanville, CA 96130
(530) 257-2151
www.fs.usda.gov/lassen/
Plumas National Forest
159 Lawrence Street
Quincy, CA 95971-6025
(530) 283-2050
www.fs.usda.gov/plumas
Shasta-Trinity National Forest
3644 Avtech Parkway
Redding, CA 96002
(530) 226-2500
www.fs.usda.gov/stnf/
Sierra National Forest
1600 Tollhouse Road
Clovis, CA 93611
(559) 297-0706
www.fs.usda.gov/sierra
Stanislaus National Forest
19777 Greenley Road
Sonora, CA 95370
(209) 532-3671
www.fs.usda.gov/stanislaus
Tahoe National Forest
631 Coyote Street
Nevada City, CA 95959
(530) 265-4531
www.fs.usda.gov/tahoe

Ranger Districts

ELDORADO NATIONAL FOREST

Pacific Ranger District
7887 US Highway 50
Pollock Pines, CA 95726-9602
(530) 644-2349

Placerville Ranger District
4260 Eight Mile Road
Camino, CA 95709
(530) 644-2324

HUMBOLDT-TOIYABE NATIONAL FOREST

Bridgeport Ranger District
HC62, Box 1000
Bridgeport, CA 93517
(760) 932-7070

Carson Ranger District
1536 South Carson Street
Carson City, NV 89701
(775) 882-2766

INYO NATIONAL FOREST

Mammoth Ranger District
Box 148
2500 CA Highway 203
Mammoth Lakes, CA 93546
(760) 924-5500

Mono Lake Ranger District
Box 429
Lee Vining, CA 93541
(760) 647-3044

Mount Whitney Ranger District
Box 8
640 South Main Street
Lone Pine, CA 93545
(760) 876-6200

White Mountain Ranger District
798 North Main Street
Bishop, CA 93514
(760) 873-2500

LASSEN NATIONAL FOREST

Almanor Ranger District
Box 767
900 East CA Highway 36
Chester, CA 96020
(530) 258-2141

Eagle Lake Ranger District
477-050 Eagle Lake Road
Susanville, CA 96130
(530) 257-4188

Hat Creek Ranger District
Box 220
43225 East CA Highway 299
Fall River Mills, CA 96028
(530) 336-5521

PLUMAS NATIONAL FOREST

Beckwourth Ranger District
Box 7
23 Mohawk Road
Blairsden, CA 96103
(530) 836-2575

Feather River Ranger District
875 Mitchell Avenue
Oroville, CA 95965-4699
(530) 534-6500

Mount Hough Ranger District
39696 CA Highway 70
Quincy, CA 95971
(530) 283-0555

SHASTA-TRINITY NATIONAL FOREST

McCloud Ranger District
Box 1620
2019 Forest Road
McCloud, CA 96057
(530) 964-2184

Mount Shasta Ranger District
204 West Alma
Mount Shasta, CA 96067
(530) 926-4511

SIERRA NATIONAL FOREST

Bass Lake Ranger District
57003 Road 225
North Fork, CA 93643
(559) 877-2218

High Sierra Ranger District
29688 Auberry Road
Prather, CA 93651
(559) 855-5355

STANISLAUS NATIONAL FOREST

Calaveras District
Box 500
5519 CA Highway 4
Hathaway Pines, CA 95233
(209) 795-1381

Groveland District
24545 CA Highway 120
Groveland, CA 95321
(209) 962-7825

Mi-Wuk District
24695 CA Highway 108
Mi-Wuk Village, CA 95346
(209) 586-3234

Summit District
1 Pinecrest Lake Road
Pinecrest, CA 95364
(209) 965-3434

TAHOE NATIONAL FOREST

American River Ranger District
22830 Foresthill Road
Foresthill, CA 95631
(530) 367-2224

Sierraville Ranger District
Box 95
317 South Lincoln Street
Sierraville, CA 96126
(530) 994-3401

Truckee Ranger District
10811 Stockrest Springs Road
Truckee, CA 96161
(530) 587-3558

Yuba River Ranger District
15924 CA Highway 49
Camptonville, CA 95922
(530) 288-3231

ACKNOWLEDGMENTS

I WOULD LIKE TO EXTEND A SPECIAL THANK-YOU to my friends, my family, my beautiful wife, and especially my ski partners for their support and understanding during the process of authoring this guidebook. I am especially grateful to other guidebook authors including John Moynier, Nate Greenberg, and Dan Mingori for sharing their knowledge and inspiring and helping others to get out and enjoy the mountains that we all love. This guidebook would not have been possible without the incredible and generous support of Flylow Gear, Pret Helmets, Leki Poles, Liberty Skis, Smith Optics, Deuter, Clif Bar, and Adventure Medical Kits.

INDEX

ABOUT THE AUTHOR

JEREMY BENSON IS A SPONSORED BACKCOUNTRY ski athlete and free-lance writer who has lived and skied in the great state of California since 2001. Originally from the East Coast, Benson transplanted to North Lake Tahoe shortly after graduating from Saint Michael's College in northern Vermont. He has back-country skied extensively throughout the incredibly diverse mountains of California with the goal of exploring as much as they have to offer. In the warmer months he trades the skin track for the singletrack and can be found mountain biking the amazing trails in Tahoe and the surrounding areas. Benson has written for numerous national and local print and internet media outlets and is the author of *Mountain Bike: Tahoe,* also published by Mountaineers Books. He currently resides in Truckee, California, with his wife, Heather.

MOUNTAINEERS BOOKS is a leading publisher of mountaineering literature and guides—including our flagship title, *Mountaineering: The Freedom of the Hills*—as well as adventure narratives, natural history, and general outdoor recreation. Through our two imprints, Skipstone and Braided River, we also publish titles on sustainability and conservation. We are committed to supporting the environmental and educational goals of our organization by providing expert information on human-powered adventure, sustainable practices at home and on the trail, and preservation of wilderness.

The Mountaineers, founded in 1906, is a 501(c)(3) nonprofit outdoor activity and conservation organization whose mission is "to explore, study, preserve, and enjoy the natural beauty of the outdoors." One of the largest such organizations in the United States, it sponsors classes and year-round outdoor activities throughout the Pacific Northwest, including climbing, hiking, backcountry skiing, snowshoeing, bicycling, camping, paddling, and more. The Mountaineers also supports its mission through its publishing division, Mountaineers Books, and promotes environmental education and citizen engagement. For more information, visit The Mountaineers Program Center, 7700 Sand Point Way NE, Seattle, WA 98115-3996; phone 206-521-6001; www.mountaineers.org; or email info@mountaineers.org.

Our publications are made possible through the generosity of donors and through sales of more than 800 titles on outdoor recreation, sustainable lifestyle, and conservation. To donate, purchase books, or learn more, visit us online:

MOUNTAINEERS BOOKS
1001 SW Klickitat Way, Suite 201 • Seattle, WA 98134

800-553-4453 • mbooks@mountaineersbooks.org • www.mountaineersbooks.org

Mountaineers Books is proud to be a corporate sponsor of the Leave No Trace Center for Outdoor Ethics, whose mission is to promote and inspire responsible outdoor recreation through education, research, and partnerships. • The Leave No Trace program is focused specifically on human-powered (nonmotorized) recreation. • Leave No Trace strives to educate visitors about the nature of their recreational impacts and offers techniques to prevent and minimize such impacts. • Leave No Trace is best understood as an educational and ethical program, not as a set of rules and regulations. • For more information, visit www.lnt.org or call 800-332-4100.

OTHER TITLES YOU MIGHT ENJOY FROM MOUNTAINEERS BOOKS

Avalanche Essentials: A Step-by-Step System for Safety and Survival
Bruce Tremper
Learn the fundamentals of avalanche safety from an expert.

Avalanche Pocket Guide: A Field Reference
Bruce Tremper
Waterproof quick reference for evaluating and managing avalanche danger

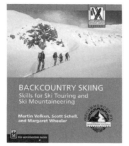

Backcountry Skiing: Skills for Ski Touring and Ski Mountaineering
Martin Volken, Scott Schell, and Margaret Wheeler
The definitive manual of backcountry skiing

Snow Travel
Mike Zawaski
Covers all the techniques for moving across snow

Don't Freeze Out There! Deck
Water-resistant playing cards with tips on safe travel in the snow